The Lease Manual

A Practical Guide to Negotiating Office, Retail, and Industrial Leases

Rodney J. Dillman

Section of Real Property,
Probate and Trust Law

Defending Liberty
Pursuing Justice

Cover design by ABA Publishing.

Library of Congress Cataloging-in-Publication Data

Dillman, Rodney J., 1952–
    The lease manual : a practical guide to negotiating office, retail, and industrial leases / by Rodney J. Dillman.
        p. cm.
    Includes index.
    ISBN-13: 978-1-59031-726-6
    ISBN-10: 1-59031-726-2
    1. Commercial leases—United States.   I. Title.

    KF593.C6D55 2006
    346.7304'3462— dc22

                                                                2006026268

Dedication

To
Laura, Brittany, and Ryan

Contents

viii   CONTENTS

PART 2
DESCRIPTION AND ANALYSIS OF RETAIL LEASE PARAGRAPHS   255

PART 3

Preface

Have you ever wondered what is holding up the signing of what seems to be a very straightforward lease transaction? Or maybe you have asked yourself, "Is there something I am missing in negotiating this lease?" Or perhaps you don't quite understand the particular importance of a lease paragraph and why one party is so insistent on not altering that paragraph. Are there times during lease negotiations when you wish you had an alternative or compromise that would be acceptable to all parties? *The Lease Manual* answers all of these questions and more. It is intended to assist lawyers, landlords, tenants, lenders, brokers, asset managers, property managers, and others involved in a commercial real estate lease transaction in the negotiation, preparation, and execution of office, retail, and industrial leases of commercial real estate.

Understanding the needs and concerns of all interested parties is the only way to effectively facilitate and complete lease negotiations. Key to this understanding is knowing who are the "interested parties." The landlord and tenant are the obvious interested parties, but that is only the beginning of the story. In the background there often is a lender whose approval is required in order to complete the lease transaction, and sometimes there may be more than one lender if the landlord has placed subordinate or mezzanine financing on the property. There may also be a ground lessor, master lessor, or sublandlord of the building if the landlord does not own the fee interest in the land and the building. There may even be other tenants in the building or retail mall whose approval is required.

In addition, the needs and concerns of these interested parties may differ depending upon the structure of their organizations. A landlord that is a publicly traded REIT (Real Estate Investment Trust) may have a different frame of reference than a landlord who is an individual. In that same vein, a landlord that is a joint venture, limited partnership, or limited liability company (LLC) may have an insurance company, pension fund, or other institutional investor as a partner, and thus may have lease requirements that differ from a landlord whose partners are local investors.

The needs and concerns of lenders may also differ depending upon their type. A local bank likely will have different lease approval parameters than those of an investment fund or the primary servicer of a Commercial

Mortgaged Backed Security (CMBS) conduit (a lender that takes pools of commercial mortgage loans, securitizes them, and sell tranches to institutional investors). Similarly, an insurance company lender may have a set of lease approval standards that differ significantly from those of a credit company or mezzanine lender.

Tenants, too, have their own needs and concerns. A tenant that has an S&P AAA credit rating and leases space for regional offices throughout the United States likely will have its own lease form and will attempt to use that form whenever and wherever market conditions permit, regardless of the amount of space leased. Similarly, big block retail stores and anchor tenants of retail malls will be able to dictate lease terms that will not be available to local tenants.

The Lease Manual examines and explores the concerns, needs, and desires of landlords, tenants, and lenders by analyzing typical lease paragraphs from each point of view. Compromises and alternatives are offered and evaluated to enable the reader to effectively negotiate a commercial lease for his or her client. In addition, forms of ancillary lease documents, such as SNDAs (Subordination, Nondisturbance, and Attornment Agreements) and Tenant Estoppel Certificates that satisfy the requirements of landlords, tenants, and lenders are provided. This Manual is reproduced on the accompanying fully searchable CD-ROM, and all sample lease paragraphs and forms are available in an easily customizable format.

Acknowledgments

The author would like to express his appreciation to the following lawyers now or formerly at Day, Berry & Howard LLP who assisted in the preparation of *The Lease Manual:*

Rosemary C. Ayers
Jonathan C. Black
Michael P. Byrne
Peter J. Duffy
Dean A. Dulchinos
C. J. Karbowicz
Margaret Kline
Jeanine M. Lynch
Leah Martin
Daniel S. Matos

Anthony J. Mavrinac
Robert McKay
Kelly G. Miley
Bruce Nicholls
Shari E. Purrington
Tina Ross
Marcia Sung
Streven M. Torkelsen
Mark C. Wilson

A special thank you also goes to Richard M. Frome, Acquisitions Editor for the American Bar Association Real Property Media/Book Products Committee.

Introduction

The Lease Manual is divided into four parts. The first three parts are a description and analysis of typical (1) office lease paragraphs, (2) retail lease paragraphs, and (3) industrial/warehouse lease paragraphs. In each of these first three parts, a "risk rating" from one to five is provided for each lease paragraph, followed by a brief summary and description of the lease paragraph and its scope. Further information on risk ratings is provided below. Then, an analysis of the lease paragraph and a critical review of the landlord's, tenant's, and lender's perspectives with respect to the lease paragraph is provided, followed by possible compromises and alternatives from each party's point of view. Miscellaneous comments, if any, are subsequently set forth, concluding with a typical lease paragraph in boldface. Finally, Part 4 is a collection of commonly used forms that are ancillary to a lease transaction. *The Lease Manual* is reproduced on the accompanying fully searchable CD-ROM, including all typical lease paragraphs and forms in an easily customizable format.

Please note that all lease paragraph cross-references refer only to the paragraphs contained in the part in which the cross-reference occurs. For example, Part 1 contains the Description and Analysis of Office Lease Paragraphs. In Paragraph 25 of Part 1, the Comments section contains a cross-reference to Paragraph 23 and Paragraph 24. Both cross-references refer to Paragraphs 23 and 24 of Part 1 (not to Part 2—Retail Lease Paragraphs or Part 3—Industrial/Warehouse Lease Paragraphs).

RISK RATINGS

The lease paragraphs analyzed in this Manual are comprehensive lease provisions that are moderate in their approach, but generally favor the landlord. Accordingly, the "risk rating" was developed from an institutional-landlord point of view. If the user of this Manual is a tenant or lender, consider assigning other risk ratings and criteria that are apropos to the user's leasing program. The following criteria were used in determining the risk ratings:

Risk Rating 1   *Giveaway.* Items rated 1 are not critical and may be negotiated.

Risk Rating 2   *Negotiable.* Care should be taken to consider the overall picture, but items rated 2 may be negotiated.

Risk Rating 3   *Very Important.* Items rated 3 are very important to the lease transaction and may have legal or business implications. These paragraphs may be the subject of negotiation, but should only be changed if a change is necessary to conclude the transaction. If the lease negotiator is not a lawyer, the negotiator may want to consult a supervisor and/or legal counsel to determine compromises and alternatives that are not readily apparent.

Risk Rating 4   *Critical.* Any item rated 4 should not be modified without the advice of legal counsel.

Risk Rating 5   *Nonnegotiable.* The substance of these items is not subject to change. It is recommended that only nonsubstantive language changes be made with the advice of legal counsel.

COMPROMISES AND ALTERNATIVES

Each lease paragraph may or may not have acceptable compromises or alternatives depending on the risk rating assigned to that paragraph and the relative leverage of the parties to the lease. A risk rating of 4 or 5 for a landlord indicates that the landlord's counsel will be involved in any negotiation and may have limited ability to compromise the terms of the paragraph. A risk rating of 4 or 5 for a tenant, however, means those paragraphs likely are to be the ones the tenant would most like to change. The size of the leased premises, the length of the term of the lease, the creditworthiness of the tenant, and market conditions will be important factors in determining whether to negotiate the terms of each lease paragraph. The landlord is more likely to compromise its position and the tenant more likely to demand concessions if the tenant is an investment-grade credit tenant leasing a significant amount of space for a long term. Another significant factor is the legal and business costs and expenses involved in protracted lease negotiations. Any changes that might impact a sale of the property or landlord's ability to control the asset will be scrutinized by the landlord. The parties should also consider any operational implications that may result from granting certain rights to tenants, including rights of first refusal, options, and rights of first offer.

COMMENTARY

Each lease paragraph may or may not have specific comments. Commentary is provided to address certain business and legal issues and to reiterate very important concepts contained in the lease paragraph or the analysis of the perspectives of the landlord, tenant, or lender.

FORMS

Form of Letter of Intent. Many lease transactions begin with a letter of intent negotiated by a broker or tenant representative or the principals to the transaction. A universal form that can be adapted to any commercial lease transaction is provided.

Form of Notice of Lease and Form of Lease Commencement Date Agreement. Many states have statutory requirements listing the information that must be contained in a recordable form of "Notice of Lease," "Memorandum of Lease," or "Short Form Lease." A form of Notice of Lease that should be adapted to the statutory requirements of the appropriate state is provided. Many leases require that a Commencement Date Agreement be executed after lease execution if a date certain for commencement of the lease term is not specified in the lease. This generally arises where either the landlord or the tenant will be performing substantial tenant improvement work at the premises, and it is the parties' intent that the commencement date and the payment of rent not begin until such work is completed. By executing a Commencement Date Agreement, the parties to the lease are able to establish and the lender is able to confirm the commencement and expiration of the lease term.

Form of Subordination, Nondisturbance, and Attornment Agreement. Both a lender form and a tenant-oriented form of SNDA are provided.

Forms of Tenant Estoppel Letters. Forms of Tenant Estoppel Letters from a lender's and a tenant's perspective are provided.

Form of Landlord's Waiver of Lien Rights. A sample Waiver of Lien form is provided to be signed by a landlord in favor of a lender requiring a first-priority lien on certain of a tenant's personal property that is already subject to a lien in favor of a landlord pursuant to the terms of the lease.

Overall, this Manual is intended to facilitate the decisions required for lease negotiations and approvals. The Manual is not static but will be updated periodically as new developments occur in leasing, and current information is needed to adequately respond to requests for changes to lease forms.

DEFINITIONS OF MOST NEGOTIATED AND LEAST UNDERSTOOD LEASE TERMS

The following definitions are the most commonly accepted usage of these terms. However, variations do exist, and it is therefore recommended that when using any of these terms in a lease, term sheet, or letter of intent, that these terms be specifically defined.

TYPES OF RENT AND ADDITIONAL RENT

Rent can be broken down into four categories: (1) net rent or triple net rent; (2) gross rent; (3) base year rent; and (4) expense stop rent. Also discussed are the terms full-service rent, additional rent, and percentage rent.

Net Rent—Net rent, or triple net rent as it is sometimes known and is at times abbreviated as NNN, does not include in the quoted base rent any allocation for maintenance and operating expenses, real estate taxes, or insurance costs. Thus, the tenant is responsible for the payment of all maintenance and operating expenses, real estate taxes, and insurance costs. Beginning on the rent commencement date, tenant pays, in addition to base rent, as "additional rent," tenant's proportionate share of *all* maintenance and operating expenses, real estate taxes, and insurance costs for the property.

Gross Rent—The opposite of net rent is gross rent. A lease that is quoted as fully gross includes in the base rent all maintenance and operating expenses, real estate taxes, and insurance costs for the entire term of the Lease. The tenant has no obligation to pay any rent other than the base rent. Gross rent is unusual today because rent is fixed for the entire term of the lease, and the landlord assumes the risk of inflationary and other increases in maintenance and operating expenses, real estate taxes, and insurance costs.

Base Year Rent—Base year rent, though often quoted as "gross rent," is really a modified gross rent. The quoted base year rent includes net rent, maintenance and operating expenses, real estate taxes, and insurance costs through the end of the base year. For each year subsequent to the base year, tenant agrees to pay as "additional rent" tenant's proportionate share of increases in maintenance and operating expenses, real estate taxes, and insurance costs over those maintenance and operating expenses, real estate taxes, and insurance costs incurred during the base year. Thus, the base year acts as a comparison year. Base year variations include tenant paying its own electricity charges or tenant paying all real estate taxes in addition to tenant's payment of tenant's proportionate share of the remaining maintenance and operating expenses and insurance costs.

Expense Stop Rent—Expense stop rent is similar to base year rent and is also a form of modified gross rent. As in base year rent, the expense stop rent quote includes maintenance and operating expenses, real estate taxes, and insurance costs. However, rather than using a base year to determine increases, tenant agrees to pay as "additional rent" tenant's proportionate share of increases above a specified amount, called a "stop." The stop is generally a fair estimate of the sum of the maintenance and operating expenses, real estate taxes, and insurance costs during the first year of the lease. Unlike base year rent, with expense stop rent, additional rent for tenant's proportionate share of maintenance and operating expenses, real estate taxes, and insurance costs may become due anytime after the rent commencement date that the stop is exceeded.

Full Service Rent—Full service rent is a term that is sometimes used by tenants or landlords when requesting or giving a rent quote. Full service rent means that the rent quoted includes all services and utilities to the premises and the building, including repairs and maintenance to the premises. Tenants under a full service lease expect that the rent quoted includes all ordinary and extraordinary repairs and replacements of fixtures and equipment in the premises, including heating, ventilation, and air-conditioning (HVAC), electrical, plumbing, and sprinkler system, in addition to ordinary janitorial cleaning.

Additional Rent—As indicated above, additional rent generally occurs in a lease containing provisions for net rent, base year rent, or expense stop rent and refers to all amounts payable to landlord that are in addition to base rent. For example, in a lease having base year rent, additional rent would generally mean tenant's proportionate share of increases in maintenance and operating expenses, real estate taxes, and insurance costs over those maintenance and operating expenses, real estate taxes, and insurance costs incurred during the base year. Many leases also contain a "catch-all" clause that states that all amounts payable to landlord under the lease shall be deemed to be "rent" or "additional rent." This type of clause would permit landlord to invoke the remedies under the lease not only for nonpayment of base year rent or the additional rent referred to above, but would also permit landlord to invoke remedies for nonpayment of charges relating to replacement of lightbulbs or other reimbursable charges due landlord under the lease. Landlord's remedies for such nonpayment of rent or additional rent would generally include the right to terminate the lease and evict tenant from the premises. See Part 1, Paragraph Number 7 for a full discussion of additional rent.

Percentage Rent—Percentage rent generally occurs in retail leases and most often requires that tenant pay to landlord a specified percentage of "gross sales" in excess of a specified "minimum gross sales" break point. For example, a retail shoe store lease at a regional mall may require that tenant pay to landlord, as percentage rent, 1% of all gross sales in excess of minimum gross sales of $1 million. Thus, in any year where tenant's gross sales exceed $1 million, percentage rent will be due to landlord. See Part 2, Paragraph Number 4 for a full discussion of percentage rent.

REAL ESTATE TAXES

Real estate taxes are determined by the municipal and/or county taxing authority where the property is located. The taxing authority first determines the "assessment," or valuation, of the property based on specific statutory criteria. In some jurisdictions this assessment occurs annually, and in others on some other periodic basis, such as every five or ten years. In some jurisdictions reassessment can also occur upon a sale or refinancing of the property, or upon the occurrence of improvements to the property. The assessment is then multiplied by the "mill rate" to determine the amount of real estate taxes due on the property. The mill rate is usually expressed as an amount per $100 or $1,000 of the assessed value.

The time for payment of real estate taxes varies from jurisdiction to jurisdiction, sometimes even within the same state. In some jurisdictions real estate taxes are paid annually, in others quarterly or semiannually. In some jurisdictions taxes are paid in arrears; in others they are paid in advance. In some jurisdictions taxes are paid and assessed on a calendar-year basis, and in other jurisdictions a special tax year is created. In every jurisdiction the vagaries of real estate taxes must be examined to determine the calculation, frequency of payment, and due date of real estate taxes.

SUBORDINATION, NONDISTURBANCE, AND ATTORNMENT

While the words "subordination," "nondisturbance," and "attornment" are often linked together in leases, they each have distinct meanings.

Subordination—Subordination relates to the priority that the lease and tenant's rights under the lease have relative to other matters affecting title to the property that have been recorded on the land records where the property is located or of which tenant has knowledge at the time of the execution of the lease. Examples of parties holding an interest in the property prior to tenant's (and therefore meaning that tenant's interest is subordinate) include: fee mortgages, ground leases, leasehold mortgages, air space leases, deeds of trust, utility easements, rights of way, and operating and reciprocal easement agreements. Subordination can also occur by agreement among parties having an interest in the property. Thus, by agreement contained within the lease document, the tenant generally agrees to subordinate the lease to any mortgage or ground lease that may come into existence after the execution of the lease. This agreement among the parties may also be restated in a Subordination, Nondisturbance, and Attornment Agreement (SNDA).

Nondisturbance—While the existence and recording of mortgages and ground leases are generally beyond the control of tenant, tenant does have means of protecting itself. The key word for a tenant is "nondisturbance." The lease and an SNDA with nondisturbance protection will generally provide that in the event of a foreclosure of a mortgage or the termination of a ground lease, lender or ground lessor agrees not to disturb tenant's possession of the premises, provided tenant is not then in default under its lease. Without nondisturbance, if the lease is subordinate to a mortgage, and if lender forecloses, lender can elect to name the tenant as party in the foreclosure action and terminate the lease. Tenant does not want to risk being left on the street if landlord defaults on its mortgage loan payments and thus tries to negotiate nondisturbance being added to the Lease or the SNDA. Lender, on the other hand, prefers to retain the option to disturb tenant's occupancy of the premises, because if tenant is paying rent below the current market, lender can terminate the lease and obtain a new tenant who will pay a market rent.

Attornment—While nondisturbance is key to tenant, attornment is crucial to lender. The attornment part of the lease and the SNDA states that upon foreclosure or deed in lieu of foreclosure, tenant will attorn to, or recognize, the new landlord (who either used to be the lender or is a third-party purchaser at a foreclosure sale) as the current landlord under the lease. Tenant further agrees to be bound by all provisions of the lease. Since in some jurisdictions, foreclosures can be beneficial to tenant, allowing tenant the opportunity to walk away from a lease to which tenant no longer wants to be bound, lender wants to make sure that this will not happen and that tenant will continue to pay rent. Attornment waives tenant's right to walk away and reaffirms the lease.

PART 1

Description and Analysis of Office Lease Paragraphs

The Parties

RISK RATING: 4

A. DESCRIPTION AND SCOPE

This Paragraph sets forth the names, addresses, and types of entities of each party to the Lease. It also serves to identify the particular entity that is the Landlord.

B. ANALYSIS

1. Landlord's Perspective

Landlord wants to ensure that the Lease lists the proper legal entity as Tenant and Tenant's state of organization in the event Landlord must sue Tenant to collect rent, enforce Tenant's obligations under the Lease, or evict Tenant.

2. Tenant's Perspective

Tenant wants to ensure that the Lease lists the proper legal entity as Landlord and Landlord's state of organization in the event Tenant must sue Landlord to enforce Landlord's obligations under the Lease.

3. Lender's Perspective

Lender wants to make sure that the Landlord described in the Lease and Lender's borrower are the same entity, or that the borrower is a successor in interest to the stated Landlord. A Lender is also interested in the name of the Tenant obligor under the Lease for purposes of underwriting the credit of that particular Tenant. Additionally, Lender will request that the Lease be assigned to the Lender as additional collateral for the mortgage loan. An "Assignment of Leases and Rents" will be recorded on the land records and Tenant may be asked to acknowledge the existence of this document.

C. COMPROMISES AND ALTERNATIVES

The proposed Tenant may want to create a judgment proof subsidiary of a rated corporate parent to execute the Lease. Consideration should thus be given as to whether a full or partial Guaranty of the Lease by the corporate parent will be required. This should be of particular concern if substantial tenant improvement dollars are being spent by the Landlord in connection with the Lease, and Tenant is an unrated subsidiary of a corporate parent that is not providing credit support via a lease guaranty.

D. COMMENTS

Information should be verified as correct and complete. It is important to specify the type of entity and state of organization for both Landlord and Tenant so that appropriate service of process and credit information can be obtained.

E. TYPICAL PARAGRAPH

1. **The Parties.**
   (a) **The name and address of Landlord is:**

   _____

   _____

   _____

   Landlord is a [corporation, limited liability company, limited partnership, etc.] organized and existing under the laws of the State of _____. The Landlord named above and its successors and permitted assigns are hereinafter referred to as "Landlord."
   (b) **The name and address of Tenant is:**

   _____

   _____

   _____

   Tenant is a [corporation, limited liability company, limited partnership, etc.] organized and existing under the laws of the State of _____. The Tenant named above and its successors and permitted assigns are hereinafter referred to as "Tenant."

PARAGRAPH **2**

Building, Premises, and Appurtenant Rights

RISK RATING: 3

A. DESCRIPTION AND SCOPE

Subparagraphs 2(a), (b) and (d) define and describe the location of the Building, the Premises, and the Common Areas and define the term "Property" as all of the foregoing. Subparagraph 2(c) describes those Rights that are "appurtenant" to the Premises, such as Tenant's right to use the parking facilities, the loading docks, and the freight elevators. This Paragraph also sets forth the rentable and usable area of the Premises (by floor and in total).

Subparagraph 2(e) requires that the "BOMA" method to be used to calculate the rentable area of the Premises and requires a remeasurement of the Premises upon completion of the Tenant improvements. Any increase or decrease in the area of the Premises will result in equitable adjustment of the Annual Base Rent, the Additional Rent (if any), and the monthly rent installment. This adjustment to the Annual Base Rent, the Additional Rent (if any), and the monthly rent installment is self-operative; however, the parties agree, for their mutual convenience, to execute a lease amendment within 30 days. Should a dispute arise over the measurement of the Premises either party may demand arbitration pursuant to Paragraph 59 of the Lease.

B. ANALYSIS

1. Landlord's Perspective

With respect to Subparagraphs 2(a), (b), (c) and (d), a correct description of the Building and the Premises is important to Landlord in enforcing the Lease. Landlord wants an expansive definition of the Common Areas for purposes of calculating Building Operating Expenses. Landlord also desires the most expansive interpretation of rentable area of the Premises so that the most Annual Base Rent and the largest possible Proportionate Share can be calculated.

Subparagraph 2(e) protects Landlord against inaccurate calculation of the rentable area of the Premises and disputes over rent adjustments brought about by changes in rentable area. In certain geographic locations, it may be more appropriate to use a measurement standard other than the BOMA standard, or a specific additional percentage common area factor may be used in the calculation of the rentable area of the Premises.

2.   Tenant's Perspective

With respect to Subparagraph 2(a), (b), (c) and (d), Tenant needs an accurate definition of the Premises for space planning purposes and estimating tenant improvement costs. Tenant wants an expansive definition of Appurtenant Rights so that it will be able to use all Building facilities outside of the Premises that Tenant will need in order to satisfy the needs of Tenant's employees. Tenant also wants a precise method of calculating the rentable area of the Premises in order to accurately budget the amount of Annual Base Rent and Additional Rent.

Subparagraph 2(e) protects Tenant against inaccurate calculation of rentable area of the Premises and against disputes arising from a rent adjustment based upon a change in the rentable area.

Tenant may request an option to increase or reduce the rentable area to facilitate Tenant's long-term planning and to protect Tenant against making a commitment to lease too much or too little space. Landlord may not be willing to consent to a reduction in rentable area if Landlord is financing the Property, since its financing is based on a certain cash flow of rental payments. Similarly, Landlord may not want to give Tenant an option to increase the area of the Premises since Landlord would have to hold such area in reserve for Tenant's possible use and in so doing remove a given amount of rentable area from the market and possibly lose a prospective tenant on the mere possibility that Tenant may opt to increase its rentable area.

With respect to Subparagraph 2(c), if the Building is equipped with fiber optic or other high-speed Internet access service, a back-up generator, uninterruptible power supply, a cafeteria, or other services or amenities that Tenant expects to use, these services and amenities should be added as appurtenances.

3.   Lender's Perspective

With respect to Subparagraphs 2(a), (b), (c) and (d), a correct description of the Building and the Premises is important to Lender, as it assures Lender that the Lease is enforceable. Lender desires certainty in the definition of Building and Premises so that cash flow available for debt service can be accurately predicted. Lender will likely resist any attempts by Tenant to obtain an option to reduce the rentable area of the Premises, since from a loan underwriting point of view, Lender must assume that Tenant will exercise the option to reduce the rentable area of the Premises at the earliest possible time. This will correspondingly reduce the fair market value of the Building and the percentage of that value that Lender will loan to Landlord. Thus both Lender and Landlord will resist granting options or rights to reduce the area of the Premises.

C. COMPROMISES AND ALTERNATIVES

With respect to Subparagraph 2(a), if the Building is under construction and the exact address of the Property is unknown at the time of execution of the Lease, the following language should be inserted: "The address of the Building shall be determined by the appropriate governmental authorities and, when determined, this Lease shall be amended to reflect the appropriate address."

D. COMMENTS

The legal description of the land where the Building is located along with a survey of the Property showing the locations of the Building and Parking Facilities should be attached as *Exhibit A-1* and a diagram of the Premises should be attached as *Exhibit A-2*.

The Common Areas include parking rights. See Paragraph 31—Parking for a more complete discussion of Parking.

In addition to the BOMA method of measuring space it should be noted that depending upon the geographic area where the Property is located, either a modified BOMA or some other measurement standard may be used, or in some cases the parties may simply agree upon the rentable square feet of the Premises without any standard or measurement.

For a discussion of the "Rent Commencement Date" see Paragraph 5—Term.

E. TYPICAL PARAGRAPH

2. **Buildings, Premises, and Appurtenant Rights.**
    (a) **The name and address of the building (the "Building") in which the Premises are located is:**

    _____

    _____

    _____

The Building is located on the land more particularly described on *Exhibit A-1* hereto (the land, the Building, the Premises, the Common Areas, the parking facilities, and any other improvements on the land are hereinafter collectively referred to as the "Property").

(b) The premises (the "Premises") covered by this Lease are as crosshatched on the attached *Exhibit A-2,* and described as approximately _____ rentable square feet of office space. The rentable and usable square foot areas occupied by Tenant are broken down as follows:

_____ FLOOR	_____ rentable square feet or _____ usable square feet
_____ FLOOR	_____ rentable square feet or _____ usable square feet
_____ FLOOR	_____ rentable square feet or _____ usable square feet
TOTAL	_____ rentable square feet or _____ usable square feet

(c) Appurtenant to the Premises (subject to the rules and regulations of Landlord promulgated from time to time) are the following rights, privileges, and licenses (the "Rights") of Tenant and its invitees:

(i) the nonexclusive right to use, in common with Landlord and other tenants and invitees of Landlord, any beneficial easements, the loading docks, the freight elevators, and all areas and passageways reasonably necessary for the use of such loading docks and freight elevators;

(ii) the nonexclusive right to use, in common with Landlord and other tenants and the invitees of Landlord and such other tenants, and the general public, the parking facilities of the Building;

(iii) the nonexclusive right to use, in common with Landlord and other tenants and invitees of Landlord and such other tenants, the Common Areas (as hereinafter defined) for all purposes for which the Common Areas are customarily used, including full, uninterrupted access to and from the Premises.

The Rights are not and are not intended to be construed to be included in the definition of the word "Premises" for any purposes whatsoever under this Lease.

(d) "Common Areas" shall mean those areas within the Property, including the Building's entrances, public lobbies, doors, windows, hallways, corridors, main elevators, freight elevators, loading docks, walkways, plazas, access ways, lavatories, roads, drives, public and fire stairways, sidewalks, exterior ramps, the parking facilities, and other areas not leased or held for lease within or contiguous to or serving the Property, but that are necessary or desirable for Tenant's full use and enjoyment of the Premises.

(e) The Annual Base Rent has been calculated on the basis of $_____ per rentable square foot per year for the office space occupied by Tenant. The rentable area of the Premises has been established using the Building Owners and Managers Association International, ANSI Z65.1 ("BOMA") method of measurement Copyright 1996, which is incorporated herein by reference. Upon completion of the Premises, the rentable area and usable area of the Premises and the Building shall be measured by authorized representatives of Landlord and Tenant in accordance with said BOMA method. If the rentable area of the Premises is increased or decreased, the Annual Base Rent, Additional Rent (if any), monthly rent installment, and Tenant's Proportionate Share shall be equitably adjusted. The adjustment to Annual Base Rent, Additional Rent (if any), monthly rent installment, and Tenant's Proportionate Share shall be self-operative, and no additional agreement between Landlord and Tenant will be necessary to effectuate such adjustment; provided, however, Landlord and Tenant shall, for their mutual convenience, execute an amendment to this Lease within thirty (30) days following Tenant's occupancy, stating the Commencement Date, the Rent Commencement Date, the rentable area and usable area of the Premises, the Annual Base Rent, the Additional Rent (if any), the monthly rent installment, and Tenant's Proportionate Share developed through the operation of this Paragraph 2(e). The failure of either party to execute and deliver such an amendment shall not affect the adjustment of the Annual Base Rent and Additional Rent. Any dispute regarding the measurement of the Premises may be settled by either party's demand for arbitration as provided for in Paragraph 59 of this Lease.

Leasing Clause

RISK RATING: 3

A. DESCRIPTION AND SCOPE

This Paragraph sets out the basic agreement of Landlord to lease the Premises to Tenant and the agreement of Tenant to lease the Premises from Landlord.

B. ANALYSIS

1. Landlord's Perspective

This Paragraph sets out the basic agreement. This is the operative Paragraph that binds Tenant to the Lease and all the covenants and conditions of Tenant set forth throughout the Lease. In addition, this Paragraph protects Landlord against a claim that the Lease creates some legal relationship other than a leasehold interest, for example, a sale of the Premises by Landlord to Tenant, a license, or some other arrangement whereby Tenant would become an occupant of the Premises.

2. Tenant's Perspective

This is the operative Paragraph that binds Landlord to the Lease. This Paragraph requires that Landlord lease the Premises to Tenant. This Paragraph also identifies Tenant as a "lessee" as opposed to Tenant having some other legal relationship to Landlord, such as a licensee or a partner. As a tenant, Tenant has certain statutory protections relating to termination and enforcement of the Lease.

11

3. Lender's Perspective

Lender wants assurance that both Landlord and Tenant are bound to the Lease. This is the operative paragraph that binds Landlord and Tenant to the Lease and all of Landlord's and Tenant's respective covenants set forth throughout the Lease.

C. COMPROMISES AND ALTERNATIVES

Tenant may request that Landlord make certain warranties and representations regarding Landlord's ownership of the Property and Landlord's right to enter into the Lease. The following may be an acceptable addition to the Lease:

> *Landlord is the owner of the Property and warrants and represents to Tenant that Landlord has full right and authority to make this Lease. Landlord further warrants and represents that, to the best of Landlord's actual knowledge, the provisions of this Lease do not conflict with or violate the provisions of existing agreements between Landlord and third parties.*

D. COMMENTS

In lieu of the warranties and representations set forth under Paragraph C above, Landlord may suggest that Tenant purchase Title Insurance if Tenant is concerned about the status of Landlord's title to Property.

E. TYPICAL PARAGRAPH

3. Leasing Clause. Landlord, for and in consideration of the rents and other charges and payments payable by Tenant and of the covenants, agreements, terms, provisions, and conditions to be kept and performed hereunder by Tenant, does hereby demise and lease to Tenant, and Tenant does hereby hire and lease from Landlord the Premises. Said demise is and shall be upon and subject to the covenants, agreements, terms, provisions, and conditions of this Lease.

Use of Premises

RISK RATING: 2

A. DESCRIPTION AND SCOPE

This Paragraph states the permitted uses of the Premises: executive and general offices and related uses.

B. ANALYSIS

1. Landlord's Perspective

Landlord has probably intended that the Building be used exclusively for office purposes and, even if zoning laws permitted, would not want the Building to be used for retail or residential purposes. This Paragraph protects Landlord against use of the Premises by Tenant for purposes other than office purposes. This paragraph also insures a successor Landlord that the use of the Building and the Premises may not be changed without its consent.

2. Tenant's Perspective

Tenant wants the broadest possible use of the Premises not only for Tenant's own operations, but also in the event that Tenant assigns the Lease or sublets the Premises to a third party. Therefore, Tenant may ask for a clause that permits Tenant to use the Premises for "any other purpose permitted by law." Tenant may also request that Landlord permit "related uses or incidental use of the Premises for other purposes."

Tenant desires the Property be in compliance with all laws and may ask for Landlord's representation that the Property is in compliance with all laws. Tenant may object to Landlord's limiting this representation to the best of

Landlord's knowledge. Also, Tenant may request that Landlord promptly take all steps necessary to bring the Property in compliance with all laws.

3.   Lender's Perspective

Lender desires to preserve the cash flow generated by the Lease as well as by the cash flow generated by leases to other tenants on the Property. Lender therefore desires that Tenant not use the Premises for purposes that would be harmful or offensive to other tenants or prospective tenants on the Property.

Because violations of legal requirements may impair the value of the Property and therefore Lender's security, Lender desires assurance that the Property is in compliance with all legal requirements.

C.   COMPROMISES AND ALTERNATIVES

If Tenant requests that Landlord represent and warrant that the Property is in compliance with all laws, the following additional provision may be acceptable:

> On the Commencement Date the Property shall, to the best of Landlord's actual knowledge, be in conformance with all applicable legal requirements, including zoning and planning ordinances, and shall, to the best of Landlord's actual knowledge, not violate applicable restrictions, if any. Landlord, upon being notified of any non-conformity with the legal requirements stated above shall: (a) take all reasonable and diligent steps to bring the Property in conformity; and (b) deliver possession of the Premises to Tenant as provided for in this Lease ready for occupancy and free of all tenants and third party equipment or personal property.

As a compromise to Tenant's request that Tenant be permitted to use the Premises for "any use permitted by law," the following use clause may be used:

> Tenant may not use and occupy the Premises other than for executive and general office purposes and other uses related thereto incidental to such purposes.

D.   COMMENTS

If the Premises are to be used for purposes other than general offices, the additional uses desired should be specified.

E.   TYPICAL PARAGRAPH

4.   Use of Premises. Tenant may use and occupy the Premises for executive and general office purposes only, and no other use of the Premises shall be permitted without the express written consent of Landlord.

Term

RISK RATING: 4

A. DESCRIPTION AND SCOPE

Subparagraph 5(a) specifies the date on which the Lease term is expected to begin ("Scheduled Commencement Date"), the date on which the Lease term will actually begin ("Commencement Date"), the date on which it ends ("Expiration Date"), and the duration of the Lease ("Term").

Subparagraphs 5(b) and (c) require Landlord to provide notice to Tenant at least 30 days prior to the Substantial Completion of the Premises. If Landlord fails to "Substantially Complete" the Premises, as defined in Subparagraph 5(c), on or before the Scheduled Commencement Date, then the Commencement Date will be postponed until a fixed number of days after the date the Premises are Substantially Complete and Landlord has given Tenant notice of completion. The fixed number of days between notice of completion and the Commencement Date should correspond to the notice requirement with which Tenant must comply under any then existing lease pursuant to which Tenant must give notice in order to terminate its occupancy.

If Substantial Completion is delayed due to an act or omission of Tenant, Landlord must notify Tenant of its act or omission within five days after the end of such delay and the Premises will be deemed to be Substantially Completed as of the date the Premises would have been Substantially Complete but for Tenant's act or omission. In addition, if the Premises cannot be Substantially Completed due to any holding-over by a prior occupant, then the Lease will remain in effect, except the Rent Commencement Date will be postponed until Substantial Completion. This Paragraph also provides that Landlord will have no liability for such holding-over.

Subparagraph 5(d) permits Landlord to agree to an earlier Scheduled Commencement Date. Subparagraph 5(e) permits Tenant, under certain conditions, to install equipment and furnishings in the Premises before taking occupancy and without paying rent, and subparagraph 5(f) provides that Landlord use commercially reasonable efforts to realize Substantial Completion on or before the Scheduled Commencement Date.

B.   ANALYSIS

1.   Landlord's Perspective

This Paragraph allows Landlord to specify a limited term to Tenant's occupancy of the Premises. This Paragraph also identifies that date from which the Rent Commencement Date will be calculated and, therefore, the date Tenant will begin paying rent.

Landlord will begin receiving rent provided Landlord has Substantially Completed the Premises by the Scheduled Commencement Date. Landlord is protected against delays in Substantial Completion caused by Tenant acts or omissions. Although Landlord may desire to shorten the thirty-day notification period prior to the date of Substantial Completion, Tenant is likely to resist this because Tenant will usually need the time to organize and plan its move to the Premises.

2.   Tenant's Perspective

For budgeting purposes, this Paragraph identifies the date after which Tenant's monetary obligations under the Lease will commence. In addition, this Paragraph protects Tenant against Tenant's not having a leasehold interest in the Premises for the desired period of time, and eliminates any doubts as to the precise duration of the tenancy.

This Paragraph protects against the various contingencies involved in the completion of the Premises by Landlord and the taking of occupancy by Tenant. It provides flexibility for Landlord but protects Tenant in that Tenant has no obligation to pay rent or occupy the Premises prior to Substantial Completion. Tenant may also desire to establish a date after which Tenant may terminate the Lease if the Premises are not Substantially Complete or are not available for possession by Tenant (a "drop dead date").

3.   Lender's Perspective

Lender will need to know the Term of the Lease to verify that borrower will have funds available to repay the loan amount for a defined period of time based on the length of the Lease Term. This paragraph also enables Lender to underwrite the lease rollover risk in connection with the loan. If the Building is new construction and Lender has made a construction loan, Lender will be interested in the definition of Rent Commencement Date, since only after that date will an income stream commence or be augmented, thus allowing the construction Lender to be assured that a takeout or permanent loan will be forthcoming.

C. COMPROMISES AND ALTERNATIVES

Landlord will generally desire that the Commencement Date coincide with the date of Substantial Completion, thereby minimizing the "free rent" period after Substantial Completion. Another alternative is for the Commencement Date to "occur on the earlier of (i) ___ days after Substantial Completion, or (ii) Tenant's commencement of business operations at the Premises."

From Tenant's point of view, the thirty day period for notification of Tenant prior to Substantial Completion could be reduced if Tenant's planning schedule so permits. If Tenant insists upon a drop-dead date for Substantial Completion of the Premises, Landlord will likely want a very lengthy period after which Tenant has the right to terminate the Lease. It would not be unusual for Landlord to require nine months or even one year. The following may be an acceptable addition to the Lease:

> *If the Premises are not Substantially Complete within _____ (____) days after the Scheduled Commencement Date, then Tenant shall have the right to terminate this Lease by giving Landlord _____ (____) days' advance written notice of Tenant's intent to terminate.*

D. COMMENTS

Rely solely on this Paragraph 5 for determining the Commencement Date.

E. TYPICAL PARAGRAPH

5. **Term.**
   (a) **Except as hereinafter provided, the Term (as hereinafter defined) of this Lease shall begin on _____ (the "Scheduled Commencement Date"). The first day of the Term shall be known as the "Commencement Date." The Term shall end on the later to occur of _____, or the date that is the last day of the _____ (____) month following the Commencement Date (the "Expiration Date"), unless: (i) sooner terminated in accordance with the terms and conditions contained in this Lease; or (ii) extended pursuant to the provisions of this Lease.**

The initial term of this Lease, plus any applicable renewal term(s), collectively shall be called, the "Term."

(b) Landlord shall notify Tenant in writing at least thirty (30) days prior to the anticipated date of Substantial Completion (as hereinafter defined) of the Premises. If Landlord fails to Substantially Complete the Premises in a good and workmanlike manner on or before the Scheduled Commencement Date, then the Commencement Date will be postponed until that date _____ (____) days after the later of the actual date of Substantial Completion or the anticipated date of Substantial Completion as set forth in Landlord's notice to Tenant.

Notwithstanding the foregoing provisions of this Paragraph, if Substantial Completion of the Premises by Landlord is delayed due to any act or omission of Tenant, and Landlord gives written notice to Tenant within five (5) days after such delay ends stating the cause of the delay and the length of time of any postponement caused by the delay, then the Premises shall be deemed to have been Substantially Completed on the date the Premises would have been Substantially Complete if such Tenant act or omission had not occurred. Without limiting the foregoing, if the Premises are not Substantially Completed prior to the Scheduled Commencement Date because of the fault of Tenant, then the Rent Commencement Date (as hereinafter defined) shall not be postponed on account thereof.

Additionally, if Landlord is unable to Substantially Complete the Premises on or before the Scheduled Commencement Date because of the holding-over by any occupant of the Premises, this Lease shall continue in effect and Landlord shall not be liable to Tenant or any third party for such inability; provided, however, that the Rent Commencement Date shall be postponed (provided Tenant is not responsible for its inability to take possession) until the date of Substantial Completion. If Landlord fails to Substantially Complete the Premises within one year after the Scheduled Commencement Date, this Lease shall be null and void.

(c) "Substantial Completion," "Substantially Complete," and "Substantially Completed" shall mean that all of the following conditions have been satisfied: (i) Landlord has secured and delivered to Tenant a Temporary Certificate of Occupancy (or the substantial equivalent thereof under applicable state or local law) to permit use and occupancy of the Building, the Premises and the Common Areas and construction of the improvements to the Premises have been completed in accordance with Tenant's plans and specifications as certified by the Building architect, subject only to normal punch list items such as minor or insubstantial details of construction, mechanical adjustment, or decoration, which items Landlord agrees to use its best efforts to correct as soon as reasonably practicable; (ii) delivery to Tenant of a certification by the Building architect, consented to and approved by Landlord, that: (A) the Premises, the Building, and the Common Areas have been substantially completed in accordance with the plans and specifications therefore; (B) the proper federal, state, county, regional, and local authorities, including those having jurisdiction over applicable zoning, building, health, safety, and environmental regulations, have issued all licenses, permits, approvals, and consents necessary in connection with the construction and lawful occupancy by Tenant of the Premises for the purposes permitted in this Lease (collectively, the "Permits"); and (C) the rentable area of the Premises and the Building are as shown on the schedule to such certification, and that such areas have been calculated in accordance with the BOMA method (or such alternative method approved by Landlord), based on the supporting calculation attached to such certification; and (iii) delivery to Tenant of a copy of all Permits and a copy of any certificates of inspection related thereto.

(d) Except as provided in Paragraph (e) below, if Landlord gives Tenant permission to enter into possession of the Premises prior to the Scheduled Commencement Date, such possession shall be deemed to be upon all the terms, covenants, conditions, and provisions of this Lease, including payment of Annual Base Rent and of Additional Rent, together with any other monies due Landlord under this Lease.

(e) Landlord, at Landlord's discretion, may permit Tenant and Tenant's agents to enter the Premises prior to the Scheduled Commencement Date to permit Tenant to do such other work as may be required by Tenant to make the Premises ready for Tenant's use and occupancy. If Landlord permits such entry prior to the Scheduled Commencement Date, such permission is conditioned upon Tenant and its agents, contractors, employees, and invitees working in harmony and not interfering with Landlord and its agents, contractors and employees in doing Landlord's Work, in the Premises or for other tenants and occupants of the Building. If at any time such entry shall cause or threaten to cause disharmony or interference, Landlord shall have the right to withdraw such permission upon twenty-four (24) hours notice to Tenant. Tenant agrees that any such entry into and occupation of the Premises shall be deemed to be under all of the terms, covenants, conditions and provisions of the Lease except as to the covenant to pay Base Rent or Additional Rent, and further agrees that Landlord shall not be liable in any way for any injury, loss or damage that may occur to any of Tenant's work and installations made in the Premises or to properties placed therein prior to the Scheduled Commencement Date, the same being at Tenant's sole risk.

(f) Landlord will use commercially reasonable efforts to Substantially Complete the Building, the Premises and the Common Areas on or before the Scheduled Commencement Date.

(g) Landlord and Tenant agree to execute a Commencement Date Certificate in the form of Exhibit 5.1 hereto specifying the Commencement Date.

PARAGRAPH **6**

Base Rent

RISK RATING: 3

A. DESCRIPTION AND SCOPE

This Paragraph sets forth the Annual Base Rent, which is calculated by multiplying the rentable square footage of the Premises by the cost per rentable square foot, and specifies that such rent is to be paid in equal installments beginning on the "Rent Commencement Date" and on the first day of each month thereafter throughout the Term.

B. ANALYSIS

1. Landlord's Perspective

Landlord is concerned with making a clear and accurate statement of the Annual Base Rent. Landlord also wants to state exactly when each installment of Annual Base Rent is due, and that each installment is due without any demand by Landlord. If any free rent period is given, Landlord may want to limit such free rent period to the Annual Base Rent so that Tenant is paying at least its applicable share Building Operating Expenses and Real Estate Taxes during the free rent period. If the Tenant's credit or business prospects are not certain, Landlord may want to layer in the free rent period over several months or years. In addition, should Tenant default under the Lease, Landlord may want the right to recapture the free rent. The Typical Paragraph requires that the first month's rent be paid at the time of the execution of the Lease, rather than on the Rent Commencement Date. This requirement may be waived for Tenants with a credit rating satisfactory to Landlord.

2. Tenant's Perspective

Tenant is similarly concerned with making a clear and accurate statement of the Annual Base Rent; however, Tenant is also concerned with stating that no installment of Annual Base Rent is due before the Rent Commencement Date, and that the Rent Commencement Date can be determined with specificity.

3. Lender's Perspective

A Lender's primary concern is to confirm Tenant's obligation to pay Annual Base Rent in the stated amount and to determine whether Tenant is entitled to any free rent period or reduced rent period so that Lender can properly underwrite the cash flow from the Property and project a satisfactory debt service coverage ratio. Lender will want to make sure the Lease contains a provision similar to Paragraph 6(b) so as to insure that Tenant has no rights of offset or deduction against Annual Base Rent and thus no diminution in the net income available for debt service.

C. COMPROMISES AND ALTERNATIVES

The initial installment of Annual Base Rent could be payable on the Rent Commencement Date rather than upon the execution of the Lease.

D. COMMENTS

"Commencement Date" and "Rent Commencement Date," while usually the same, may sometimes differ so as to permit Tenant to take possession of the Premises on a Commencement Date, which is prior to the "Rent Commencement Date," thus providing a free rent period, a move-in period, or a period during which Tenant may construct Tenant Improvements.

E. TYPICAL PARAGRAPH

6. **Base Rent.**
   (a) **The Annual Base Rent is _____ and __/100 Dollars ($ _____), based on _____ rentable square feet of office space and $_____ per rentable square foot, and shall be payable in equal monthly installments of _____ and __/100 Dollars ($ _____), commencing on the Rent Commencement Date (as hereinafter defined), and on the first day of each month through and including the Expiration Date. All monthly rent installments shall be made without any prior demand. Each of the monthly installments shall be payable at**

Landlord's office in the Building, or at such other place as Landlord may designate in writing, upon the first day of each and every calendar month throughout the Term. The "Rent Commencement Date," as used herein, shall mean that date which is _____ (____) days after the Commencement Date. Rent for the first full calendar month of the Term shall be due and payable simultaneously with the execution and delivery of this Lease.

(b) Except as otherwise specifically provided for in this Lease, Tenant covenants to pay when due and without setoff the Annual Base Rent, Additional Rent (as hereinafter defined) and all other payments due Landlord under this Lease.

Additional Rent
(Base Year*)

A. DESCRIPTION AND SCOPE

This Paragraph requires Tenant to pay a monthly estimate of the Operating Expense Payment and the Tax Payment equal to 1/12 of Landlord's reasonable estimate of increases in Building Operating Expenses and Real Estate Taxes for the current year over the Base Year.

This Paragraph establishes the Lease as a "Base Year" lease and it (a) sets forth the means by which Tenant pays its fair share of increases in Real Estate Taxes and Building Operating Expenses over the Real Estate Taxes and Building Operating Expenses for the Base Year based upon the proportion of space it occupies in the Building, (b) defines certain items included within and certain items excluded from Real Estate Taxes and Building Operating Expenses, (c) requires Tenant to pay a monthly estimate of Additional Rent equal to 1/12 of Landlord's reasonable estimate of the sum of increases in Building Operating Expenses and Real Estate Taxes for the current year over the Base Year, (d) provides a reconciliation mechanism at the end of each Computation Year following the Base Year whereby Tenant receives a credit toward future Additional Rent for any excess or makes a payment for any deficiency in its payments of Additional Rent, and (e) provides Tenant with the right to verify and, if necessary, to dispute Landlord's statements of Real Estate Taxes and Building

---

See the Introduction to this Lease Manual for a discussion of base year rent, expense stop rent, and net rent. An alternative for each such type of additional rent is set forth in the pages that follow.

Operating Expenses for up to 60 days following the receipt of Landlord's statement for each Computation Year and for the Base Year. Any such dispute of Landlord's statements of Real Estate Taxes or Building Operating Expenses will be resolved by an independent accounting firm if Landlord and Tenant cannot reconcile their differences.

Additional Rent is calculated by multiplying Tenant's Proportionate Share by increases in Building Operating Expenses and Real Estate Taxes over Building Operating Expenses and Real Estate Taxes for the Base Year. Real Estate Taxes and Building Operating Expenses for the Base Year and each Computation Year that the Building is not at least 90% leased and occupied are based upon an estimate of the Real Estate Taxes and Building Operating Expenses that would have been paid assuming the Building was 90% leased and occupied and the Property was fully assessed.

Tenant must pay a monthly estimate of Additional Rent equal to 1/12 of Landlord's reasonable estimate of the sum of the Tax Payment and the Operating Expense Payment for the current year. An appropriate adjustment is made at the end of each Computation Year to account for under or over-payments of Additional Rent by Tenant.

B. ANALYSIS

1. Landlord's Perspective

Generally, this paragraph protects Landlord from having to absorb any increases in the costs of Real Estate Taxes or any increases in the cost of the maintenance and operation of the Property after the Base Year, which increases are passed through to Tenant on a prorated basis.

Landlord will want to designate the year in which the Lease is executed as the Base Year since that is the year for which Landlord has the best information in order to estimate the Real Estate Taxes and Building Operating Expenses. In quoting the Annual Base Rent for the Premises, Landlord has presumably loaded into the Annual Base Rent Landlord's Base Year estimate of Real Estate Taxes and Building Operating Expenses.

With respect to the definition of Tenant's Proportionate Share, Landlord may require that the denominator of the ratio be the "leased" area of the Building rather than the "rentable" area of the Building. Such a change shifts the risk of the fixed costs of vacant space in the Building to the tenants in the Building.

The "gross up" of Building Operating Expenses and Real Estate Taxes during the Base Year and each Computation Year means that for a Building that is less than 90% leased and occupied, Landlord will not be able to charge Tenant for variable Building Operating Expenses that increase as occupancy of the Building increases. For example, assume the Building is

50% leased and has an annual electricity bill of $100,000 during the Base Year, and further assume that in the first Computation Year the occupancy increases to 90% and the annual electricity bill increases to $180,000, if the "gross up" requirement for the Base Year and the Computation Year is contained in the Lease, then Landlord rather than Tenant will absorb the $80,000 increase in the electricity charges component of the Building Operating Expenses. If the "gross up" provision is not included in the Lease, Tenant will be obligated to pay its pro rata share of the $80,000 increase in Building Operating Expenses.

With respect to Paragraph 7(j) and Tenant's right to audit Landlord's books and records relating to Building Operating Expenses and Real Estate Taxes, a recent trend has been for Tenants to retain auditors who specialize solely in these types of audits and are compensated on a contingent fee basis only. The fee to these auditors is a percentage of any refund due Tenant or reduction in Additional Rent that results from such audit. Many Landlords now include a provision in the Lease that prohibits Tenant's use of such contingent fee auditors.

2. Tenant's Perspective

While imposing the obligation upon Tenant of paying its proportionate share of increases in Real Estate Taxes and Building Operating Expenses over said expenses for the Base Year and to make estimated payments of said increases on a monthly basis based upon Landlord's reasonable estimate thereof, this Paragraph also protects Tenant against having to pay more than its fair share of those expenses. This Paragraph permits Tenant to audit Landlord's statement of Real Estate Taxes and Building Operating Expenses and to obtain a credit for any overpayments. To the extent the audit indicates an overstatement of actual Real Estate Taxes or Building Operating Expenses in excess of 5%, Landlord will be liable for the cost of the audit. Tenant will likely want to negotiate this percentage to 2–3% rather than 5%.

Tenant may object to a Base Year definition that designates the year in which the Lease is signed as the Base Year if the Rent Commencement Date occurs in the last half of that year or if the Rent Commencement Date occurs in the year after the Lease is executed. Tenant may argue that Annual Base Rent should include the expense load for a full calendar year after the Rent Commencement Date and therefore, the Base Year should be the "first full calendar year that occurs after the Rent Commencement Date."

Tenant may object to the inclusion of capital expenditures in the definition of Building Operating Expenses since capital enhancements to the Property will benefit the Landlord long after the expiration date of Tenant's Lease. Tenant will therefore argue that such capital costs are the sole responsibility of Landlord. Tenant may also object to capital expenditures incurred by Landlord in complying with laws and regulations since these capital improvements also add long term value to the Building.

Subparagraph 7(a)(v)(F) of the Typical Paragraph provides that property management fees and asset management fees may be included in Building Operating Expenses. Tenant may want to limit property management fees to a specified percentage of gross revenues based on market conditions in the area where the Property is located. Tenant may also object to asset management fees since it can be argued that such fees do not directly benefit the operation of the Property, but rather benefit only Landlord.

Tenant may object to the all-inclusive nature of the definition of Building Operating Expenses and request that only the items expressly set forth in Subparagraph 7(a)(v) be included in Building Operating Expenses. Tenant may also object to the inclusion of depreciation in the definition of Building Operating Expenses since depreciation of the capital improvements is a tax benefit that accrues only to Landlord and actual depreciation of the Property does not generally occur.

Tenant may also request that any successful contest of Real Estate Taxes result in a proportionate refund to Tenant of the applicable Real Estate Tax Payment. Tenant may request that Landlord have an affirmative obligation to contest any unreasonable increase in Real Estate Taxes. The likelihood of success of this request generally depends upon the degree of leverage that Tenant has in the Lease transaction. Landlord will be concerned about losing control of the Real Estate Tax appeal procedure and the impact such an appeal may have on future valuation and assessment of the Building.

Finally, Tenant may request that Landlord's failure to provide the statement of Operating Expenses and Real Estate Taxes required under Paragraph 7(f) within 6–12 months after the end of a Computation Year will terminate Tenant's obligation to pay Additional Rent for that Computation Year. This would permit Tenant to close its books for the prior year and not have to be concerned about a substantial and unexpected Additional Rent bill in the later years of the Lease Term.

3.   Lender's Perspective

Lender's primary concern is that Tenant be obligated to pay its share of increases in Real Estate Taxes and Operating Expenses so that cash flow designated for debt service will not be burdened with increases in Building Operating Expenses and Real Estate Taxes, and that any dispute between Landlord and Tenant relating to that obligation (i) can be resolved quickly, and (ii) will not in any case result in Tenant having the right to withhold payments of Additional Rent.

Lender wants to be able to determine a net effective rent during the term of its loan so that it can calculate the net cash flow available for debt service. Lender may also object to any rights of offset for any overpayments of Additional Rent. Rather such overpayment should be credited against the next due installment of Additional Rent.

C.   COMPROMISES AND ALTERNATIVES

The following alternative methods of having Tenant contribute to the payment of Real Estate Taxes and Building Operating Expenses may also be used: (a) a "net lease" approach, in which all expenses for Real Estate Taxes and Building Operating Expenses are passed through to Tenant as Additional Rent, as provided for in Alternative 3 of Paragraph Number 7; and (b) an "Expense Stop" approach, in which a specified amount of Building Operating Expenses and Real Estate Taxes is included in Annual Base Rent on the Commencement Date, with Tenant paying Tenant's Proportionate Share of increases over that fixed amount anytime after the Commencement Date that such Expense Stop is exceeded, as provided for in Alternative 2 of Paragraph Number 7.

Tenants with sufficient leverage and/or creditworthiness will most likely want to pay its proportionate share of Building Operating Expenses and Real Estate Taxes monthly based solely on actual costs incurred by Landlord for the previous year, or pay its proportionate share of Building Operating Expenses and Real Estate Taxes annually in arrears.

D.   COMMENTS

The method of calculating and determining Real Estate Taxes and Building Operating Expenses is likely to be one of the most negotiated provisions of the Lease. A clear understanding of the ramifications of any changes is imperative.

E.   TYPICAL PARAGRAPH

7.   **Additional Rent (Base Year).**
   (a)   **For purposes of this Paragraph 7:**
      (i)   *Base Year* **shall mean the calendar year 2_ _ _, which is the calendar year during which this Lease was executed.**
      (ii) *Computation Year* **shall mean each consecutive full twelve (12) calendar months subsequent to the Base Year through the end of the Term, as the same may be extended, except that the last Computation Year of the Term shall mean a partial calendar year equal to the remaining months of the**

Term for such last calendar year if this Lease does not expire on December 31.

(iii) *Tenant's Proportionate Share* means the ratio, expressed as a percentage, of the rentable square feet in the Premises, to the entire rentable area in the Building, which is _____ rentable square feet. Tenant's Proportionate Share as of the date of this Lease is ___%. The numerator of Tenant's Proportionate Share is subject to adjustment if the rentable square foot area of the Premises changes pursuant to the provisions of this Lease, and the denominator of Tenant's Proportionate Share is subject to adjustment if the rentable square foot area of the Building changes.

(iv) *Real Estate Taxes* shall mean all taxes, assessments, levies, and other charges, general and special, ordinary and extraordinary, foreseen and unforeseen, of any kind and nature whatsoever, which shall or may be during the Term assessed, levied, charged, confirmed, or imposed upon or become payable out of or become a lien on the Property, but shall not include any municipal, state or federal capital levy, estate, succession, inheritance, transfer, sales, use, or franchise taxes, or any income, profits, or revenue tax, assessment, or charge imposed upon the rent received as such by Landlord under this Lease; provided, however, that if at any time during the Term, the present method of real estate taxation or assessment shall be changed so that there shall be substituted for the whole or any part of such taxes, assessments, levies, impositions, or charges now or hereafter levied, assessed, or imposed on real estate and improvements, a capital tax or other tax imposed on the rents or income received by Landlord from the Property or the rents or income reserved herein, or any part thereof, then all such capital taxes or other taxes shall, to the extent that they are so substituted, be deemed to be included within the term "Real Estate Taxes." For the Base Year and each Computation Year if the Building is not at least 90% leased and occupied during the Base Year and each Computation Year, Real Estate Taxes shall be deemed to mean the Real Estate Taxes that are or would have been incurred during the Base Year or each Computation Year, as applicable, if the Building during the Base Year and such Computation Year was 90% leased and occupied and the Property was fully assessed.

(v) *Building Operating Expenses* means the total expenses incurred by Landlord for the operation, maintenance, and repair of the Property during any calendar year or portion thereof. For the Base Year only if the Building is not at least 90% leased and occupied during the Base Year, Building Operating Expenses shall be deemed to mean the total expenses incurred by Landlord for the operation, maintenance, and repair of the Property that would have been incurred during the Base Year if the Building was 90% leased and occupied. Building Operating Expenses shall include but not be limited to:

(A) janitorial services and supplies;

(B) maintenance and engineering services and supplies;

(C) fire and extended coverage, rental interruption, liability insurance, earthquake insurance, terrorism insurance, and such other insurance as is actually maintained in connection with Landlord or the Property;

(D) water, gas, and other fuels and other utilities;

(E) electricity used by Landlord in the operation and maintenance of the Property;

(F) salaries and wages of employees involved in the operation of the Property, together with administration expenses, which shall include property management fees and asset administration fees;

(G) expenses incurred in connection with providing security to the Property and emergency systems and systems for policing and protecting the Property;

(H) other expenses including capital expenditures incurred and paid to fulfill Landlord's obligations under this Lease, provided the cost of such capital expenditure, amortized over the useful life of such expenditure, shall not exceed the reduction in Building Operating Expenses as projected by Landlord's accountant for the relevant year of the amortized term as it relates to said capital expenditures;

(I) a reasonable reserve for the repair or replacement of capital improvements on the Property, and the depreciation actually claimed by Landlord for capital improvements on the Property;

(J) all costs and expenses incurred in complying with all laws, rules, and regulations affecting the Property, such costs to be amortized over the useful life of the equipment or improvements purchased or constructed as a result thereof as determined by Landlord's accountant; and

(K) all costs and expenses incurred in connection with any Real Estate Tax appeal affecting the Property.

Notwithstanding anything in this Lease to the contrary, the following expenses are excluded from Building Operating Expenses:

(i) expenses for painting, redecorating, or other work that Landlord performs for any other tenant of the Building;

(ii) expenses for repairs or other work occasioned by fire, windstorm, or other casualty to the extent such expenses are reimbursed by Landlord's insurer;

(iii) expenses incurred in leasing or procuring new tenants;

(iv) legal expenses incurred in enforcing the terms of any lease; and

(v) interest or amortization payments on a mortgage or loan and rental payments under any ground lease or master lease and all costs and expenses associated with any such mortgage, loan, ground lease, or master lease.

(b) In addition to the Annual Base Rent, for each Computation Year during the Term, Tenant shall pay Landlord the following sums (collectively, "Additional Rent"):

(i) Tenant's Proportionate Share of any increase in Real Estate Taxes over Real Estate Taxes for the Base Year (the "Tax Payment"). The Tax Payment shall be made by Tenant in accordance with the terms of Paragraphs 7(d) and 7(e) and shall be subject to adjustment as provided for in this Paragraph 7; and

(ii) Tenant's Proportionate Share of any increase in Building Operating Expenses over Building Operating Expenses for the Base Year (the "Operating Expense Payment"). The Operating Expense Payment shall be made by Tenant in accordance with the terms of Paragraphs 7(d) and 7(e) and shall be subject to adjustment as provided for in this Paragraph 7.

(c) Tenant shall pay to Landlord the Tax Payment and the Operating Expense Payment as provided herein.

(d) For each Computation Year, Tenant shall pay, at the time of payment of each monthly installment of Annual Base Rent, an amount equal to one-twelfth (1/12) of Landlord's reasonable estimate of the sum of the Operating Expense Payment and the Tax Payment to be due for the then current Computation Year, if any. Said monthly payments shall be an estimate of the Oper-

ating Expense Payment and the Tax Payment for the then current Computation Year and shall be subject to adjustment
based upon the final calculation of the Operating Expense Payment and the Tax Payment as provided for in this Paragraph 7.

(e) After the end of each Computation Year, Tenant shall make or
receive for any Computation Year, an Additional Rent payment
or an Additional Rent credit equal to any excess or deficiency
between the actual Additional Rent, if any, owed by Tenant for
the most recent Computation Year and the amounts paid by
Tenant as an estimate of the Operating Expense Payment and
the Tax Payment, if any, in accordance with Paragraph 7(d).
Tenant shall pay such Additional Rent or receive such credit
against future Additional Rent within fifteen (15) days following receipt of notice thereof and receipt of the statement
described in Paragraph 7(f).

(f) Within ninety (90) days after the end of the Base Year and the
end of each Computation Year, Landlord shall furnish to Tenant a written statement setting forth the Real Estate Taxes and
Building Operating Expenses for the Base Year or for the most
recently completed Computation Year, as the case may be, and
Tenant's Tax Payment and Operating Expense Payment.

(g) So long as Tenant has paid the Tax Payment and the Operating
Expense Payment in full and in a timely manner, within sixty
(60) days after receipt of any statement, Tenant shall have the
right, by notice to Landlord, to dispute the inclusion and
amounts of any item or items in any statement for the immediately preceding Computation Year or, with respect to the first
such statement, for the Base Year. In the event that Tenant disputes the inclusion or amounts of any item or items, and such
dispute is not settled by agreement between Landlord and Tenant within thirty (30) days after notice has been delivered to
Landlord, the dispute as to whether such item, items or
amounts have been properly included in any such statement
shall be determined by a firm of independent certified public
accountants (the "Accountants"), said firm to be mutually
acceptable to Landlord and Tenant. The Accountants, Landlord, and Tenant all shall be entitled to review all records relating to the disputed items, and the parties shall be granted a
hearing before the Accountants prior to the rendering of a
determination by the Accountants. The determination of any
such matter by the Accountants shall be final and binding upon
both Landlord and Tenant and the expenses involved in such

determination shall be borne by the party against whom the decision is rendered by the Accountants; provided, that if more than one item is disputed and the decision shall be against each party in respect of any item or items so disputed, the expenses shall be apportioned based on the weighted average dollar amounts allocated to such items. If, at the time of such disagreement, Landlord and Tenant have not agreed upon and selected the Accountants, Landlord and Tenant shall each select an Accountant and said Accountants shall select a Third Accountant. The Third Accountant shall act as the "Accountant" for purposes of this Section 7(g). If the Accountants selected by Landlord and Tenant cannot agree upon a Third Accountant within ten (10) days after being so selected, either Landlord or Tenant may request that the Accountant be appointed by an arbitrator in accordance with the provisions of Paragraph 59 of this Lease.

If a dispute by Tenant of the items in said statements is decided against Tenant, then Tenant shall, to the extent such item remains unpaid, promptly pay to Landlord the amount of such item.

To the extent that Tenant has made estimated payments to Landlord of Additional Rent in accordance with Paragraph 7(d) in excess of the actual Additional Rent, Tenant shall receive a credit against future Additional Rent in the amount of such overpayment of Additional Rent.

(h) Tenant's obligation with respect to the Operating Expense Payment and the Tax Payment shall survive the expiration or early termination of the Lease and all such payments shall be prorated to reflect the actual term of this Lease.

(i) Landlord's failure to render a statement with respect to increases in Building Operating Expenses or Real Estate Taxes for any Computation Year shall not prejudice Landlord's right to thereafter render a statement with respect thereto or with respect to any other Computation Year.

(j) Tenant shall have the right, not more often than once a year, to examine, to copy and to have an audit conducted of all books and records of Landlord as shall pertain to Building Operating Expenses and Real Estate Taxes. Such audit shall be conducted by an accounting/auditing firm retained by Tenant. All expenses of such audit shall be borne by Tenant unless such audit shall disclose an overstatement of Building Operating Expenses or Real Estate Taxes of five percent (5%) or more, in which case all expenses of such audit shall be borne by Landlord, and Tenant's Operating Expense Payment or Tax Payment shall be adjusted accordingly. In the event Landlord disputes the findings of said audit, and Landlord and Tenant are unable to reach an agreement with respect to any difference in such Building Operating Expenses or Real Estate Taxes, then Landlord and Tenant agree to submit the matter to the Accountants for resolution pursuant to the terms of Paragraph 7(g).

Additional Rent (Expense Stop)

RISK RATING: 4

A. DESCRIPTION AND SCOPE

The primary difference between this Paragraph and Typical Paragraph 7 (Alternative 1) is that this Paragraph incorporates the "Expense Stop" concept whereby Tenant pays its proportionate share of increases in Building Operating Expenses and Real Estate Taxes over a predetermined amount, rather than using the "Base Year" concept whereby Tenant pays its proportionate share of increases in Building Operating Expenses and Real Estate Taxes over said expenses for a Base Year. As an "Expense Stop" lease, this Lease (a) establishes a means by which Tenant pays its fair share, based upon the proportion of space it occupies in the Building, of increases in Real Estate Taxes and Building Operating Expenses over a predetermined expense stop amount; (b) defines certain items included within and certain items excluded from Real Estate Taxes and Building Operating Expenses; (c) requires Tenant to pay a monthly estimate of Additional Rent equal to 1/12 of Landlord's reasonable estimate of the sum of increases in Building Operating Expenses and Real Estate Taxes for the current year over the expense stop amount; (d) provides a reconciliation mechanism at the end of each Computation Year whereby Tenant receives a credit toward future Additional Rent for any excess or makes a payment for any deficiency in its payments of Additional Rent; and (e) provides Tenant with the right to verify and, if necessary, to dispute Landlord's statements of Real Estate Taxes and Building Operating Expenses for up to 60 days following the receipt of Landlord's statement for each Computation Year. Any such dispute of Landlord's statements of Real Estate Taxes or Building Operating Expenses will be resolved by an independent accounting firm if Landlord and Tenant cannot reconcile their differences.

Additional Rent is calculated by multiplying Tenant's Proportionate Share by increases in Building Operating Expenses and Real Estate Taxes over predetermined fixed amounts per rentable square foot. The Tax Payment and the Operating Expense Payment are payable in monthly installments based upon Landlord's reasonable estimate of the Tax Payment and the Operating Expense Payment. The Tax Payment and the Operating Expense Payment are subject to adjustment at the end of each Computation Year, based upon Landlord's actual increase in expenses for Real Estate Taxes and Building Operating Expenses over the estimated amounts paid by Tenant.

B. ANALYSIS

1. Landlord's Perspective

Generally, this paragraph protects Landlord from having to absorb any increases in the costs of Real Estate Taxes or any increases in the cost of the maintenance and operation of the Property in excess of predetermined amounts, which increases are passed through to Tenant on a prorated basis.

With respect to the definition of Tenant's Proportionate Share, Landlord may require that the denominator of the ratio be the "leased" area of the Building rather than the "rentable" area of the Building. Such a change shifts the risk of the fixed costs of vacant space in the Building to the tenants in the Building.

2. Tenant's Perspective

While imposing the obligation upon Tenant to pay its proportionate share of increases in Real Estate Taxes and Building Operating Expenses over the predetermined amounts and to make estimated payments of the increase in Building Operating Expenses based upon Landlord's reasonable estimate of said increase, this Paragraph also protects Tenant against having to pay more than its fair share of those expenses. This Paragraph permits Tenant to audit Landlord's statement of Real Estate Taxes and Building Operating Expenses and to obtain a credit for any overpayments. To the extent the audit indicates an overstatement of actual Real Estate Taxes or Building Operating Expenses in excess of 5%, Landlord will be liable for the cost of the audit. Tenant will likely want to negotiate this percentage to 2–3% rather than 5%.

Tenant may object to the inclusion of capital expenditures in the definition of Building Operating Expenses since capital enhancements to the Property will benefit the Landlord long after the expiration date of Tenant's Lease. Tenant will therefore argue that such capital costs are the sole responsibility of Landlord. Tenant may also object to capital expenditures incurred by Landlord in complying with laws and regulations since these capital improvements also add long-term value to the Building.

Subparagraph 7(a)(iv)(F) of the Typical Paragraph provides that property management fees and asset management fees may be included in Building Operating Expenses. Tenant may want to limit property management fees to a specified percentage of gross revenues based on market conditions in the area where the Property is located. Tenant may also object to asset management fees since it can be argued that such fees do not directly benefit the operation of the Property, but rather benefit only Landlord.

Tenant may object to the all-inclusive nature of the definition of Building Operating Expenses and request that only the items expressly set forth in Subparagraph 7(a)(iv) be included in Building Operating Expenses. Tenant may also object to the inclusion of depreciation in the definition of Building Operating Expenses since depreciation of the capital improvements is a tax benefit that accrues only to Landlord and actual depreciation of the Property does not generally occur.

Tenant may also request that any successful contest of Real Estate Taxes result in a proportionate refund to Tenant of the applicable Real Estate Tax Payment. Tenant may request that Landlord have an affirmative obligation to contest any unreasonable increase in Real Estate Taxes. The likelihood of success of this request generally depends upon the degree of leverage that Tenant has in the Lease transaction. Landlord will be concerned about losing control of the Real Estate Tax appeal procedure and the impact such an appeal may have on future valuation and assessment of the Building.

Finally, Tenant may request that Landlord's failure to provide the statement of Operating Expenses and Real Estate Taxes required under Paragraph 7(f) within 6–12 months after the end of a Computation Year will terminate Tenant's obligation to pay Additional Rent for that Computation Year. This would permit Tenant to close its books for the prior year and not have to be concerned about a substantial and unexpected Additional Rent bill in the later years of the Lease Term.

3. Lender's Perspective

Lender's primary concern is that Tenant be obligated to pay its share of increases in Real Estate Taxes and Operating Expenses so that cash flow designated for debt service will not be burdened with increases in Building Operating Expenses and Real Estate Taxes, and that any dispute between Landlord and Tenant relating to that obligation (i) can be resolved quickly, and (ii) will not in any case result in Tenant having the right to withhold payments of Additional Rent.

Lender wants to be able to determine a net effective rent during the term of its loan so that it can calculate the net cash flow available for debt service. Lender will subtract the amount of the Expense Stop from the Annual Base Rent in determining the net effective rent and thus the net cash flow available for debt service. Lender may also object to any rights of offset for any overpayments of Additional Rent. Rather such overpayment should be credited against the next due installment of Additional Rent.

C. COMPROMISES AND ALTERNATIVES

The following alternative methods of having Tenant contribute to the payment of Real Estate Taxes and Building Operating Expenses may be considered for any particular lease after having consulted with counsel: (a) a "net lease" approach, in which all expenses for Real Estate Taxes and Building Operating Expenses are passed through to Tenant as Additional Rent, as provided for in Alternative 3 of Paragraph Number 7; and (b) a "Base Year lease" approach, in which Tenant pays its proportionate share of increases in Real Estate Taxes and Building Operating Expenses over Landlord's expenses for the same in the Base Year, as provided for in Alternative 1 of Paragraph Number 7.

D. COMMENTS

The method of calculating and determining Real Estate Taxes and Building Operating Expenses is likely to be one of the most negotiated provisions of this Lease. A clear understanding of the ramifications of any changes is imperative.

E. TYPICAL PARAGRAPH

7.   Additional Rent (Expense Stop).
    (a) **For purposes of this Paragraph 7:**
        (i)   *Tenant's Proportionate Share* **means the ratio, expressed as a percentage, of the rentable square feet in the Premises, to the entire rentable area in the Building, which is _____ rentable square feet. Tenant's Proportionate Share as of the date of this Lease is ___%. The numerator of Tenant's Proportionate Share is subject to adjustment if the rentable square foot area of the Premises changes pursuant to the provisions of this Lease, and the denominator of Tenant's Proportionate Share is subject to adjustment if the rentable square foot area of the Building changes.**

(ii) *Computation Year* shall mean the first 12 full calendar months after the Commencement Date and each 12-month period thereafter.

(iii) *Real Estate Taxes* shall mean all taxes, assessments, levies, and other charges, general and special, ordinary and extra-ordinary, foreseen and unforeseen, of any kind and nature whatsoever, which shall or may be during the Term assessed, levied, charged, confirmed, or imposed upon or become payable out of or become a lien on the Property, but shall not include any municipal, state, or federal capital levy, estate, succession, inheritance, transfer, sales, use, or fran-chise taxes, or any income, profits, or revenue tax, assess-ment or charge imposed upon the rent received as such by Landlord under this Lease; provided, however, that if at any time during the Term, the present method of real estate taxation or assessment shall be so changed that there shall be substituted for the whole or any part of such taxes, assessments, levies, impositions, or charges now or here-after levied, assessed, or imposed on real estate and improve-ments, a capital tax or other tax imposed on the rents or income received by Landlord from the Property or the rents or income reserved herein, or any part thereof, then all such capital taxes or other taxes shall, to the extent that they are so substituted, be deemed to be included within the term "Real Estate Taxes."

(iv) *Building Operating Expenses* means the total expenses incurred by Landlord for the operation, maintenance and repair of the Property during any calendar year or portion thereof. Building Operating Expenses shall include but not be limited to:

(A) janitorial services and supplies;

(B) maintenance and engineering services and supplies;

(C) fire and extended coverage, rental interruption, liabil-ity insurance, earthquake insurance, terrorism insur-ance, and such other insurance as is actually main-tained by Landlord in connection with the Property;

(D) water, gas, and other fuels and other utilities;

(E) electricity used by Landlord in the operation and maintenance of the Property;

(F) salaries and wages of employees involved in the opera-tion of the Property, together with administration expenses which shall include property management fees and asset administration fees;

(G) expenses incurred in connection with providing security to the Property and emergency systems and systems for policing and protecting the Property;

(H) other expenses including capital expenditures incurred and paid to fulfill Landlord's obligations under this Lease provided the cost of such capital expenditure, amortized over the useful life of such expenditure, shall not exceed the reduction in Building Operating Expenses as projected by Landlord's accountant for the relevant year of the amortized term as it relates to said capital expenditures;

(I) a reasonable reserve for the repair or replacement of capital improvements on the Property, and the depreciation actually claimed by Landlord for capital improvements on the Property;

(J) all costs and expenses incurred in complying with all laws, rules, and regulations affecting the Property, such costs to be amortized over the useful life of the equipment or improvements purchased or constructed as a result thereof as determined by Landlord's accountant; and

(K) all costs and expenses incurred in connection with any Real Estate Tax appeal affecting the Property.

Notwithstanding anything in this Lease to the contrary, the following expenses are excluded from Building Operating Expenses:

(i) expenses for painting, redecorating, or other work that Landlord performs for any other tenant of the Building;

(ii) expenses for repairs or other work occasioned by fire, windstorm, or other casualty to the extent such expenses are reimbursed by Landlord's insurer;

(iii) expenses incurred in leasing or procuring new tenants;

(iv) legal expenses incurred in enforcing the terms of any lease; and

(v) interest or amortization payments on a mortgage or loan, and rental payments under any ground lease or master lease and all costs and expenses associated with any such mortgage, loan, ground lease, or master lease.

(b) In addition to the Annual Base Rent, for each Computation Year during the Term, Tenant shall pay Landlord the following sums (collectively, "Additional Rent"):

(i) Tenant's Proportionate Share of any increase in Real Estate Taxes (calculated on a per rentable square foot per annum basis) over $_____ per rentable square foot per annum (the "Tax Payment"). The Tax Payment shall be made by Tenant in accordance with the terms of Paragraphs 7(d) and 7(e) and shall be subject to adjustment as provided for in this Paragraph 7; and

(ii) Tenant's Proportionate Share of any increase in Building Operating Expenses (calculated on a per rentable square foot per annum basis) over $_____ per rentable square foot per annum (the "Operating Expense Payment"). The Operating Expense Payment shall be made by Tenant in accordance with the terms of Paragraphs 7(d) and 7(e) and shall be subject to adjustment as provided for in this Paragraph 7.

(c) Tenant shall pay to Landlord the Tax Payment and the Operating Expense Payment as provided herein.

(d) For each Computation Year, Tenant shall pay, at the time of payment of each monthly installment of Annual Base Rent, an amount equal to one-twelfth (1/12) of Landlord's reasonable estimate of the sum of the Operating Expense Payment and the Tax Payment to be due for the then current Computation Year, if any. Said monthly payments shall be an estimate of the Operating Expense Payment and the Tax Payment for the then current Computation Year and shall be subject to adjustment based upon the final calculation of the Operating Expense Payment and the Tax Payment as provided for in this Paragraph 7.

(e) After the end of each Computation Year, Tenant shall make or receive for any Computation Year, an Additional Rent payment or an Additional Rent credit equal to any excess or deficiency between the actual Additional Rent, if any, owed by Tenant for the most recent Computation Year and the amounts paid by Tenant as an estimate of the Operating Expense Payment and Tax Payment, if any, in accordance with Paragraph 7(d). Tenant shall pay such Additional Rent or receive such credit against future Additional Rent within fifteen (15) days following receipt of notice thereof and receipt of the statement described in Paragraph 7(f).

(f) Within ninety (90) days after the end of each Computation Year, Landlord shall furnish to Tenant a written statement setting forth the Real Estate Taxes and Building Operating Expenses for the most recently completed Computation Year and Tenant's Tax Payment and Operating Expense Payment.

(g) So long as Tenant has paid the Tax Payment and the Operating Expense Payment in full and in a timely manner, within sixty (60) days after receipt of any statement, Tenant shall have the right, by notice to Landlord, to dispute the inclusion and amounts of any item or items in any statement for the immediately preceding Computation Year or, with respect to the first such statement, for the Base Year. In the event that Tenant disputes the inclusion or amounts of any item or items, and such dispute is not settled by agreement between Landlord and Tenant within thirty (30) days after notice has been delivered to Landlord, the dispute as to whether such item, items, or amounts have been properly included in any such statement shall be determined by a firm of independent certified public accountants (the "Accountants"), said firm to be mutually acceptable to Landlord and Tenant. The Accountants, Landlord, and Tenant all shall be entitled to review all records relating to the disputed items, and the parties shall be granted a hearing before the Accountants prior to the rendering of a determination by the Accountants. The determination of any such matter by the Accountants shall be final and binding upon both Landlord and Tenant, and the expenses involved in such determination shall be borne by the party against whom the decision is rendered by the Accountants; provided, that if more than one item is disputed and the decision shall be against each party in respect of any item or items so disputed, the expenses shall be apportioned based upon the weighted average dollar amounts allocated to such items. If, at the time of such disagreement, Landlord and Tenant have not agreed upon and selected the Accountants, Landlord and Tenant shall each select an Accountant and said Accountants shall select a Third Accountant. The Third Accountant shall act as the "Accountant" for purposes of this Section 7(g). If the Accountants selected by Landlord and Tenant cannot agree upon a Third Accountant within ten (10) days after being so selected, either Landlord or Tenant may request that the Accountant be appointed by an arbitrator in accordance with the provisions of Paragraph 59 of this Lease.

If a dispute by Tenant of the items in said statements is decided against Tenant, then Tenant shall, to the extent such item remains unpaid, promptly pay to Landlord the amount of such item.

To the extent that Tenant has made estimated payments to Landlord of Additional Rent in accordance with Paragraph 7(d) in excess of the actual Additional Rent, Tenant shall receive a credit against future Additional Rent in the amount of such overpayment of Additional Rent.

(h) Tenant's obligation with respect to the Operating Expense Payment and the Tax Payment shall survive the expiration or early termination of the Lease, and all such payments shall be prorated to reflect the actual term of this Lease.

(i) Landlord's failure to render a statement with respect to increases in Building Operating Expenses or Real Estate Taxes for any Computation Year shall not prejudice Landlord's right to thereafter render a statement with respect thereto or with respect to any other Computation Year.

(j) Tenant shall have the right, not more often than once a year, to examine, to copy, and to have an audit conducted of all books and records of Landlord as shall pertain to Building Operating Expenses and Real Estate Taxes. Such audit shall be conducted by an accounting/auditing firm retained by Tenant. All expenses of such audit shall be borne by Tenant unless such audit shall disclose an overstatement of Building Operating Expenses or Real Estate Taxes of five percent (5%) or more, in which case all expenses of such audit shall be borne by Landlord, and Tenant's Operating Expense Payment or Tax Payment shall be adjusted accordingly. In the event Landlord disputes the findings of said audit, and Landlord and Tenant are unable to reach an agreement with respect to any difference in such Building Operating Expenses or Real Estate Taxes, then Landlord and Tenant agree to submit the matter to the Accountants for resolution pursuant to the terms of Paragraph 7(g).

Additional Rent
(Net Lease)

RISK RATING: 4

A. DESCRIPTION AND SCOPE

The primary difference between this Paragraph and Typical Paragraph 7 (Alternative 1) is that this Paragraph incorporates the "net lease" concept whereby Tenant pays its proportionate share of all Real Estate Taxes and Building Operating Expenses, rather than using the "Base Year" concept whereby tenant pays only its proportionate share of any *increases* in Real Estate Taxes and Building Operating Expenses over said expenses for a Base Year. As a "net lease," the Lease should (a) establish a means by which Tenant pays its fair share of Real Estate Taxes based upon the proportion of space it occupies in the Building; (b) defines certain items included within and certain items excluded from Real Estate Taxes and Building Operating Expenses; (c) require Tenant to pay a monthly estimate of Additional Rent based upon Landlord's reasonable estimate of the Real Estate Taxes and the Building Operating Expenses for the Partial Year and thereafter, based upon the Landlord's reasonable estimate of Real Estate Taxes and Building Operating Expenses; (d) provides a reconciliation mechanism at the end of each calendar year whereby Tenant receives a credit toward future Additional Rent for any excess or makes a payment for any deficiency in its payments of Additional Rent; and (e) provides Tenant with the right to verify and, if necessary, to dispute Landlord's statements of Real Estate Taxes and Building Operating Expenses for up to 60 days following the receipt of Landlord's statement for each calendar year. Any such dispute of Landlord's statements of Real Estate Taxes or Building Operating Expenses will be resolved by an independent accounting firm if Landlord and Tenant cannot reconcile their differences.

Additional Rent is calculated by multiplying Tenant's Proportionate Share by Building Operating Expenses and Real Estate Taxes for the Building. Additional Rent is payable in monthly installments. Tenant must pay a monthly estimate of Additional Rent equal to 1/12 of Landlord's reasonable estimate of the sum of the Tax Payment and the Operating Expense Payment for the current year. Additional Rent is subject to adjustment at the end of each calendar year, based upon Landlord's actual expenses for Building Operating Expenses and Real Estate Taxes in the prior year.

B.   ANALYSIS

1.   Landlord's Perspective

Generally, this paragraph protects Landlord from having to absorb any of the costs of Real Estate Taxes or of the maintenance and operation of the Building and the Premises, which costs are passed through to Tenant on a prorated basis.

With respect to payments of Tenant's Proportionate Share of Building Operating Expenses, Landlord may desire that any free rent period not be applicable to such Additional Rent payments and therefore may require that Tenant begin paying such installments on the Commencement Date rather than on the Rent Commencement Date.

With respect to the definition of Tenant's Proportionate Share, Landlord may require that the denominator of the ratio be the "leased" area of the Building rather than the "rentable" area of the Building. Such a change shifts the risk of the fixed costs of vacant space in the Building to the tenants in the Building.

With respect to Paragraph 7(j) and Tenant's right to audit Landlord's books and records relating to Building Operating Expenses and Real Estate Taxes, a recent trend has been for Tenants to retain auditors who specialize solely in these types of audits and are compensated on a contingent fee basis only. The fee to these auditors is a percentage of any refund due Tenant or reduction in Additional Rent that results from such audit. Many Landlords now include a provision in the Lease that prohibits Tenant's use of such contingent fee auditors.

2.   Tenant's Perspective

While imposing the obligation upon Tenant of paying its proportionate share of Real Estate Taxes and Building Operating Expenses, this Paragraph also protects Tenant against having to pay more than its fair share of those expenses. This Paragraph permits Tenant to audit Landlord's statement of Real Estate Taxes and Building Operating Expenses and to obtain a credit for any overpayments. To the extent the audit indicates an over-statement of actual Real Estate Taxes or Building Operating Expenses in excess of 5%, Landlord will be liable for the cost of the audit. Tenant will likely want to negotiate this percentage to 2–3% rather than 5%.

Tenant may object to the inclusion of capital expenditures in the definition of Building Operating Expenses since capital enhancements to the Property will benefit the Landlord long after the expiration date of Tenant's Lease. Tenant will therefore argue that such capital costs are the sole responsibility of Landlord. Tenant may also object to capital expenditures incurred by Landlord in complying with laws and regulations since these capital improvements also add long-term value to the Building.

Subparagraph 7(a)(iv)(F) of the Typical Paragraph provides that property management fees and asset management fees may be included in Building Operating Expenses. Tenant may want to limit property management fees to a specified percentage of gross revenues based on market conditions in the area where the Property is located. Tenant may also object to asset management fees since it can be argued that such fees do not directly benefit the operation of the Property, but rather benefit only Landlord.

Tenant may object to the all-inclusive nature of the definition of Building Operating Expenses and request that only the items expressly set forth in Subparagraph 7(a)(iv) be included in Building Operating Expenses. Tenant may also object to the inclusion of depreciation in the definition of Building Operating Expenses since depreciation of the capital improvements is a tax benefit that accrues only to Landlord, and actual depreciation of the Property does not generally occur.

Tenant may also request that any successful contest of Real Estate Taxes result in a proportionate refund to Tenant of the applicable Real Estate Tax Payment. Tenant may request that Landlord have an affirmative obligation to contest any unreasonable increase in Real Estate Taxes. The likelihood of success of this request generally depends upon the degree of leverage that Tenant has in the Lease transaction. Landlord will be concerned about losing control of the Real Estate Tax appeal procedure and the impact such an appeal may have on future valuation and assessment of the Building.

Finally, Tenant may request that Landlord's failure to provide the statement of Operating Expenses and Real Estate Taxes required under Paragraph 7(f) within 6–12 months after the end of a Computation Year will terminate Tenant's obligation to pay Additional Rent for that calendar year. This would permit Tenant to close its books for the prior year and not have to be concerned about a substantial and unexpected Additional Rent bill in the later years of the Lease Term.

3.   Lender's Perspective

Lender's primary concern is that Tenant be obligated to pay its share of increases in Real Estate Taxes and Operating Expenses so that cash flow designated for debt service will not be burdened with increases in Building Operating Expenses and Real Estate Taxes, and that any dispute between Landlord and Tenant relating to that obligation (i) can be resolved quickly; and (ii) will not in any case result in Tenant having the right to withhold payments of Additional Rent.

Lender wants to be able to determine a net effective rent during the term of its loan so that it can calculate the net cash flow available for debt service. Lender may also object to any rights of offset for any overpayments of Additional Rent. Rather such overpayment should be credited against the next due installment of Additional Rent.

C.   COMPROMISES AND ALTERNATIVES

The following alternative methods of having Tenant contribute to the payment of Real Estate Taxes and Building Operating Expenses may also be used: (a) a "Base Year" approach, in which expenses for Real Estate Taxes and Building Operating Expenses are included as an element of Annual Base Rent for the first year of Tenant's occupancy, with Tenant paying its proportionate share of increases in those expenses as Additional Rent, as provided in Alternative 1 of Paragraph Number 7; and (b) an "Expense Stop" approach, in which a specified amount of Building Operating Expenses and Real Estate Taxes is included in the Annual Base Rent on the Commencement Date, with Tenant paying Tenant's Proportionate Share of increases over that fixed amount anytime after the Commencement Date that such Expense Stop is exceeded, as provided for in Alternative 2 of Paragraph Number 7.

D.   COMMENTS

The method of calculating and determining Real Estate Taxes and Building Operating Expenses is likely to be one of the most negotiated provisions of this Lease. A clear understanding of the ramifications of any changes is imperative.

E.   TYPICAL PARAGRAPH

7.   **Additional Rent (Net Lease).**
    (a) **For purposes of this Paragraph 7:**

(i) *Partial Year* shall mean that portion of the Term commencing on the Commencement Date and ending on December 31 of the calendar year in which the Commencement Date occurs.

(ii) *Tenant's Proportionate Share* means the ratio, expressed as a percentage, of the rentable square feet in the Premises, to the entire rentable area in the Building, which is _____ rentable square feet. Tenant's Proportionate Share as of the date of this Lease is ___%. The numerator of Tenant's Proportionate Share is subject to adjustment if the rentable square foot area of the Premises changes pursuant to the provisions of this Lease, and the denominator of Tenant's Proportionate Share is subject to adjustment if the rentable square foot area of the Building changes.

(iii) *Real Estate Taxes* shall mean all taxes, assessments, levies and other charges, general and special, ordinary and extraordinary, foreseen and unforeseen, of any kind and nature whatsoever, which shall or may be during the Term assessed, levied, charged, confirmed, or imposed upon or become payable out of or become a lien on the Property, but shall not include any municipal, state, or federal capital levy, estate, succession, inheritance, transfer, sales, use, or franchise taxes, or any income, profits, or revenue tax, assessment or charge imposed upon the rent received as such by Landlord under this Lease; provided, however, that if at any time during the Term, the present method of real estate taxation or assessment shall be so changed that there shall be substituted for the whole or any part of such taxes, assessments, levies, impositions, or charges, now or hereafter levied, assessed, or imposed on real estate and improvements, a capital tax or other tax imposed on the rents or income received by Landlord from the Property or the rents or income reserved herein, or any part thereof, then all such capital taxes or other taxes shall, to the extent that they are so substituted, be deemed to be included within the term "Real Estate Taxes."

(iv) *Building Operating Expenses* means the total expenses incurred by Landlord for the operation, maintenance and repair of the Property during any calendar year or portion thereof. Building Operating Expenses shall include but not be limited to:

(A) janitorial services and supplies;

(B) maintenance and engineering services and supplies;

(C) fire and extended coverage, rental interruption, liability insurance, earthquake insurance, terrorism insurance, and such other insurance as is actually maintained in connection with Landlord or the Property;

(D) water, gas, and other fuels and other utilities;

(E) electricity used by Landlord in the operation and maintenance of the Property;

(F) salaries and wages of employees involved in the operation of the Property, together with administration expenses which shall include property management fees and asset administration fees;

(G) expenses incurred in connection with providing security to the Property and emergency systems and systems for policing and protecting the Property;

(H) other expenses including capital expenditures incurred and paid to fulfill Landlord's obligations under this Lease provided the cost of such capital expenditure, amortized over the useful life of such expenditure, shall not exceed the reduction in Building Operating Expenses as projected by Landlord's accountant for the relevant year of the amortized term as it relates to said capital expenditures;

(I) a reasonable reserve for the repair or replacement of capital improvements on the Property, and the depreciation actually claimed by Landlord for capital improvements on the Property;

(J) all costs and expenses incurred in complying with all laws, rules, and regulations affecting the Property, such costs to be amortized over the useful life of the equipment or improvements purchased or constructed as a result thereof as determined by Landlord's accountant; and

(K) all costs and expenses incurred in connection with any Real Estate Tax appeal affecting the Property.

Notwithstanding anything in this Lease to the contrary, the following expenses are excluded from Building Operating Expenses:

(i) expenses for painting, redecorating or other work that Landlord performs for any other tenant of the Building;

(ii) expenses for repairs or other work occasioned by fire, windstorm or other casualty to the extent such expenses are reimbursed by Landlord's insurer.

(iii) expenses incurred in leasing or procuring new tenants;

(iv) legal expenses incurred in enforcing the terms of any lease; and

(v) interest or amortization payments on a mortgage or loan and rental payments under any ground lease or master lease, and all costs and expenses associated with any such mortgage, loan, ground lease, or master lease.

(b) In addition to the Annual Base Rent set forth in Paragraph 6, Tenant shall pay Landlord the following sums (collectively, "Additional Rent"):

(i) Tenant's Proportionate Share of Real Estate Taxes (the "Tax Payment"). The Tax Payment shall be made by Tenant in accordance with the terms of Paragraphs 7(d) and 7(e) and shall be subject to adjustment as provided for in this Paragraph 7; and

(ii) Tenant's Proportionate Share of Building Operating Expenses (the "Operating Expense Payment"). The Operating Expense Payment shall be made by Tenant in accordance with the terms of Paragraphs 7(d) and 7(e) and shall be subject to adjustment as provided for in this Paragraph 7.

(c) Any payments by Tenant of the Tax Payment and the Operating Expense Payment during the Partial Year shall be prorated to reflect only the actual period after the Commencement Date that such Real Estate Taxes and Building Operating Expenses accrue.

(d) Beginning on the Commencement Date, for each calendar month during the Term, Tenant shall pay, together with the monthly installment of Annual Base Rent, an amount equal to one-twelfth (1/12) of the sum of the annual estimated Operating Expense Payment and Tax Payment for the Partial Year or calendar year in which such payment occurs. Said payments shall be reasonably estimated by Landlord and shall be subject to adjustment based upon the final calculation of the Operating Expense Payment and Tax Payment, as provided for in this Paragraph 7.

(e) Tenant shall make or receive for the Partial Year and for each calendar year thereafter, an Additional Rent payment or a credit equal to any excess or deficiency between the actual Additional Rent owed by Tenant for said period and the estimated Operating Expense Payments and Tax Payments made by Tenant in accordance with this Paragraph 7 for the Partial Year or the most recent calendar year, as the case may be. Tenant shall pay such Additional Rent or receive such credit against future

Additional Rent within fifteen (15) days following receipt of notice thereof and receipt of the statement described in Paragraph 7(f).

(f) Within ninety (90) days after the end of the Partial Year and the end of each calendar year during the Term, Landlord shall furnish to Tenant a written statement setting forth the Real Estate Taxes and Building Operating Expenses for the Partial Year or for the most recently completed calendar year, as the case may be, and Tenant's Tax Payment and the Operating Expense Payment.

(g) So long as Tenant has paid the Tax Payment and the Operating Expense Payment in full and in a timely manner, within sixty (60) days after receipt of any statement, Tenant shall have the right, by notice to Landlord, to dispute the inclusion and amounts of any item or items in any statement for the immediately preceding calendar year. In the event that Tenant disputes the inclusion or amounts of any item or items, and such dispute is not settled by agreement between Landlord and Tenant within thirty (30) days after notice has been delivered to Landlord, the dispute as to whether such item, items, or amounts have been properly included in any such statement shall be determined by a firm of independent certified public accountants (the "Accountants"), said firm to be mutually acceptable to Landlord and Tenant. The Accountants, Landlord, and Tenant all shall be entitled to review all records relating to the disputed items, and the parties shall be granted a hearing before the Accountants prior to the rendering of a determination by the Accountants. The determination of any such matter by the Accountants shall be final and binding upon both Landlord and Tenant, and the expenses involved in such determination shall be borne by the party against whom the decision is rendered by the Accountants; provided, that if more than one item is disputed and the decision shall be against each party in respect of any item or items so disputed, the expenses shall be apportioned based on the weighted average dollar amounts allocated to such items. If, at the time of such disagreement, Landlord and Tenant have not agreed upon and selected the Accountants, Landlord and Tenant shall each select an Accountant and said Accountants shall select a Third Accountant. The Third Accountant shall act as the "Accountant" for purposes of this Section 7(g). If the Accountants selected by Landlord and Tenant cannot agree upon a Third Accountant within ten (10) days after being so selected, either Landlord or Tenant may request that the Accountant be appointed by an arbitrator in accordance with the provisions of Paragraph 59 of this Lease.

If a dispute by Tenant of the items in said statements is decided against Tenant, then Tenant shall, to the extent such item remains unpaid, promptly pay to Landlord the amount of such item.

To the extent that Tenant has made estimated payments to Landlord of Additional Rent in accordance with Paragraph 7(d) in excess of the actual Additional Rent, Tenant shall receive a credit against future Additional Rent in the amount of such overpayment of Additional Rent.

(h) Tenant's obligation with respect to the Operating Expense Payment and the Tax Payment shall survive the expiration or early termination of the Lease and all such payments shall be pro-rated to reflect the actual term of this Lease.

(i) Landlord's failure to render a statement with respect to increases in Building Operating Expenses or Real Estate Taxes for the Partial Year or for any calendar year shall not prejudice Landlord's right to thereafter render a statement with respect thereto or with respect to any subsequent calendar year.

(j) Tenant shall have the right, not more often than once a year, to examine, to copy, and to have an audit conducted of all books and records of Landlord as shall pertain to Building Operating Expenses and Real Estate Taxes. Such audit shall be conducted by an accounting/auditing firm retained by Tenant. All expenses of such audit shall be borne by Tenant unless such audit shall disclose an overstatement of Building Operating Expenses or Real Estate Taxes of five percent (5%) or more, in which case all expenses of such audit shall be borne by Landlord, and Tenant's Operating Expense Payment or the Tax Payment shall be adjusted accordingly. In the event Landlord disputes the findings of said audit, and Landlord and Tenant are unable to reach an agreement with respect to any difference in such Building Operating Expenses or Real Estate Taxes, then Landlord and Tenant agree to submit the matter to the Accountants for resolution pursuant to the terms of Paragraph 7(g).

Gross-Up of Building Operating Expenses

RISK RATING: 3

A. DESCRIPTION AND SCOPE

This Paragraph establishes an assumed level of Building Operating Expenses for the Base Year and each Computation Year that will be used for the term of the Lease to calculate Tenant's Proportionate Share of Building Operating Expenses in excess of the Base Year expenses. The necessity of this Paragraph arises from the fluctuation of the expenses that Landlord will incur as the Building is leased up and Landlord's variable expenses increase due to the increased occupancy rate in the Building. The intent of this Paragraph is to create an expense level in the Base Year that equitably accounts for such increases in Building Operating Expenses. Generally, only variable expenses that will change as occupancy in the Building changes should be grossed-up. For example, electricity expenses and cleaning expenses would usually be grossed-up, while insurance and landscaping expenses would not be grossed-up.

B. ANALYSIS

1. Landlord's Perspective

This gross-up Paragraph is needed only if a similar paragraph, such as Additional Rent (Base Year) Paragraph 7(a)(v), on gross-up is not included in the Additional Rent Paragraph.

Since this gross-up Paragraph benefits Tenant during the Base Year and the Landlord during the Computation Years, some Landlord forms of Leases will not include the Base Year gross-up provisions of this Paragraph.

If the "gross-up" paragraph includes only a Base Year gross-up and not a Computation Year gross-up, Landlord should be concerned with establishing a gross-up factor for the Base Year that does not exceed the likely expense level and occupancy level for the Building. For example, if the assumed occupancy level is 95% and Landlord only achieves a 70% occupancy for the entire term of a five-year lease, Landlord may never be entitled to collect any portion of actual increases in Building Operating Expenses from Tenant. Many tenants will insist upon grossing-up Base Year Building Operating Expenses to an assumed occupancy level of 100%. Landlord may want to resist this change if it gives Tenant an artificially high Base Year calculation of Building Operating Expenses.

2.   Tenant's Perspective

A Tenant in a multitenant building should always request a Base Year gross-up provision in a Lease that uses a Base Year.

Most Tenants will negotiate for the highest possible Base Year gross-up percentage. Tenants may also resist the inclusion of a Computation Year gross-up percentage or any alternative provision that would permit the Base Year level of Building Operating Expenses to be reduced if occupancy levels in the Building fall. Tenants will also likely request that the assumed occupancy level for the Base Year be 100%. This assumption, if agreed to by Landlord, may give Tenant a benefit if normal vacancy rates rise in the future.

3.   Lender's Perspective

A mortgage Lender's primary concern is that Landlord not risk being in a position where Tenant is not required to pay its proportionate share of real increases in Building Operating Expenses. Lenders will look favorably upon a gross-up provision if both the Base Year and each Computation Year are grossed up or if the provision permits Landlord to decrease the Base Year Building Operating Expenses if occupancy levels in the Building fall. Lender will not want Landlord/borrower to absorb Building Operating Expense increases that cannot be passed on to Tenant due to grossing up the Base Year.

C.   COMPROMISES AND ALTERNATIVES

The assumed level of occupancy during the Base Year and each Computation Year is likely to be the point of negotiation with most Tenants. 90% to 100% is generally the negotiating range for most compromises.

D. COMMENTS

In smaller buildings with smaller tenants, Landlord may be able to use a form Lease that does not provide for grossing-up Building Operating Expenses for the Base Year. In larger Leases, this Paragraph is likely to be one of the most heavily negotiated sections of the Lease.

E. TYPICAL PARAGRAPH

8.   Gross-Up of Building Operating Expenses. If the Building is not at least [90%] leased and occupied during the Base Year, the Building Operating Expenses for the Base Year shall be adjusted to project the Building Operating Expenses as if the Building were [90%] leased and occupied. If, during any Computation Year, the Building shall be less than [90%] leased and occupied, the Building Operating Expenses for that Computation Year shall be deemed to be increased to [90%].

Adjustments to Rent

RISK RATING: 4

A. DESCRIPTION AND SCOPE

In order to keep up with inflation and expenses, and maintain a steady return on investment, the market will permit landlords in some regions of the United States (including Washington, D.C.) to periodically increase rents as the CPI (Consumer Price Index) increases. To the extent that the fixed rent does not increase, particularly over a Lease term in excess of five years, Landlord's income and Lender's security may be eroded by inflation. Common methods of providing for increased rent include:

(1) Step-up Rent. The fixed rent is graduated periodically over the lease term in predetermined amounts known as "bumps" or "steps." Leases with terms greater than five years may impose rent bumps, in addition to a CPI escalation.

(2) Indexed Rent. The fixed rent fluctuates (or only increases) as a function of an external standard or index, usually an economic indicator. The most commonly used index is the Consumer Price Index (often called the CPI or the cost-of-living index), published by the Bureau of Labor Statistics of the U.S. Department of Labor. While the CPI does not necessarily reflect changes in real property values, it is commonly used because it is widely published and easy to administer. CPI rent adjustments were incorporated in many commercial office leases during the years of high inflation in the late 1970s. The CPI was established during World War I to measure cost-of-living increases for wage earners in major industrial areas. This wage earner index, the Urban Wage Earners and Clerical Workers Index, commonly designated CPI-W, currently represents the buying habits of about a third of the population. Broader use

of the cost-of-living index brought about the introduction in 1978 of the All Urban Consumers Index, known as the CPI-U. The CPI-U currently reflects the spending patterns of about 80 percent of the population.

Both the CPI-W and the CPI-U are published monthly for five major metropolitan areas and four regions, known collectively as the U.S. City Average. The standard reference base period for the two indices was updated in 1988 from 1967 to the 1982 through 1984 average, denominated as "1982 − 84 = 100." Until such time as the indices are revised again, the 1982 − 84 = 100 reference base should be used.

Another method of increasing rents is known as the porters' wage escalation, named that because it raises rents based on increase in a class of building workers' wages. Rent increases tied to the porters' wage escalation are used in New York City.

Usually, porters' wage escalation requires an increase of one cent, or one and one-half cents, per square foot for each one-cent increase in the porters' wage.

(3) Market Rent Adjustment. The fixed rent is redetermined periodically by a broker or appraiser during the lease term based on market rents for similar properties at the time of the adjustment. The method of determining the market rent and instructions to a broker or appraiser should be carefully examined. This method may or may not accurately reflect cost increases due to inflation. For example, there could be external factors relating to supply and demand that cause rent adjustments that have nothing at all to do with inflation. Also, this method of adjusting rent is generally more time-consuming and costly than using an index adjustment.

B. ANALYSIS

1. Landlord's Perspective

Landlord is interested in making sure that the rent is adjusted upward sufficiently to cover any inflation; either CPI indexing or step-ups can accomplish this, but CPI may be a more accurate measure; it may be that Landlord thinks rental rates are on the rise and will want step ups in rent to account for increases in the fair market rental rates over time. The longer the lease term, the more important this rental provision becomes. Landlord will want to provide only for adjustments to increase rent, not decrease rent; the CPI provision will usually be set up so that the initial rent payable is a floor, regardless of any decreases based on CPI. Any decrease in rent would reduce cash flow and would be resisted by both Landlord and Lender.

Paragraph 9(c) may be resisted by Landlord, since a third party is needed to determine the rent and additional costs will be incurred for lawyers and arbitrators.

2.   Tenant's Perspective

Tenant should accept a CPI rent increase clause only in those markets where the majority of Landlords are quoting rents on this basis.

Tenant would prefer a fixed rent for the entire term of the Lease because, generally, fluctuations in the cost of living and inflation will cause rental values to creep up. If Tenant thinks the CPI will increase dramatically or if the CPI index is unstable and unpredictable, Tenant may request a cap on the annual amount of any CPI increase or may request that the Annual Base Rent be increased by a fixed percentage (e.g., 30%) of the amount of the CPI increase, or Tenant may prefer a step-up provision for its certainty and because it can be negotiated ahead of time and thus planned for. Tenant would like a floorless CPI provision, which would account for decreases as well as increases. Tenant may feel more comfortable with a shorter term in an unstable market so as to avoid wide rent fluctuations.

3.   Lender's Perspective

Lender's perspective is generally similar to Landlord's, in that Lender will want to make sure that its security is protected against inflation. If the interest rate Lender charges is variable and tied to an index, the Annual Base Rent increase may be similarly tied to the same index to permit Landlord to pass along to the Tenants Landlord's increase in debt service costs. Usually, Lender will prefer longer-term leases, at least as long as the term of its mortgage, and will want to make sure that the rent payable at the end of the term is enough for Landlord to cover monthly debt service payments by at least 1.2 times.

C.   COMPROMISES AND ALTERNATIVES

The parties have a choice among a fixed step-up in rent, a CPI, or other index-based adjustment or setting a market-based rent. If the parties agree on CPI, there are two methods generally used for increasing rent according to the CPI: The first is the prior-year method, so called because it increases rent annually by an agreed-upon percentage of the increase in the CPI over the previous year. The formula for the prior-year method is as follows:

New Monthly Rent =

$$\text{Monthly Rent in Prior Year} \times \frac{Current\ CPI - Prior\ Year\ CPI}{Prior\ Year\ CPI} \times \underline{}\%$$

The second method for increasing rent according to the CPI is the base-year method, so called because it increases rent annually by an agreed-upon percentage of the total increase in the CPI since the Lease commencement date. The formula for base-year method is as follows:

New Monthly Rent =

$$\text{Original Monthly Rent} \times \frac{Current\ CPI - Base\ Year\ CPI}{Base\ Year\ CPI} \times \underline{}\%$$

Arithmetically, the prior-year and base-year methods of calculating increases yield the same results if Tenant pays 0 percent or 100 percent of the CPI increase. Otherwise, for percentages in between 0 percent and 100 percent peaking at about 50 percent, the prior-year method imposes lesser increases than the base-year method. The differential is relatively modest during the early years of the Lease Term, but becomes more significant thereafter. If Landlord refuses to alter the formula in the form Lease for administrative reasons of Lease management, Tenant can calculate the present value of the projected difference over the Lease term, and request that Landlord offer that amount to Tenant in another form, such as an increase in the tenant improvement allowance.

If Tenant is faced with a Lease imposing both CPI and fixed-dollar increases, Tenant may wish to either ask to eliminate the CPI escalation in years with bumps on the ground that both increases in the same year are excessive, or, if Tenant is unable to eliminate the CPI escalation in a year with a bump, Tenant may seek to have the escalation calculated before the addition of the bump. Note, however, that under the base-year method, total rent, including the bump, will increase the following year by the aggregate increase in the CPI since Lease commencement. In this way, Landlord is able to utilize an entire Lease Term of escalation to increase a rent bump only a year old. Tenant may argue that this results in an unduly high rent increase.

Two methods are proposed for modifying this result. First, in the year following the bump, the CPI base could be revised so that it refers to the reference period immediately preceding the bump year, not the corresponding period at the beginning of the Lease. Alternatively, the year after the bump is imposed, a separate CPI reference period can be used to escalate the bump. The result would then be added to the original base rent, as escalated by the base year method. Total escalated rent under this method would equal the sum of the separately escalated bump and base rent. Using either of these methods permits the bump to remain at the agreed amount, but escalates the bump based upon increases in the CPI since the bump year, not since inception of the Lease.

D. COMMENTS

Language referring to CPI increases should be as specific as possible. A clause that states, "base rent is to be increased by 30 percent of the increase in CPI," should be changed to read, "base rent is to be increased annually by 30 percent of the increase in the CPI from the CPI for the last reference period prior to the Lease Commencement Date." The Lease should address the issue of any "caps" or "floors" on escalations, and whether the excess over a limit on rent increases allowable in any one year will carry forward. In some markets a CPI increase is used in lieu of Building Operating Expense pass-throughs.

Assuming an increase in base rent is imposed separately, and in addition to an increase in operating expenses, then Tenant may argue that the base rent should go up by no more than a fraction of the total annual CPI increase, say 25% or 30% since the purpose of the increase is to preserve Landlord's equity and not to provide a windfall to Landlord.

The CPI clause must specify when the first rent increase and subsequent increases will take place, whether on a calendar basis or based on Landlord's fiscal year.

E. TYPICAL PARAGRAPH

9.   **Adjustments to Rent.**
   (a) **As provided for below, the Monthly Rent (as hereinafter defined) shall be adjusted on each May 1 during the Term, commencing with the Initial CPI Escalation Date (as hereinafter defined), to reflect any increase during the prior calendar year in the index known as "United States Bureau of Labor Statistics, Consumer Price Index for Urban Wage Earners and Clerical Workers," for Washington, D.C.-MD-VA (1982–84 = 100) (hereinafter referred to as the "Index"). Said adjustment shall be hereinafter referred to as "CPI Escalation." If the Index is changed so that a base year other than 1982–1984 is used, the Index used herein shall be converted in accordance with the conversion factor published by the Bureau of Labor Statistics.**
   (b) **The "Monthly Rent" shall initially mean and be equal to the Annual Base Rent specified herein, divided by 12. Beginning on each June 1 after the Commencement Date, Monthly Rent shall mean and be equal to Monthly Rent for the immediately**

preceding April (as previously adjusted by the CPI escalation) multiplied by the CPI Fraction (as defined herein). The "CPI Fraction" shall be a fraction (A) whose numerator is the difference between (x) the first published monthly Index for the calendar year for which the adjustment to Monthly Rent is being made, less (y) the first published monthly index for the immediately preceding calendar year; and (B) whose denominator is the aforesaid first published monthly Index for the immediately preceding calendar year. The adjusted Monthly Rent shall remain in effect until the next succeeding first day of June, when a new adjusted Monthly Rent fixed pursuant to this section becomes effective. In no event shall the amount of Monthly Rent as adjusted pursuant to this section be less than the amount of Monthly Rent in effect for the immediately preceding month of April.

(c) If the Index is discontinued with no successor or comparable successor Index, the parties shall attempt to agree upon a substitute formula, but if the parties are unable to agree upon a substitute formula, then the matter shall be determined by arbitration in accordance with the terms of this Lease.

Quiet Enjoyment

RISK RATING: 2

A. DESCRIPTION AND SCOPE

This Paragraph sets out Landlord's covenant that so long as Tenant is not in default under its Lease, Tenant is entitled to uninterrupted use of the Premises during the Term.

B. ANALYSIS

1. Landlord's Perspective

The Paragraph establishes the obligation of Landlord to provide Tenant with quiet enjoyment of the Premises. Contrary to popular belief, that Paragraph has nothing to do with the level of noise that may be generated by Tenant's neighbors in the Building. Rather "quiet enjoyment" refers to quality of Landlord title to the Premises and Building. In this Paragraph Landlord is covenanting that Landlord has good title to the Building and Premises and that no other person or entity has any interest in the Building or Premises that could interfere or interrupt Tenant's use of the Building or Premises.

2. Tenant's Perspective

The Paragraph protects against Tenant having to enforce its rights under the Lease against third parties claiming an interest in or legal title to the Premises or Building. Tenant may also request that this Paragraph be modified to also require Landlord to "maintain the Building in a first-class condition." This additional covenant would protect Tenant against Landlord permitting the character of the Building to deteriorate, and may serve as an important legal protection to Tenants claiming untenantability of premises.

3. Lender's Perspective

Lender will want assurances that Landlord has good and marketable title to the Building and Premises. In addition, Lender will likely favor a "first-class" Building covenant. Lender is concerned that its collateral, the Building, is maintained by Landlord in accordance with an objective standard. This will be one of the few instances in the Lease where interests of Lender and Tenant are aligned.

C. COMPROMISES AND ALTERNATIVES

In those situations where Landlord desires narrower definition of a "first-class office building," a reference could be made to particular buildings in the geographic area where the Premises are located, or a general reference to similar buildings in the area where the Premises are located could be added. In addition, there may be situations where Landlord or Tenant will lease space in a Building other than a "first-class" Building; in those situations, a different standard will be appropriate.

D. COMMENTS

Generally, this Paragraph should not be controversial.

E. TYPICAL PARAGRAPH

10. Quiet Enjoyment. Subject to the terms and conditions of this Lease, so long as Tenant is not in default under this Lease, Landlord covenants and agrees that Tenant is entitled to quiet enjoyment of the Premises during the Term.

PARAGRAPH **11**

Assignment or Sublease

RISK RATING: 4

A. DESCRIPTION AND SCOPE

This Paragraph prevents Tenant from assigning the Lease or subletting the Premises without Landlord's prior written consent, unless the assignee or subtenant is an affiliate of Tenant, in which case Landlord's consent is not required. This Paragraph states very specific criteria that Tenant must satisfy in order to obtain Landlord's consent. This Paragraph also gives Landlord the option of taking back the space Tenant proposes to assign or sublet, thus relieving the Tenant of its obligations with respect to the space and permitting Landlord to re-lease the space to a third party. In the event Landlord consents to the assignment or sublease, or does not respond to Tenant's offer to reconvey the space to be assigned or sublet, this Paragraph provides that Tenant shall have the right to enter into a sublease or assignment.

B. ANALYSIS

1. Landlord's Perspective

Generally, any right to assign or sublet favors Tenant and will thus diminish Landlord's rights to the Premises. From Landlord's point of view, the most favorable provision of the Typical Paragraph is the first sentence of Paragraph 11(a)(i), and Landlord would prefer that Paragraph 11(a) begin and end with the first sentence. However, many Tenants will request that Landlord not unreasonably withhold consent to assignment or subletting, and in such case the remainder of Paragraph 11(a)(i) is preferable to a clause that simply states that "Landlord will not unreasonably withhold consent to any assignment or subletting."

In some states, the courts will impose upon Landlord a "commercially reasonable" standard even though this standard is not so stated in the Lease. In such situations, it is preferable to Landlord to define, as in the case of the Typical Paragraph, what is "reasonable" with respect to consenting to assignments and subletting.

Landlord wants to retain Tenant as the party liable under this Lease since Landlord has evaluated the financial condition of Tenant.

Landlord will likely insist that the right to "recapture" the Premises be retained in the Lease, since Landlord's ability to accept reconveyance enables Landlord to capture net gains due to increases in market rents.

With respect to Subparagraph 11(c), Landlord may want 100% of the net gain from the transaction, particularly if any such subletting or assignment would directly compete with Landlord's efforts to lease the remainder of the Building.

Landlord may also want to limit the applicability of this Paragraph so that only the original Tenant and not any assignee or subtenant has assignment or subletting rights under the Lease.

2.   Tenant's Perspective

Tenant wants flexibility to deal with the Premises as its space needs change. Tenant may want to provide that Landlord's consent will not be unreasonably withheld or delayed to protect itself from Landlord employing delay tactics in approving Tenant's proposed assignment or sublease.

Corporate Tenants with many affiliates should insist that Paragraph 11(a)(ii) and (iii) be included in the Lease so that Tenant has maximum flexibility in permitting other divisions, affiliates, or corporate partners of Tenant to use the Premises. These paragraphs also will permit Tenant to complete a merger or acquisition without having to worry about obtaining Landlord's consent or risk being declared in default under the Lease.

Tenant should resist granting Landlord the "recapture" rights under Paragraph 11(b), since this limits Tenant's flexibility and also transfers to Landlord any increase in the value of the Premises. The Lease rights to the Premises could become very valuable if substantial increases in market rents occur during the Term of the Lease. With respect to Paragraph 11(c), Tenant may also argue that 100% of the excess rents received from any assignment or subletting should be retained by Tenant, since Tenant is assuming 100% of the risk that rents will decrease during the Term of the Lease.

3. Lender's Perspective

A Lender wants to be able to analyze the income generated by the Lease. In the event that Tenant assigns or sublets, a Lender wants assurances that (i) the assignee or sublessee will have the financial strength to meet its obligations under the Lease; (ii) the proposed assignee's or sublessee's business will not conflict with exclusive clauses in other tenants' leases; and (iii) the quality and character of such assignee's or sublessee's business is similar to that of other tenants of the Building.

Lender will likely insist that no Tenant be released of any liability in connection with any assignment or subletting without Lender's consent, since the credit of each Tenant in the Building is viewed by Lender as a potential source of repayment of Lender's mortgage loan so long as that Tenant is liable for the payment of rent under the Lease.

C. COMPROMISES AND ALTERNATIVES

Additional criteria could be added for proposed subleases or assignments that do not require Landlord's prior approval. In Paragraph 11(a)(iii), Landlord may desire that the terms "affiliate and subsidiary" be restricted or defined so as to limit affiliates and subsidiaries to those entities which are 100% owned or controlled by Tenant.

With respect to Paragraph 11(c), a typical compromise requires that Tenant pay to Landlord 50% of any "excess" rents. Tenant may, however, insist that only a percentage of the "net" excess rents be paid to Landlord. Tenant should be permitted to deduct brokerage commissions, free rent periods, tenant improvements or tenant improvement allowances, and any other concessions that Tenant is obligated to provide to the subtenant, so that only a percentage of the net excess rents are paid over to the Landlord. Landlord will likely agree to this request, but will require that Tenant amortize these costs over the term of the sublease, rather than deducting these costs from the first rents received by Tenant from the subtenant.

D. COMMENTS

Landlord will likely require that any agreement to assign or sublet be conditioned upon Landlord's right to accept a reconveyance of the Premises within 30 days of said offer. The parties may want to agree on the form of reconveyance in advance and attach it as an Exhibit to the Lease so as to avoid any disagreement as to the form of such reconveyance in the future. Should Landlord consent to an assignment or subletting, Landlord may want to condition that consent on Landlord's prior approval of the "Assignment of Lease" or the "Sublease" document.

E. TYPICAL PARAGRAPH

11. Assignment or Sublease.

(a) (i) Tenant will not assign this Lease or hypothecate or mortgage the same or sublet the Premises or any part thereof. For the purposes of this Paragraph 11, Landlord agrees that it will not withhold its consent to an assignment or subletting, so long as the proposed subtenant or assignee, in the reasonable determination of Landlord, (1) is of a character and quality similar to that of other tenants in the Building or in other first-class office buildings of similar age, size, and quality in [insert geographic area]; (2) has the financial net worth to enable it to meet its obligations under this Lease; and (3) the total area of the Premises subject to a sublease shall not exceed ____% of the Premises.

(ii) Notwithstanding the provisions of Paragraph 11(a)(i), if Tenant is a corporation, the assignment or transfer of this Lease, and the term and estate hereby granted, to any corporation into which Tenant is merged or with which Tenant is consolidated, which corporation shall have a net worth at least equal to that of Tenant immediately prior to such merger or consolidation, (such corporation being hereinafter called "New Corp.") without the prior written consent of Landlord shall not be deemed to be prohibited hereby if, and upon the express condition that, New Corp. and Tenant shall promptly execute, acknowledge and deliver to Landlord an agreement in form and substance satisfactory to Landlord whereby New Corp. shall agree to be bound by and upon all the covenants, agreements, terms, provisions, and conditions set forth in this Lease on the part of Tenant to be performed, and whereby New Corp. shall expressly agree that the provisions of this Paragraph shall, notwithstanding such assignment or transfer, continue to be binding upon it with respect to all future assignments and transfers.

(iii) This Lease may be assigned, or the Premises may be sublet to any corporation that is a parent, subsidiary, or affiliate of Tenant provided that, such parent, subsidiary, or affiliate and Tenant shall promptly execute, acknowledge, and deliver to Landlord an agreement in form and substance satisfactory to Landlord whereby such parent, subsidiary, or affiliate shall agree to be bound by and upon all the covenants, agreements, terms, provisions, and conditions set forth in this Lease on the part of Tenant to be performed; and whereby such parent, subsidiary, or affiliate shall expressly agree that the provisions of this Paragraph shall, notwithstanding such assignment or transfer, continue to be binding upon it with respect to all future assignments and transfers. For the purpose of this Subparagraph 11(a)(iii), "parent" shall mean a corporation that owns directly or through any other entity that it controls, directly or indirectly, not less than fifty percent (50%) of the outstanding stock of Tenant; "subsidiary" shall mean any corporation not less than fifty percent (50%) of whose outstanding stock shall be owned by Tenant, directly or through any other entity that it controls, directly or indirectly; and "affiliate" shall mean any corporation not less than fifty percent (50%) of whose outstanding stock shall be owned by Tenant or Tenant's parent.

(b) No less than thirty (30) days prior to the effective date of a proposed assignment or sublease (other than one made pursuant to Paragraph 11(a)(ii) or (iii)), Tenant shall offer to reconvey to Landlord, as of the effective date, that portion of the Premises that Tenant is seeking to assign or sublet. Landlord, in its absolute discretion, shall accept or reject the offered reconveyance within thirty (30) days of the offer and if Landlord accepts, the reconveyance shall be evidenced by an agreement reasonably acceptable to Landlord and Tenant. If Landlord fails to accept or reject the offer within the thirty (30) day period, Landlord shall be deemed to have rejected the offer. If Landlord rejects or is deemed to have rejected Tenant's offer, then Tenant shall have the right to enter into said assignment or sublease subject to the consent of Landlord as described in Paragraph 11(a)(i) above.

(c) Notwithstanding the foregoing, in the event Landlord consents to an assignment or subletting, ____% of all rent, property, or other consideration received by Tenant that is in excess of the Base Rent provided hereunder, shall be paid by Tenant to Landlord as and when received as Additional Rent.

Inspection and Repair of Premises

RISK RATING: 3

A. DESCRIPTION AND SCOPE

This Paragraph permits Landlord to enter the Premises with prior notice to, but not the consent of, Tenant at reasonable times (including during business hours when necessary) to inspect, make repairs, bring in materials for the purpose of making such repairs and, during the last twelve (12) months of the Term, to show the Premises to prospective tenants and other interested parties. Emergency repairs do not require prior notice to Tenant.

B. ANALYSIS

1. Landlord's Perspective

Landlord wants authority to enter the Premises at all times to maintain, inspect, or show the Premises as well as immediate access without prior notice in the event of emergency. Landlord should resist having to obtain Tenant's prior consent to enter the Premises, and if Landlord does agree to obtain Tenant's consent, then Tenant's consent should not be unreasonably withheld or delayed.

2. Tenant's Perspective

Tenant desires protection against Landlord's unwarranted intrusions and protection against damages and disruption from Landlord's warranted intrusions. Accordingly, Tenant will want (i) Landlord to obtain Tenant's consent prior to Landlord entering the Premises (except for emergencies);

and (ii) to restrict Landlord's entry to after normal business hours. If Landlord's entry is required during normal business hours, then Tenant will want Landlord to use its best efforts not to materially interfere with Tenant's use of the Premises or normal business routine. Tenant may also object that the twelve (12) month period allowed to show the space to new or prospective tenants is too long.

3. Lender's Perspective

Lender will want to insure that the parties permitted to inspect the Premises include Lender. Also, in the event Lender forecloses and takes title to the Premises, Lender will want to assure there is access to the Premises in order to make any repairs to the Building and Premises that were neglected by Landlord.

C. COMPROMISES AND ALTERNATIVES

Landlord may agree to use reasonable efforts not to enter the Premises during Tenant's normal business hours, and if Landlord enters the Premises during Tenant's normal business hours, not to unreasonably interfere with Tenant's business routine. If the rentable square footage of the Premises is such that it could take less than twelve months to market and lease such space, then Landlord may agree that a period of nine, six, or even three months may be a more reasonable period during which Landlord may show the Premises. This time period should "dovetail" with the amount of lead time provided for exercise of any Option to Renew.

D. COMMENTS

None.

E. TYPICAL PARAGRAPH

12. Inspection and Repair of Premises. Tenant shall permit Landlord and its agents, representatives, and contractors to enter the Premises at all reasonable times with prior notice for any reasonable purpose, including to (a) inspect the same; (b) show the Premises to prospective tenants or interested parties such as prospective lenders and purchasers; (c) enforce the rules and regulations, clean, repair, alter, or improve the Premises or the Building; (d) discharge Tenant's obligations when Tenant has failed to do so within a reasonable time after written notice from Landlord; (e) post notices of non-responsibility and similar notices or "For Sale" signs, and (f) place "For Lease" signs upon or adjacent to the Building or the Premises

at any time within twelve (12) months of the expiration of the Term. Tenant shall permit Landlord and its agents to enter the Premises at any time and without prior notice in the event of an emergency. When reasonably necessary for repair of the Premises or Building; Landlord may temporarily close entrances, doors, corridors, elevators, or other facilities in the Premises or the Building, all without liability to Landlord. Landlord shall have no liability for disrupting Tenant's business if Landlord or its agents enter the Premises as provided above.

Damage to Premises

A. DESCRIPTION AND SCOPE

This Paragraph sets out alternative responses and procedures in the event of damage to the Property, including Landlord's obligation to restore, abatement of Annual Base Rent and Additional Rent, time limits for restoration, and termination of the Lease. The termination provision is usually extensively negotiated by Landlord and Tenant.

B. ANALYSIS

1. Landlord's Perspective

Landlord wants to protect itself from having to repair or restore the Building or the Premises following a casualty if repair or restoration would not be in the best economic interest of Landlord. Landlord also wants to be able to terminate the Lease if restoration costs more than available insurance proceeds. Landlord should never agree to pay restoration costs in excess of insurance proceeds. Landlord does not want to be responsible for repair or replacement of Tenant's furnishings, removable fixtures and equipment or improvements to the Premises made by Tenant in the event of casualty damage. Landlord wants to lock Tenant into the Lease and not permit Tenant to re-think the economics of the deal. There is no economic loss to the parties because Tenant is protected by business interruption insurance and Landlord can obtain rent loss insurance to protect itself and assure its Lender that it will keep making its mortgage payments.

2. Tenant's Perspective

Tenant does not want to be inflexibly locked into the Lease when the Premises have been partially or totally damaged. Tenant may want to condition Landlord's right to terminate the Lease upon Landlord's election also to terminate the leases of all other tenants in the Building, in order to prevent Landlord from using casualty damage as an excuse for terminating an unfavorable lease. Tenant will want the same rights as Landlord to terminate the Lease. Tenant's rights to terminate should be limited, because Lender will object to unusual termination rights by Tenant (see Lender's Perspective below).

If Landlord will restore the Premises and the Building, Tenant will want Landlord to complete restoration within the shortest possible time period. In very large projects involving substantial damage, Landlord may require at least 180 to 365 days to complete restoration. Tenant will resist a long restoration time, since its operations at the site will be shut down or transferred to a temporary location during such restoration. If such restoration period is too long (e.g., beyond 120 days), then it may be more appropriate for Tenant to negotiate a lease at a new location and terminate the Lease. Tenant will want a provision that permits Tenant to terminate the Lease for damage rendering the Premises untenantable during the last 6 or 12 months of the Lease Term. Landlord will likely resist such a provision if the Term is less than five years.

3. Lender's Perspective

Lender will usually object to Tenant having the right to terminate the Lease as a result of damage to the Premises or the Building, if the damage can be repaired within a short period of time (e.g., less than six months).

Termination of the Lease affects cash flow from the Property and may adversely affect Landlord's ability to pay debt service to Lender from the cash flow of the Property. Lender also wants to control insurance proceeds from any casualty.

Lender may require that casualty proceeds be used to reduce or pay off Landlord's indebtedness to Lender. In addition, requiring Landlord to use insurance proceeds to restore the Premises or the Building may not be acceptable to Lender, if (i) Tenant has the right to terminate the Lease if Landlord does not timely complete the restoration, or (ii) the abatement of rent following a casualty does not allow Landlord to pay debt service to Lender. Lender will want to make sure that Landlord has at least 12 months (some Lenders will require 18–24 months) of rent loss insurance so that debt service payments will not be interrupted during the restoration period.

It should be noted that any provision of the Lease that obligates Landlord to use insurance proceeds to restore the Building and Premises will likely be subordinate to Lender's rights to use insurance proceeds to pay down the mortgage loan by virtue of the automatic subordination provisions of the Lease or a separate Subordination, Nondisturbance, and Attornment Agreement that Lender requires Tenant to execute.

C. COMPROMISES AND ALTERNATIVES

Variations in the language would require significant revision of the entire Paragraph and should only be undertaken on a comprehensive basis.

D. COMMENTS

(1) The Lease terminates at the option of Landlord if the Building is totally destroyed.

(2) Annual Base Rent and Additional Rent are abated in proportion to untenantable area of the Premises. It should be noted that this may not be satisfactory to Tenant if there are areas of the Premises that are critical to Tenant's operations. For example, if the "computer room" and "telephone closets" are the lifeblood of Tenant's business operations, yet only comprise 5% of the rentable area of the Premises, if these areas are destroyed, but the remainder of the Premises is tenantable, then Tenant would be required to continue paying 95% of the Annual Base Rent and Additional Rent even though Tenant could not open for business. For damage to such critical areas, Tenant should require that the entire rent for the Premises be abated.

(3) Landlord determines in its sole discretion whether to restore the Premises and the Building, and restoration is limited to insurance proceeds received by Landlord.

(4) In a single-tenant build-to-suit Building, the Landlord right to terminate contained in subparagraph (f) should be deleted.

E. TYPICAL PARAGRAPH

13. **Damage or Destruction of Premises.**

(a) **If the Premises are destroyed or rendered untenantable, either wholly or in part, by fire or other casualty, then Landlord may, at its option, (i) terminate this Lease effective as of the date of such damage or destruction; or (ii) restore the Premises to their** previous condition, and in the meantime Annual Base Rent and Additional Rent shall abate in the same proportion as the untenantable portion of the Premises bears to the whole thereof, and this Lease shall continue in full force and effect. If the damage is caused, directly or indirectly, by the fault, neglect, or negligence of Tenant, or its officers, contractors, licensees, agents, servants, employees, guests, invitees, or visitors, then there shall be no abatement of Annual Base Rent and Additional Rent, except to the extent Landlord receives proceeds from any applicable insurance policy of Tenant to compensate Landlord for loss of Annual Base Rent and Additional Rent.

(b) If the Building is destroyed or damaged by fire or other casualty insured against under Landlord's fire and extended coverage insurance policy to the extent that more than fifty percent (50%) thereof is rendered untenantable, or if the Building is materially destroyed or damaged by any other casualty other than those covered by such insurance policy, notwithstanding that the Premises may be unaffected directly by such destruction or damage, then Landlord may in its sole discretion terminate this Lease by giving written notice to Tenant within sixty (60) days after such destruction or damage. Termination pursuant to such notice shall be effective thirty (30) days after receipt thereof by Tenant.

(c) Other than abatement of Annual Base Rent and Additional Rent as provided in Paragraph 13(a), no damages, compensation, or claim shall be payable by Landlord to Tenant for any inconvenience to or loss of Tenant's business arising from or in connection with any repair or restoration of the Property or portion thereof.

(d) If Landlord elects to repair the Building or the Premises, then Landlord's obligations shall be limited to the base Building and the Common Areas and the Tenant Work. Anything herein to the contrary notwithstanding, if the Premises are destroyed or damaged in whole or in part during the last twelve (12) months of the Term, then Landlord may, at its option, cancel and terminate this Lease as of the date of the occurrence of such damage.

(e) Tenant understands that Landlord will not carry insurance of any kind on Tenant's furniture and furnishings or on any fixtures or equipment removable by Tenant under the provisions of this Lease nor any improvements to the Premises other than the Tenant Work and that Landlord shall not be obligated to repair any damage thereto or to replace the same.

(f) A total destruction of the Building shall, at Landlord's option, permit Landlord to terminate this Lease.

(g) In the event of the termination of this Lease in accordance with the provisions of this Paragraph 13, any Annual Base Rent or Additional Rent paid in advance as of the date of such occurrence shall be immediately refunded to Tenant and this refund obligation shall survive such termination.

(h) Landlord and Tenant do each hereby release and discharge the other party and any officer, agent, employee, or representative of such party of and from any liability whatsoever hereafter arising from loss, damage, or injury caused by fire, or other insurable casualty for which insurance (permitting waiver of liability and containing waiver of subrogation) is required to be carried by the injured party by the terms of this Lease at the time of such loss, damage, or injury.

Eminent Domain

A. DESCRIPTION AND SCOPE

This Paragraph describes arrangements to be made in the event that any material portion of the Premises, the Building, or the Land is "taken" by a public authority under power of eminent domain, including a proportionate reduction in Annual Base Rent and Additional Rent if the Lease is not terminated, and an allocation of the compensation award.

B. ANALYSIS

1. Landlord's Perspective

Landlord wants the Term to continue so long as the project remains economically viable after a taking. Landlord may therefore want to define a material taking by reference to some higher percentage of damage. Landlord also does not want to risk losing to Tenant a portion of Landlord's condemnation award.

2. Tenant's Perspective

Tenant does not want to be inflexibly obligated under the Lease when a material portion of the Premises, the Building, or the Land has been taken and wants protection against the risk of having to pursue its respective rights in the Premises against Landlord in an adversarial court action. Tenant will be concerned with the Landlord's termination clause, especially if Tenant is constructing or adding improvements in the Premises. In that case Tenant, in addition to its claim for moving expenses, will want the Lease to provide for Tenant's recovery of the unamortized cost of its improvements upon condemnation. An agreement to apportion the award may be made, perhaps capping Tenant's portion at Tenant's unamortized cost. If such agreement is not made subject to the rights of a Lender, a Lender will ordinarily object to it, since it might reduce the security (i.e., the condemnation award in lieu of the real property) available to Lender.

If the Lease is not terminated due to an immaterial taking, Tenant should require that Landlord reconstruct the Building, Premises, or Common Areas within a specified period of time after the taking. One hundred twenty (120) days would be a reasonable period of time for an immaterial taking.

3.   Lender's Perspective

Lender wants (i) to be paid in full before any proceeds are available to Landlord, Tenant, or Tenant's leasehold mortgagee; and (ii) to hold the proceeds if a partial taking has occurred and reconstruction is to occur.

C.   COMPROMISES AND ALTERNATIVES

Tenant may be concerned if a portion of the parking area is taken in condemnation. That is actually the most likely to occur of most condemnation scenarios, since a road widening could result in a loss of parking areas. In such case, Tenant may want to require that Landlord provide substitute parking either on site, if available, or off site if not. Should Landlord be unable to provide substitute parking, Tenant should have a right to terminate the Lease. Tenant may also want some definition of "material" and a right of Tenant to terminate the Lease if a "material" taking occurs. A "material" taking may be any taking that affects parking or Tenant's ingress and egress to the Property, Building, or Premises or any taking that affects any utilities or other services to the Building or Premises.

Variations in the language would require significant revision of the entire Paragraph and should only be undertaken on a comprehensive basis.

D.   COMMENTS

  (1) The damage award will be property of Landlord.
  (2) Tenant may assert a claim for moving expenses.
  (3) If the Lease is not terminated, then Tenant will receive a proportionate abatement of Annual Base Rent and Additional Rent.

E.   TYPICAL PARAGRAPH

14.   Eminent Domain. If fifty percent (50%) or more of the Premises or of such portions of the Building or the Land as Landlord determines are material for Tenant's reasonable use of the Premises are taken by emi-

nent domain or sale under threat of condemnation by eminent domain and Landlord is unable to relocate Tenant to another area of the Building, then this Lease shall, upon Landlord giving written notice to Tenant, terminate as of the date title vests in the condemning authority. All Annual Base Rent and Additional Rent and other sums payable by Tenant hereunder shall accrue up to and including such date and shall be paid by Tenant to Landlord on such date. Landlord reserves all rights to any awards or damages in connection with any such full or partial taking by eminent domain. Tenant hereby assigns to Landlord any right Tenant may have to such damages or awards and waives all claims against Landlord and the condemning authority in connection with such taking, including all claims for termination of Tenant's leasehold interest hereunder and interference with Tenant's business. Notwithstanding the foregoing, Tenant shall have the right to claim and recover from the condemning authority compensation for any loss which Tenant may incur for Tenant's moving expenses or the taking of Tenant's personal property (excluding Tenant's leasehold interest hereunder), provided such claim by Tenant does not reduce Landlord's claim. If this Lease does not terminate as aforesaid, then Landlord shall proceed to make all necessary repairs to the Property in order to render and restore the same to the condition they were in prior to the taking, but in no event shall Landlord be required to expend more than the condemnation proceeds received by Landlord with respect to such taking, and Tenant shall continue in possession of the portion of the Premises not so taken upon the same terms and conditions as are herein provided, except that Annual Base Rent and Additional Rent shall be reduced in direct proportion to the area of the Premises so taken.

Tenant's Obligations (Including Alterations and Insurance)

A. DESCRIPTION AND SCOPE

This Paragraph sets forth specific obligations of Tenant under the Lease, including the obligations of Tenant to use the Premises in a quiet, lawful, and orderly manner; to surrender the Premises to Landlord; to adhere to Landlord's rules and regulations; to notify Landlord of any material damage to the Premises; to make improvements, alterations, and additions in accordance with certain conditions; to maintain appropriate insurance coverage; and to pay rent.

B. ANALYSIS

1. Landlord's Perspective

Landlord prefers an expansive definition of Tenant's obligations in order to ensure that Tenant will use the Premises in the manner Landlord expects and in order to be able to enforce Tenant's compliance with the terms of the Lease. With respect to Paragraph (a), Landlord may request Tenant to comply with all laws affecting the use of the Premises and not just those limited to "Tenant's manner of use of the Premises." With respect to Paragraph (b), Landlord will likely want to add the right on the part of Landlord to require that Tenant restore the Premises to their original condition. This would include a law that is passed that requires a substantial retrofit of the Premises. Tenant will argue that in such an event, capital expenditures for such a retrofit are more properly allocated to Landlord than to Tenant. With respect to Paragraph (c), Landlord may request the right to revise the rules and regulations at Landlord's discretion and Tenant will argue that Tenant should have the right to approve any changes in the rules and regulations that may affect the Tenant.

With respect to Paragraph (f), Landlord may want to require that Tenant use only contractors approved by Landlord.

2.   Tenant's Perspective

Tenant wants to ensure that its obligations are set forth precisely to protect Tenant against the risk of uncertainty in fulfilling its obligations. Tenant also seeks to have its obligations narrowly defined in order to ensure that Tenant will be able to comply with the terms of the Lease more readily. With respect to Paragraph (a), Tenant should require Landlord to warrant and represent that the Property, Building, and Premises are in compliance with all laws on the Commencement Date and that Tenant's permitted use complies with all Zoning Laws. Should Landlord refuse to make these representations, Tenant should independently confirm zoning and compliance with law requirements. With respect to Paragraph (e), Tenant will want Landlord to specify its excess-hours charge for at least the first year of the Lease Term. With respect to Paragraph (f) and Tenant's right to make changes or improvements to the Premises with the consent of Landlord, Tenant may object or at least want the right to make any nonstructural changes without the consent of Landlord.

3.   Lender's Perspective

Lender will want Tenant to be responsible for as much of the maintenance and other costs as possible; also, obligations must be clear and uniform among Tenants so there are no gaps in obligations.

C.   COMPROMISES AND ALTERNATIVES

If Landlord and Tenant agree on specific additional obligations, they should be added here.

D.   COMMENTS

Insurance coverage limits should be cleared with Tenant's risk manager or insurance agent. Landlord should confirm the coverages and limits.

See Paragraph 25 for a complete discussion of compliance with laws issues.

See Paragraph 46 for complete discussion of insurance issues.

See Paragraph 55 for a discussion of Tenant's repair and restoration obligations upon expiration of the Lease.

E. TYPICAL PARAGRAPH

15. Tenant's Obligations.

(a) Tenant will not conduct its business in other than a quiet, lawful, and orderly manner. Tenant shall promptly comply with all laws, rules, ordinances, lawful orders, and regulations pertaining to Tenant's particular use or manner of use of the Premises and Common Area Facilities, and Tenant shall not use or permit the use of any portion of the Premises for any unlawful purpose. Tenant shall also pay the cost of complying with all laws, rules, ordinances, lawful orders, and regulations in connection with any changes or alterations to the Premises initiated by Tenant. Tenant shall not perform any act or carry on any practice that materially injures the Property.

(b) At the end of the Term, Tenant may remove only its personal property from the Premises including any security, telephone, and computer systems installed by Tenant and will surrender the Premises without further notice and in substantially as good condition as when entered, except for loss or damages resulting from hostile or warlike action in time of peace or war, casualty, condemnation, ordinary wear and tear, or perils covered by standard forms of fire and extended coverage insurance policies. Upon the expiration or sooner termination of the Term, Tenant shall have no liability to Landlord on account of alterations, additions, or improvements, provided Tenant surrenders the Premises in the condition in which Tenant was using the Premises immediately before the expiration or termination.

(c) Tenant will obey the rules and regulations provided for in this Lease.

(d) Tenant will promptly notify Landlord of any material damage to the Premises, upon becoming aware of the same.

(e) Tenant shall pay for any excess-hours usage for services after business hours that Tenant has requested. If more than one tenant requests these additional services, then the cost of providing the services during nonbusiness hours shall be allocated proportionately between or among those tenants requesting additional services based upon the amount of time each tenant benefits, and the square footage of each tenant's premises. The cost for these services shall not exceed Landlord's actual costs.

(f) During the Term, Tenant may not make any improvements, alterations, and additions to the Premises without the prior written consent of Landlord. Should Landlord consent to such improvements, alterations, or additions, then the same shall be completed in a first-class and workmanlike manner with materials and finishes that are comparable to those then existing in the Premises, and Tenant agrees to:

(i) furnish Landlord with plans of said improvements, alterations, and additions;

(ii) comply with all insurance requirements and all laws, ordinances, rules, and regulations of all governmental authorities, and Landlord shall cooperate with Tenant in securing any necessary building and other permits, the cost thereof being borne by Tenant;

(iii) Tenant shall discharge by payment, bond, or otherwise, mechanics' liens filed against the Property for work, labor, services, or materials claimed to have been performed at or furnished to the Premises for or on behalf of Tenant within 15 days after the filing thereof; and

(iv) within 15 days after completion of such work, furnish to Landlord contractors' releases and full and final waivers of liens.

(g) Tenant shall maintain, at its expense, and keep in effect during the entire Term:

(i) Commercial General Liability Insurance with a Broad Form Comprehensive General Liability endorsement in a form and with such renewals as is acceptable to Landlord. The limits of liability of such insurance shall be an amount not less than ___ Million Dollars ($_____) per occurrence, Bodily Injury including death and ___ Million Dollars ($_____) per occurrence, Property Damage Liability or ___ Million Dollars ($_____) combined single limit for Bodily Injury and Property Damage Liability. Such polices shall name Landlord as additional insured. Tenant shall deliver a certificate of insurance evidencing said coverage not earlier than thirty (30) days prior to the Commencement Date and not later than the Commencement Date, and at such other time, within thirty (30) days of Landlord's written request. The policies providing said coverage will provide that they shall not be canceled without at least thirty (30) days' prior written notice of cancellation to Landlord; and

(ii) "special form" property insurance on Tenant's personal property on such forms and with such insurers as shall be acceptable to Landlord. This insurance shall include, but not be limited to, fire and extended coverage perils. Such property insurance policy will contain appropriate provisions or endorsements waiving the insurer's right of subrogation against the Landlord. Tenant shall deliver a certificate of insurance evidencing said coverage not earlier than thirty (30) days prior to the Commencement Date and not later than the Commencement Date, and at such other time, within thirty (30) days of Landlord's written request. Tenant will renew such policies or provide replacement policies prior to their expiration, and the policies providing said coverage must provide that they will not be canceled without at least thirty (30) days' prior written notice of cancellation to Landlord.

Landlord's Obligations (Insurance, Repairs, and Services)

RISK RATING: 3

A. DESCRIPTION AND SCOPE

This Paragraph sets forth specific obligations of Landlord under the Lease, including the obligations of Landlord to insure, maintain, and repair the Property; to furnish services to Tenant ranging from heating, ventilating, and air-conditioning to landscaping and to comply with all laws, rules, and regulations relating to the Property.

B. ANALYSIS

1. Landlord's Perspective

Most Landlords will be extremely reluctant to assume the range of obligations set forth in this paragraph, and many Landlords' forms of Leases will not have this Paragraph. However, if such a Paragraph does exist in the Lease, or if a Tenant requests this type of Paragraph, Landlord wants to limit its obligation to provide services of any kind to Tenant and prefers that any such requirements be specifically defined.

With respect to Subparagraph 16(a)(iii), Landlord will generally require that Tenant maintain insurance on the improvements to the Premises, even though it is likely to be more cost effective for Landlord to maintain this insurance and pass the cost through to Tenant as a reimbursable item.

With respect to Paragraph 16(b), the maintenance obligations of Landlord are broad. Landlord will want to limit maintenance obligations to the structural components and Common Areas of the Building and will want to delete the "without limiting the generality of the foregoing" language.

With respect to Subparagraph 16(c)(ii), most buildings do not have humidification control systems, and therefore the reference to "humidification" should be deleted. In addition if the regular business hours of Tenant differ from those included in other Leases in the Building, Landlord may request additional payment for the increased operating costs associated with such hours. Landlord wants to minimize its obligations, restrict the opportunities for it to be in default under the Lease, and strictly limit rights of self-help or offset.

2.   Tenant's Perspective

Tenant wants an expansive definition of Landlord's obligations in order to ensure that Landlord will provide the services necessary for Tenant to fully use the Premises. Tenant wants to be able to accurately predict the cost of using the Premises and wants to be able to enforce Landlord's compliance with the terms of the Lease. With respect to Subparagraph 16(a)(iii), Tenant wants to ensure that all improvements and betterments in the Premises are insured by Landlord. In order to ensure that the Premises always look in a first-class condition without additional cost to Tenant, Tenant may request that Landlord periodically repaint the Premises and in which case the following provision may be an acceptable insert to Paragraph 16(c):

> *(xi) Such repainting as is necessary to maintain the Building in a first-class condition; the complete repainting of all paintable surfaces in the Premises at the end of the third (3rd) and fifth (5th) years of the Term, and also at the end of the seventh (7th) year of the Term, provided Tenant has exercised its option to renew the Term as provided for Paragraph __ of this Lease. All painting in the Premises will be done in standard colors of Tenant's selection.*

3.   Lender's Perspective

Since Lender could succeed to the responsibilities of Landlord, it wants to limit Landlord's obligations, Tenant's self-help cure rights and rights of offset, as well as minimize potential for Landlord defaults.

C.   COMPROMISES AND ALTERNATIVES

The repainting suggested under Tenant's Perspective is convertible to a monetary obligation of Landlord and could be eliminated in exchange for some other monetary concession. The definition of regular business hours contained in Subparagraph 16(e)(ii), if changed, could require substantial Additional Rent payments by Tenant for excess operating hours. Landlord may request that a provision be added requiring Tenant to pay a per-hour charge for excess operating hours.

D. COMMENTS

Insurance limit changes or modifications should be discussed with Landlord's insurance agent or risk manager.

E. TYPICAL PARAGRAPH

16. Landlord's Obligations.
    (a) Landlord shall maintain, at its expense, and keep in effect during the entire Term:
        (i) Commercial General Liability Insurance with a Broad Form Comprehensive General Liability endorsement. The limits of liability of such insurance shall be an amount not less than $_____ per occurrence, Bodily Injury including death $_____ per occurrence, Property Damage Liability $_____ combined single limit for Bodily Injury and Property Damage Liability. Such polices shall name Tenant as additional insured; and
        (ii) "special form" property insurance on the Building, the Premises, and the Common Areas insuring one hundred percent (100%) of the replacement value thereof. This insurance shall include fire and extended coverage perils; and
        (iii) the property to be insured by Landlord in accordance with Paragraph 16(a)(ii) shall also be deemed to include all improvements and betterments in the Premises.
    (b) Throughout the Term, Landlord shall make all repairs and replacements to the Building, the Common Areas, the Premises, any appurtenant structures, and all other portions of the Property and all service systems for the same, except when the obligation to do so is specifically imposed upon Tenant by the provisions of this Lease. Without limiting the generality of the foregoing, Landlord shall maintain, repair, and replace, as necessary, and keep in good order, safe and clean condition:
        (i) the plumbing, sprinkler, heating, ventilating, and air-conditioning system; building electrical and mechanical lines and equipment associated therewith; and elevators

and boilers, all of which either are located in or serve the Premises or Common Areas;

(ii)   broken or damaged glass and damage by vandals;

(iii) the exterior and interior structure of the Building, including the roof, exterior walls, bearing walls, support beams, foundation, columns, exterior doors and windows, and lateral support to the Building and the Common Areas;

(iv)   the interior walls, ceilings, floors, and floor coverings (including carpets and tiles) of the Common Areas; and

(v)   the exterior improvements to the land, including ditches, shrubbery, landscaping, and fencing.

Nothing in this Paragraph 16 shall require Landlord to maintain or repair Tenant's personal property.

(c) Landlord will furnish the following facilities, maintenance, and services using first-class materials and in a first-class manner;

(i)   Elevator service for both passengers and freight;

(ii)   Heating, ventilation, humidification, and air-conditioning when the same are necessary for the comfortable occupancy and use of the Premises, during Tenant's regular business hours from 9:00 a.m. to 5:00 p.m. on Monday through Friday, and 9:00 a.m. to 1:00 p.m. on Saturday;

(iii) At Tenant's additional expense, as reasonably determined by Landlord, all services normally provided by Landlord during regular business hours, and any parking facilities provided for in this Lease, to permit use of the Premises by Tenant after Tenant's aforesaid regular business hours, twenty-four (24) hours per day, seven (7) days per week;

(iv)   Toilet facilities and all necessary toilet supplies, hot and cold water, and sewage disposal;

(v)   Refrigerated drinking water;

(vi)   Clearing of ice, snow, and debris from the Common Areas;

(vii) Vermin extermination, and repair and replacement of any property damaged by vermin;

(viii) Electricity for standard office uses such as lighting, vending machines, and customary office machines up to _____ watts per rentable square foot;

(ix)   Janitorial services as provided for in Exhibit ___ attached; at Tenant's expense, Landlord will provide such reasonable additional janitorial services as may be requested by Tenant in writing; and

(x) Landscaping maintenance and services as necessary to maintain the plants, shrubs, flower beds, and grounds of both the interior and exterior of the Building and the Common Areas in first-class condition.

(d) Landlord shall be responsible for all repairs to the Property necessitated by the negligence of the Landlord, its agents, contractors, or employees.

(e) In performing any service, maintenance, or repair work pursuant to this Lease, Landlord shall use its reasonable efforts to protect Tenant's property and personnel from loss or injury and to minimize disrupting Tenant's regular business routine.

Indemnification

RISK RATING: 4

A. DESCRIPTION AND SCOPE

This Paragraph sets forth the conditions under which Tenant agrees to indemnify Landlord. The indemnity is a broad, one-sided indemnity in favor of Landlord. The purpose of the one-sided indemnity is to require Tenant's insurance company to pay for damages relating to the Premises because the Premises are in Tenant's exclusive control.

B. ANALYSIS

1. Landlord's Perspective

This Paragraph protects Landlord against liability for the negligent acts, omissions, or failures of Tenant (even if Landlord is also negligent) for anything occurring in or about the Premises. Landlord does not want to use its time and resources in a legal fight over who was negligent, and if both Landlord and Tenant were negligent, each party's respective share of negligence. Landlord is also concerned with the out-of-pocket cost of the deductible amount of its insurance. With respect to Tenant's obligations to defend, Landlord may prefer to retain its own counsel and require a reimbursement of legal fees and expenses from Tenant.

Tenant may object that the indemnity is too one-sided in favor of Landlord. Landlord should resist carving out Landlord's negligence from Tenant's obligation to indemnify since (i) Landlord and Tenant should avoid dissipating their time and energy in legal proceedings determining whose liability insurance will pay for any given claim; and (ii) Tenant's insurance should pay for damage or injury arising in the areas which Tenant exclusively controls. If Landlord deletes the parenthetical regarding

Landlord's negligence, then the purpose of the indemnity paragraph is negated. The goal of both parties should be to create in the Lease clear demarcation lines as to which party's liability insurance will be responsible for any given third-party negligence claim. A demarcation line based on the standard of who is negligent does nothing to improve the status quo. If Tenant is paying Additional Rent, then Tenant is in effect paying for Landlord's insurance. Any increase in Landlord's insurance due to such claims will be passed on to Tenant. If Landlord and Tenant both are required to make claims against their respective insurance carriers (because the parenthetical is deleted from the Paragraph), then Tenant will be the ultimate loser, since it will pay for any increase in its insurance premiums directly and for increases in Landlord's insurance premiums indirectly as Additional Rent.

2. Tenant's Perspective

Tenant should request a reciprocal indemnity from Landlord. With respect to Paragraph 17(b), Tenant will want the indemnity limited to acts occurring at the Premises, since Tenant cannot control invitees and contractors once they leave the Premises. Tenant should confirm with its insurance agent or risk manager that its liability insurance adequately covers this indemnity.

3. Lender's Perspective

Lender wants Tenant's indemnity to be broad enough to cover Lender's acts and omissions in the event Lender takes control or possession of the Premises either prior to or after foreclosure.

C. COMPROMISES AND ALTERNATIVES

Due to the contingent liability that arises with the giving of any indemnity, any changes requested by Landlord should be made on a comprehensive basis and discussed with counsel. If Landlord agrees to a mutual indemnity, then Landlord's indemnity must be limited to damages arising in connection with areas under Landlord's exclusive control, such as the Common Areas when the Building is a multi-tenant Building and that are covered by Landlord's standard insurance. For example, environmental related damages to the Common Areas or host liquor liability not covered by Landlord's insurance but caused by Tenant should be paid for by Tenant. In order for a mutual indemnity to be meaningful, it must allocate the liability regardless of who was negligent, except as noted above when the liability is not covered by Landlord's standard insurance coverage. If Landlord self-insures, then it should reject this approach because it may have to pay out of pocket a large amount of damages that result solely from the negligence of Tenant. The following paragraph is an alternative to Paragraph 17 if a mutual indemnity is required:

> *Tenant will indemnify and hold harmless Landlord and Landlord's agents, employees, officers, directors, partners, members, and shareholders from any and all liability, loss, cost, or expense arising from a third-party claim respecting an incident that occurred within the Premises and that resulted in personal injury or property damage even if resulting from the negligent acts or omissions of Landlord or Landlord's agents, employees, officers, directors, partners, members, and shareholders. Landlord will indemnify and hold Tenant and Tenant's agents, employees, officers, directors, partners, members, and shareholders harmless from any and all liability, loss, cost, or expense arising from a third-party claim respecting an incident that occurred within the Common Areas of the Building or upon the Land and that resulted in personal injury or property damage even if resulting from the negligent acts or omissions of Tenant or Tenant's agents, employees, officers, directors, partners, members, and shareholders. If any action or proceeding is brought against Landlord or Landlord's agents, employees, officers, directors, partners, members, and shareholders, and such claim is a claim for which Tenant is obligated to indemnify Landlord pursuant to this Paragraph, then Tenant, upon notice from Landlord, shall resist and defend such action or proceeding (by counsel reasonably satisfactory to Landlord). Tenant shall carry insurance that covers its obligations under this Paragraph 17 and shall deliver evidence of such insurance to Landlord. The obligation of Tenant under this Paragraph 17 shall survive the expiration or earlier termination of this Lease. In case any action or proceeding is brought against Tenant or Landlord's agents, employees, officers, directors, partners, members, and shareholders, and such claim is a claim for which Landlord is obligated to indemnify Tenant pursuant to this Paragraph 17, Landlord, upon notice from Tenant, shall resist and defend such action or proceeding (by counsel reasonably satisfactory to Tenant). The obligation of Landlord under this Paragraph 17 shall survive termination of this Lease.*

D. COMMENTS

Even though Paragraph 17 requires Tenant to carry insurance that covers Tenant's indemnity obligations, Landlord should carry its own insurance because Tenant may let its insurance lapse despite Landlord's monitoring Tenant's insurance. When a mutual indemnity is used, Landlord should resist naming Tenant as an additional insured on Landlord's policy unless Landlord can pass along to Tenant any additional premium caused thereby. Landlord should obtain separate indemnities from Tenant for matters not insurable at normal rates and for environmental matters caused by Tenant.

Due to the increase in the use of limited liability companies for the ownership of real estate, the possible "members" of Landlord should be an indemnified party.

E. TYPICAL PARAGRAPH

17. Indemnification. Tenant shall indemnify and hold harmless Landlord and all superior mortgagees and its and their respective agents, employees, officers, directors, partners, members, and shareholders, from and against any and all liabilities, judgments, demands, causes of action, claims, losses, damages, costs, and expenses, including, without limitation, reasonable attorneys' fees and costs arising out of or in any way connected with (a) the conduct or management of the Premises or any business therein, or any work or thing whatsoever done, or any condition created (even if due to Landlord's negligence or breach of this Lease) in or about the Premises during the Term or during the period of time, if any, prior to the Commencement Date that Tenant may have been given access to the Premises; (b) any act, omission, or negligence of Tenant or any of its subtenants or licensees or its or their partners, directors, officers, agents, employees, invitees, or contractors (c) any accident, injury, or damage whatever (even if caused by Landlord's negligence) occurring in, at, or upon the Premises; and (d) any breach or default by Tenant in the full and prompt payment and performance of Tenant's obligations under this Lease. In case any action or proceeding is brought against Landlord or any superior mortgagee or its or their agents, employees, officers, directors, parties, members, and shareholders and such claim is a claim for which Tenant is obligated to indemnify Landlord pursuant to this Paragraph 17, Tenant, upon notice from Landlord or such superior mortgagee, shall resist and defend such action or proceeding (by counsel reasonably satisfactory to Landlord or such superior mortgagee). Tenant shall carry insurance that covers its obligations under this Paragraph 17 and shall deliver evidence of such insurance to Landlord. The obligations of Tenant under this Paragraph 17 shall survive the expiration or earlier termination of this Lease.

PARAGRAPH **18**

Default by Tenant

RISK RATING: 4

A. DESCRIPTION AND SCOPE

This Paragraph describes the conditions under which Tenant may be in default under the Lease (including failure to pay rent, bankruptcy, and failure to comply with Lease covenants) and establishes a notice and cure period for certain defaults.

B. ANALYSIS

1. Landlord's Perspective

This Paragraph enables Landlord to take appropriate remedial action should Tenant fail to comply with its Lease obligations. The Paragraph does not require Landlord to give written notice for rental defaults. Since Landlord's mortgage loan obligation likely would be due on the first day of the month, requiring Landlord to give Tenant written notice of default each month would cause delay in the payment of Landlord's mortgage loan obligation and perhaps subject it to default interest, late charges, or foreclosure. Such an argument may be countered by the Tenant, depending upon its credit rating and its history of paying its obligations when due. The Paragraph also sets an outside date on nonmonetary defaults that Tenant is not capable of curing within thirty (30) days.

2. Tenant's Perspective

Tenant should require Landlord to give written notice of a monetary default. A ten (10) day notice and cure period for monetary default is typical and reasonable since most Lenders will give Landlord similar notice or grace period and Tenant should not risk a forfeiture of the Lease if the check truly was "lost in the mail" or, through oversight or inadvertence, Tenant fails to make a timely rental payment.

In the event that Tenant does not comply with its obligations under the Lease, the notice provisions allow Tenant to remedy a potential nonmonetary default without losing its rights under the Lease. Tenant will likely request that the ninety (90) day maximum period to cure nonmonetary defaults be changed to an unlimited period, provided Tenant continues to diligently cure such nonmonetary default.

With respect to Paragraph 18(c), Tenant should request a ninety (90) day period to dismiss an involuntary bankruptcy.

With respect to Paragraph 18(e) and (h), Tenant should not be in default for failing to occupy nonretail Premises as long as Tenant continues to pay rent.

With respect to Paragraph 18(g), if Tenant expects to use venture capital financing that may require transfers of ownership interests in Tenant, this paragraph should be modified accordingly. In addition, if Tenant expects to sell its business during the Term of the Lease, this event should be expressly permitted. It is also advisable that transfers to a family trust or by bequest to family members be permitted for estate planning purposes.

3. Lender's Perspective

The notice and cure periods are reasonable and should not be objectionable to Lender.

C. COMPROMISES AND ALTERNATIVES

If Tenant requests that Landlord give notice upon monetary default, one alternative would be that Landlord shall not be required to give such notice more than two times in any twelve-month period. Another alternative would be that Landlord shall use good faith efforts to notify Tenant, although Landlord is not obligated to do so and will have no liability to Tenant for not doing so.

D. COMMENTS

Since procedures for declaring and enforcing a Lease default are State-specific, Landlord should discuss with local counsel the validity of this Paragraph in the jurisdiction where the Property is located.

E.   TYPICAL PARAGRAPH

18.   Default by Tenant. The occurrence of any of the following events shall constitute a "Default" under this Lease: (a) the failure of Tenant to pay when due any installment of Annual Base Rent, Additional Rent, or other charge due under this Lease; or (b) the failure of Tenant to fulfill any of the other covenants or provisions of this Lease on its part to be performed and such default is not remedied within thirty (30) days (or if such default cannot reasonably be remedied within such thirty (30) days, within such time as may reasonably be required to remedy the default up to an aggregate of ninety (90) days, provided Tenant diligently commences curing such default within the first thirty (30) days and diligently proceeds to cure such default) after Landlord shall have given Tenant written notice of such default; or (c) any bankruptcy, insolvency, or similar proceeding shall be filed by or against Tenant and the same shall not be dismissed within thirty (30) days; or (d) if Landlord shall give to Tenant within any period of twelve (12) consecutive months during the term of this Lease, three (3) notices of Default; or (e) if Tenant shall abandon or fail to occupy the Premises for a period of thirty (30) consecutive days; or (f) if Tenant shall fail to take possession of the Premises on the Commencement Date; or (g) if Tenant is not a publicly traded corporation or entity, and any part or all of its shares or ownership interests shall be transferred by sale, assignment, bequest, inheritance, operation of law, or other disposition so as to result in a change in the present voting control of Tenant by the person or entity owning a majority of said shares or ownership interests on the date of this Lease; or (h) if Tenant removes all or substantially all of its furniture, fixtures, and equipment from the Premises other than by reason of an assignment or subletting of the Premises permitted under this Lease.

Remedies of Landlord

RISK RATING: 4

A. DESCRIPTION AND SCOPE

This Paragraph describes Landlord's remedies upon Tenant's default and permits Landlord to pursue concurrently any remedy provided under the Lease, at law or in equity. The Lease remedies include terminating the Lease, recovery of the present value of the rental and other charges payable by Tenant for the remainder of the Lease term, or collection of the monthly rent and charges as and when due less the proceeds of reletting the Premises.

B. ANALYSIS

1. Landlord's Perspective

Since remedies for a Lease default are State-specific, Landlord should discuss with local counsel the enforceability of this Paragraph in the jurisdiction where the Property is located. In many States, this Paragraph will provide Landlord with an adequate choice of remedies for a Default by Tenant under the Lease. Generally, a Landlord will be reluctant to negotiate or alter the remedies provisions of the Lease. In Subparagraph 19(e) Landlord has a right to relet the Premises, but should not be obligated to do so. Landlord should generally not agree to mitigate damages since if Tenant so chooses, Tenant can locate a subtenant and mitigate Tenant's damages. However, some states do require that Landlord use commercially reasonable efforts to re-lease the Premises and mitigate damages. An additional remedy that Landlord may want to add is the right to take possession of the Premises without terminating the Lease, since in some jurisdictions, recovery of damages may be limited if the Lease is terminated.

111

2. Tenant's Perspective

Credit Tenants or other Tenants with significant leverage may be in a position to negotiate some changes to the remedies of Landlord. In such case, Tenant may want Landlord to covenant to mitigate Landlord's damages.

Tenant may also want to provide that Landlord's remedy after taking possession or termination is limited to an alternative definition of "Liquidated Final Damages" that is equal to the amount of the positive difference, if any, between the present value of the Annual Base Rent due for the remainder of the Lease Term, less the present value of the current market rental value of the Premises for the remainder of the Lease Term. Thus, if the current market rental value is greater than the stated Annual Base Rent under the Lease, Tenant will not be liable for any damages. However, if the rental market has declined, Tenant will be liable for the difference. This remedy assumes that Landlord will be able to relet the Premises immediately after termination. A more likely compromise is that Tenant remains liable for the full amount of the stated Annual Base Rent for a specified lease-up period of six (6) months to one (1) year and that the aforesaid present value calculation be for the Lease Term remaining after the lease-up period.

With respect to Paragraph 19(b), Tenant should object to any recovery of the Premises "by force."

With respect to Paragraph 19(f), credit Tenants may want to limit liability for Landlord's reletting costs, since if the Lease Term had expired normally at the end of the Lease Term, Tenant would not have been liable for Landlord's reletting costs, and since Tenant will be liable for the economic equivalent of the Annual Base Rent due for the remainder of the Term, Tenant should not be also liable for such reletting costs.

3. Lender's Perspective

Since Lender may become the future Landlord should Lender foreclose on the Property, Lender will want to make sure the Lease contains strong Landlord remedies.

C. COMPROMISES AND ALTERNATIVES

Since Landlord may be required to mitigate damages under local law, adding an express provision to the Lease may not be objectionable.

D. COMMENTS

None.

E. TYPICAL PARAGRAPH

19. **Remedies of Landlord.**

    (a) In the event of any Default under this Lease, Landlord may, at Landlord's option and without prejudice to its rights hereunder, terminate this Lease upon notice to Tenant. No act by Landlord other than its giving written notice to Tenant shall terminate this Lease. Acts of maintenance, efforts to relet the Premises, or the appointment of a receiver on Landlord's initiative to protect Landlord's interest under this Lease shall not constitute a termination of this Lease or Tenant's right to possession of the Premises. In the event of such termination, all of the right, title, and interest of Tenant under this Lease, including any renewal or extension privileges, shall end, and Tenant shall quit and surrender the Premises to Landlord. Tenant's liability under all of the provisions of this Lease shall continue notwithstanding any termination or surrender, and notwithstanding Landlord's pursuit of any other remedy under this Lease, at law or in equity.

    (b) Upon termination of this Lease pursuant to this Paragraph 19, Landlord may recover possession of the Premises by summary proceedings, by force, by any suitable action or proceeding at law, or otherwise. Landlord may also enter the Premises and execute reentry of the Premises at any time after such termination and remove all persons and property therefrom without being deemed guilty of trespass or becoming liable for any loss or damage that may be occasioned thereby and may have, hold, and enjoy the Premises.

    (c) If this Lease is terminated pursuant to this Paragraph 19, Tenant shall pay to Landlord, in addition to all Annual Base Rent, Additional Rent and other charges due and payable by Tenant on the date of such termination, as current damages for Tenant's default, the equivalent of the amount of Annual Base Rent, Additional Rent, and all other charges Tenant would have been required to pay until the date this Lease would have expired had such termination not occurred, minus the proceeds of any reletting. Tenant shall pay such current damages (the "Deficiency Damages") to Landlord monthly on the days on which rent would have been payable under this Lease if this Lease were still in effect and Landlord shall be entitled to recover each month from Tenant Deficiency Damages as the same shall arise. Any suit brought to collect the Deficiency

Damages for any month shall not prejudice in any way the right of Landlord to collect Deficiency Damages for any subsequent month by a similar proceeding.

(d) If this Lease is terminated pursuant to this Paragraph 19, and if Landlord so elects, Tenant shall pay in addition to all Annual Base Rent, Additional Rent and all other charges due and payable by Tenant on the date of such termination, "Liquidated Final Damages." As used herein, "Liquidated Final Damages" shall mean the present value of an amount equivalent to the Annual Base Rent, Additional Rent, and other charges that would have been payable by Tenant from the date of such election to the date this Lease would have expired had it not been so terminated. Said Liquidated Final Damages shall become due and payable to Landlord immediately upon Landlord's notice to Tenant of such election.

(e) In the event of termination of this Lease or a reentry into the Premises pursuant to this Paragraph 19, Landlord may relet the whole or any part of the Premises in the name of Landlord, Tenant, or otherwise, for a period equal to, greater, or less than the remainder of the then term of this Lease, at such rental and upon such terms and conditions as Landlord shall deem reasonable, including, without limitation, concessions of free rent. In no event shall the making of any alterations to and/or remodeling of the Premises operate or be construed to release Tenant from liability hereunder as aforesaid. Landlord's failure to relet the Premises or in the event of such reletting, Landlord's failure to collect the rent thereunder, shall not release or affect Tenant's liability for damages hereunder, and Landlord in any event shall not be liable in any way whatsoever for said failures. Any sums received by Landlord on a reletting shall belong to Landlord.

(f) Tenant hereby indemnifies Landlord for all of Landlord's expenses incurred or paid in connection with repossessing or reletting the Premises in the event of Tenant's Default hereunder, including, without limitation, the costs of recovering possession of the Premises; the costs of removing and storing the property of Tenant or any other occupant; the costs of repairing, altering, remodeling, cleaning, or otherwise putting the Premises into condition acceptable to a new tenant or tenants; brokerage and management fees; operating and security expenses of the Premises; and reasonable attorneys' fees and disbursements.

(g) In the event of any Default or any threatened default by Tenant of any of the agreements, terms, covenants, or conditions contained in this Lease, Landlord shall be entitled to enjoin such Default or threatened default and shall have the right to invoke any right and remedy allowed at law or in equity or by statute or otherwise even if not specifically provided for in this Lease.

(h) The rights and remedies of Landlord set forth herein shall be in addition to any other right and remedy now or hereafter provided by law or in equity. All rights and remedies shall be cumulative and not exclusive of each other. Landlord may exercise its rights and remedies at any time, in any order, to any extent, and as often as Landlord deems advisable without regard to whether the exercise of one right or remedy precedes, concurs with, or succeeds the exercise of any other. A single or partial exercise of a right or remedy shall not preclude a further exercise thereof or the exercise of another right or remedy from time to time. No delay or omission by Landlord in exercising a right or remedy shall exhaust or impair the same or constitute a waiver of, or acquiescence to, any Default by Tenant. No waiver of any Default by Tenant shall extend to or affect any other Default or impair any right or remedy with respect thereto. No action or inaction by Landlord shall constitute a waiver of any Default by Tenant. No waiver of any Default by Tenant shall be effective, unless it is in writing and signed by both Landlord and Tenant.

(i) Tenant hereby expressly waives its right to any notice to quit under any statutes relating to summary process or any statutes that may be enacted for recovery of possession of leased premises or other formalities of any nature.

PARAGRAPH **20**

Self-Help

RISK RATING: 2

A. DESCRIPTION AND SCOPE

This Paragraph describes the conditions under which Landlord may invoke self-help remedies and establishes Tenant's obligation to reimburse Landlord for expenses in connection therewith.

B. ANALYSIS

1. Landlord's Perspective

This Paragraph enables Landlord, without notice to Tenant, to take appropriate remedial action should Tenant fail to comply with its Lease obligations.

2. Tenant's Perspective

In the event that Tenant does not comply with its obligations under the Lease, it will be liable to Landlord for the costs incurred by Landlord in ensuring compliance. However, Tenant usually would like a notice and cure period prior to Landlord's taking remedial action since the Tenant is responsible for the costs incurred by Landlord, plus interest.

Tenant would also like a reciprocal paragraph that would permit Tenant to have self-help rights should Landlord fail to perform its Lease obligations. Both Landlord and Lender typically object to granting Tenant such self-help rights. However, if Tenant is the largest Tenant in the Building, or if there are only a few Tenants in the Building, then such self-help rights on the part of Tenant may be available.

117

3. Lender's Perspective

Lenders like this Paragraph for the additional leverage it provides as well as the ability to recoup the costs associated with remedial expenses.

Lender will typically object to any reciprocal self-help rights granted to Tenant. However, if such rights are granted to Tenant, Lender will want notice of Tenant's intended self-help and an opportunity to cure.

C. COMPROMISES AND ALTERNATIVES

If Tenant requests that Landlord give notice prior to remedying the default, alternatives would be a short notice period and/or that Landlord shall not be required to give such notice in an emergency or more than twice in any twelve-month period. The parties may also negotiate the rate at which interest accrues on Landlord's expenditures.

D. COMMENTS

None.

E. TYPICAL PARAGRAPH

20. Self-Help. In the event Tenant defaults in fulfilling any of Tenant's covenants or provisions of this Lease on its part to be performed, Landlord may, at Landlord's sole option, at any time, without notice, cure such default for the account and at the expense of Tenant. If Landlord at any time so elects, or is compelled, to cure any such default and incurs any expense in connection therewith or is compelled to incur any other expense because of any such default (including, without limitation, reasonable attorneys' fees and disbursements in instituting, prosecuting, or defending any suits, actions, or proceedings to enforce Landlord's rights under this Lease or otherwise), the sum or sums so paid by Landlord plus all costs and damages, with interest at the lesser of the maximum legal rate of interest or eighteen percent (18%) per annum from the date Landlord incurs any expense under this Paragraph 20 until Landlord has been reimbursed by Tenant for all such expenses, costs, and damages, shall be paid by Tenant to Landlord, as Additional Rent, upon demand therefor by Landlord.

Lien Rights of Landlord

A. DESCRIPTION AND SCOPE

This Paragraph establishes a lien in favor of Landlord for rent and other charges payable by Tenant, but also provides that the lien is subordinate to the interests of certain creditors of Tenant necessary to conduct Tenant's business.

B. ANALYSIS

1. Landlord's Perspective

This Paragraph enables Landlord to enjoy the status of a secured creditor with respect to payments that the Tenant is obligated to make under the Lease, provided Landlord takes steps to perfect the lien, such as the filing of a UCC-1 Financing Statement in the appropriate filing offices. This Paragraph does not work in all jurisdictions. In some states, purchase money liens will take priority over Landlord's lien.

2. Tenant's Perspective

This Paragraph may be appropriate for a Tenant that has a single location, but for Tenants with multiple offices or stores, this Paragraph will likely conflict with other credit facilities maintained by Tenant. Tenant's primary lender may have a blanket lien on all of Tenant's fixtures and equipment, and Tenant may be prohibited from granting any other liens on such property. In addition, if Tenant is a credit Tenant, there should not be any need to grant a Landlord's lien.

If Tenant does grant a Landlord's lien and Landlord files a UCC-1 Financing Statement, upon expiration of the Lease Term, Tenant will need to obtain a UCC-3 Termination Statement from the Landlord in order to extinguish Landlord's lien, and a provision should be added to this Paragraph requiring Landlord to execute such a Termination Statement.

3.   Lender's Perspective

Lenders like this Paragraph for the additional collateral it can provide to secure Tenant's obligations under the Lease.

C.   COMPROMISES AND ALTERNATIVES

The parties may negotiate the rate at which interest accrues on Landlord's expenditures.

D.   COMMENTS

See Part 4 of this Lease Manual for a Form of Landlord's Waiver of Lien Rights.

E.   TYPICAL PARAGRAPH

21.   Lien Rights of Landlord. In consideration of the mutual benefits arising under this Lease, Tenant hereby grants to Landlord a lien on all property Tenant now or hereafter placed in or upon the Premises (except such part of any property as may be exchanged, replaced, or sold from time to time in the ordinary course of business operations or trade of Tenant), and such property shall be and remain subject to such lien of Landlord for payment of all rent and other sums agreed to be paid by Tenant herein. Said lien shall be in addition to and cumulative upon Landlord's liens provided by law. Said lien shall be second in priority to the rights of the lessor of, or the mortgagee of, any equipment or personal property under any equipment lease or mortgage, the rights of the seller under any conditional sales contract, or the rights of the lender under any leasehold mortgage consented to by Landlord. Landlord agrees not to unreasonably withhold or delay its consent to a request for a waiver of Landlord's lien by any such mortgagee, lender, or lessor, provided such mortgagee, lender, or lessor agrees to repair and restore the Premises or reimburse Landlord for the costs of repair and restoration of the Premises and the Building arising from damage to the Premises and the Building caused by the removal of any equipment or other prop-

erty secured hereunder. Tenant shall pay Landlord, as Additional Rent, all costs and expenses, including reasonable attorneys' fees, that Landlord incurs by reason of or in connection with any request by any such mortgagee, lender, or lessor for a waiver of Landlord's lien hereunder or enforcement of Landlord's rights hereunder, together with interest thereon at the lesser of the maximum legal rate of interest or eighteen percent (18%) per annum from the date Landlord incurs any expense under this Paragraph 21 until Landlord has been reimbursed therefore by Tenant, upon demand thereof by Landlord. Tenant agrees to execute such financing statements and other documents reasonably requested by Landlord to evidence and perfect such lien.

Mortgagee Protection

A. DESCRIPTION AND SCOPE

This Paragraph requires Tenant to provide any mortgagee of Landlord with notice of any Landlord default and to allow the mortgagee the opportunity to cure such default.

B. ANALYSIS

1. Landlord's Perspective

This Paragraph is critical to Landlord's ability to obtain financing for the Property, since potential mortgage Lenders will want the protections provided for in this Paragraph in the event of a Landlord default.

2. Tenant's Perspective

Tenant may require that the provisions of this Paragraph be limited to institutional mortgagees or mortgagees unaffiliated with Landlord, since to permit the provisions of this Paragraph to be extended to affiliates of Landlord is tantamount to giving Landlord an additional cure period.

In some jurisdictions, judicial foreclosure can take up to a year to complete, and in such case Tenant may insist that Lender's cure period be limited (e.g., no more than 60 or 90 days).

3. Lender's Perspective

This Paragraph is of utmost importance to Lender, and Lender's review of the Lease will focus on the terms and conditions of this Paragraph. Since the income stream from the Lease is the repayment mechanism for Lender's mortgage loan, a Lender wants to make sure that Tenant cannot terminate the Lease due to Landlord's default without permitting Lender the opportunity to cure such default. Any limitation on the cure period should allow Lender enough time to complete a foreclosure, take possession of the Property and Premises, and then cure any defaults. Lender will generally resist any alterations of this Paragraph.

C. COMPROMISES AND ALTERNATIVES

Lender's cure period could be limited to a certain period of time.

D. COMMENTS

See the Introduction to this Lease Manual for a discussion of Subordination, Nondisturbance, and Attornment, and Part 4 for Forms of Subordination, Nondisturbance, and Attornment Agreements.

E. TYPICAL PARAGRAPH

22. Mortgagee Protection. Tenant agrees to give each of Landlord's mortgagees and deed of trust holders ("Holder") a copy of any notice of default served upon Landlord (which copy shall be given in accordance with the provisions of this Lease), provided that Tenant has been notified in writing of the name and address of such Holder. Tenant agrees that if Landlord shall have failed to cure such default within the time provided for in this Lease, then each Holder shall have an additional thirty (30) days within which to cure such default, or if such default cannot be cured within that time, then such additional time as may be necessary to cure such default, if within such thirty (30) days, any such Holder has commenced and is diligently pursuing the remedies necessary to cure such default (including, but not limited to, commencement of foreclosure proceedings, if necessary to effect such cure), in which event this Lease shall not be terminated while such remedies are being diligently pursued.

Environmental Compliance

RISK RATING: 4

A. DESCRIPTION AND SCOPE

This Paragraph contains affirmative representations from Landlord regarding (a) compliance with all present and future federal, state, county, and city laws relating to the Property; (b) compliance with all Environmental Laws (which are broadly defined in the Lease) relating to the Property; (c) the existence of PCBs, asbestos, or Hazardous Materials at the Property; and (d) the fact that Landlord has received no notices of any violation of the laws referred to in this Paragraph and that there are no lawsuits pending or threatened against the Property.

This Paragraph also prohibits Tenant from using, storing, generating, or disposing of Hazardous Materials at the Premises and requires Tenant to indemnify Landlord and remediate any Hazardous Materials brought onto the Premises by Tenant.

B. ANALYSIS

1. Landlord's Perspective

Most Landlord forms of Leases will not contain Paragraphs 23(a) through 23(i), and Landlord is likely to resist the potential liability that the warranties and representations contained in those paragraphs could create. Landlord may claim for existing construction that Landlord is not the original owner of the Property and has no specific knowledge regarding the acts of prior owners. In addition, if Landlord has had an Environmental

Site Assessment Report prepared for the project, and such report indicates environmental problems that (i) have since been cleaned up or (ii) are exterior to the Building, Landlord may wish to take exception to the disclosures contained in the Environmental Site Assessment Report. In any event, any representations or warranties given by Landlord should be limited to Landlord's actual knowledge. It should be noted that in any event, Landlord would have continuing environmental liability under CERCLA and other state and federal environmental laws.

2. Tenant's Perspective

This Paragraph protects Tenant against potential liability for environmental problems not caused by Tenant or by Tenant's use of the Premises, and is also designed to "flush out" any potential environmental problems at the site by requiring Landlord to make certain factual representations. Tenant may want to add an affirmative requirement that Landlord provide Tenant with copies of any Environmental Site Assessments that Landlord undertakes.

With respect to Paragraph 23(j), if Tenant is a user of Hazardous Materials in the production of a product, this Paragraph should be modified to permit such use of Hazardous Materials so long as it is done in compliance with all laws.

3. Lender's Perspective

A Lender will want environmental indemnities from its borrower, the Landlord, but is also interested in having Tenant be responsible for cleanup costs for environmental problems caused by Tenant.

C. COMPROMISES AND ALTERNATIVES

If Landlord refuses to give the warranties and representations set forth in this Paragraph, Tenant should require that Landlord provide Tenant with a copy of any Environmental Site Assessment prepared on Landlord's behalf. Tenant may also want to have such Assessment updated and a reliance letter issued to Tenant by the environmental engineering firm that prepared the Assessment.

D. COMMENTS

Federal and state laws will make owners and operators liable for contamination. These provisions contain, identify, and allocate the risk of those burdens between the Lease parties.

E. TYPICAL PARAGRAPH

23. Environmental Compliance.

(a) Landlord represents and warrants that to Landlord's actual knowledge the Property and its existing and prior uses comply with, and Landlord is not in violation of, and has not violated, in connection with the ownership, use, maintenance, or operation of the Property and the conduct of the business related thereto, any applicable federal, state, county, or local statutes, laws, regulations, rules, ordinances, codes, standards, orders, licenses, and permits of any governmental authorities relating to environmental matters (being hereafter collectively referred to as the "Environmental Laws"), including (i) the Clean Air Act, the Federal Water Pollution Control Act of 1972, the Resource Conservation and Recovery Act of 1976, the Comprehensive Environmental Response, Compensation and Liability Act of 1980, and the Toxic Substances Control Act (including any amendments or extensions thereof and any rules, regulations, standards, or guidelines issued pursuant to any of said Environmental Laws); and (ii) all other applicable environmental standards or requirements.

(b) Without limiting the generality of Paragraph (a), Landlord represents and warrants that to Landlord's actual knowledge, Landlord, its agents, contractors, and employees (i) have operated the Property and have at all times received, handled, used, stored, treated, transported, and disposed of all petroleum products, asbestos, and all other toxic, dangerous, or hazardous chemicals, materials, substances, pollutants, and wastes, and any chemical, material, or substance, exposure to which is prohibited, limited, or regulated by any federal, state, county, regional, or local authority or that even if not so prohibited, limited, or regulated, pose a hazard to the health and safety of the occupants of the Property or the occupants or owners of property near the Property (all of the foregoing being hereinafter collectively referred to as "Hazardous Materials") in strict compliance with all applicable environmental, health, or safety statutes, ordinances, orders, rules, standards, regulations, or requirements; and (ii) have removed (or will remove prior to the Commencement Date) from the Property all Hazardous Materials.

(c) Landlord represents and warrants that to Landlord's actual knowledge there are no existing statutes, orders, standards, rules, or regulations relating to environmental matters requiring any remedial actions or any other work, repairs, construction, or capital expenditures with respect to the Property. Landlord has not received any notice requiring such remedial actions or other work.

(d) During the period in which Landlord has owned the Property, Landlord represents and warrants that to Landlord's actual knowledge no Hazardous Materials have been released into the environment, or deposited, spilled, discharged, placed, or disposed of at, on, or near the Property, nor has the Property been used at such time by any person as a landfill or a disposal site for Hazardous Materials or for garbage, waste, or refuse of any kind.

(e) Landlord represents and warrants that to Landlord's actual knowledge there are no electrical transformers or other equipment containing dielectric fluid containing polychlorinated biphenyls in excess of 50 parts per million nor is there any asbestos contained in, on, or under the Property.

(f) Landlord represents and warrants that to Landlord's actual knowledge there are no locations off the Property where Hazardous Materials generated by or on the Property have been treated, stored, deposited, or disposed of.

(g) Landlord represents and warrants that to Landlord's actual knowledge there is no fact pertaining to the physical condition of the Property or the area surrounding the Property (i) that Landlord has not disclosed to Tenant in writing prior to the date of this Lease; and (ii) that materially adversely affects or will materially adversely affect the Property, or the use or enjoyment or the value thereof, or Landlord's ability to perform the obligations contemplated by this Lease.

(h) Landlord represents and warrants that to Landlord's actual knowledge no notices of any violation of any of the matters referred to in Paragraphs (a) through (g) relating to the Property or its use have been received by Landlord, and there are no writs, injunctions, decrees, orders, or judgments outstanding; no lawsuits, claims, proceedings, or investigations pending or threatened, relating to the ownership, use, maintenance, or operation of the Property; nor is there any basis for such lawsuits, claims, proceedings, or investigations being instituted or filed.

(i) Nothing in these Paragraphs (a) through (i) shall in any way limit the representations and warranties contained in all other provisions of this Paragraph.

(j) Tenant shall not cause or permit any Hazardous Materials (other than those used for normal office purposes and in compliance with all Environmental Laws) to be used, stored, generated, or disposed of on or in the Premises by Tenant, Tenant's agents, employees, contractors, or invitees, without first obtaining Landlord's written consent. If Hazardous Materials are used, stored, generated, or disposed of on or in the Premises, whether with or without Landlord's consent or if the Premises become contaminated in any manner for which Tenant is legally liable, Tenant shall indemnify and hold harmless Landlord from any and all claims, damages, fines, judgments, penalties, costs, liabilities, or losses arising during or after the Term and arising as a result of such use, storage, generating, disposal, or contamination by Tenant. This indemnification includes without limitation, any and all costs incurred due to any investigation of the site or any cleanup, removal, or restoration mandated by a federal, state, or local agency or political subdivision. Without limitation of the foregoing, if Tenant causes or permits the presence of any Hazardous Materials on the Premises, and the same results in contamination, Tenant shall promptly, at its sole expense, take any and all necessary action to return the Premises to the condition existing prior to the presence of any such Hazardous Materials on the Premises. Tenant shall first obtain Landlord's approval for any such remedial action.

Americans with Disabilities Act Compliance

RISK RATING: 4

A. DESCRIPTION AND SCOPE

This Paragraph requires that Landlord cause the Building and Common Areas to be in compliance with ADA and that Tenant cause the Premises to be in compliance with ADA. Each party provides an indemnity to the other for noncompliance with ADA.

B. ANALYSIS

1. Landlord's Perspective

Compliance with ADA requirements can be extremely expensive and all parties to a Lease should be aware of the costs and allocation of risk. Some ADA requirements are "use-specific," with greater accessibility required in places of public accommodation. This gives Landlord an incentive to narrowly define Tenant's permitted uses. Each party wants to shift costs to the other, but a reasonable Landlord should take responsibility for public Common Areas. For full-floor Tenants, hallways and bathrooms should be made a part of the Premises so that Tenant and not Landlord assumes responsibility for ADA compliance.

2. Tenant's Perspective

A Tenant should take responsibility for alterations required as a result of its own particular use of space, or special needs of its customers or employees, but not for bringing the base building to general accessibility standards. If Tenant is moving into space but not performing significant alterations, then Tenant may want to require that Landlord represent that the Premises are currently in compliance with ADA. If Landlord, rather than Tenant, is required to construct the improvements to the Premises, then Landlord should assure ADA compliance in connection with such improvements. Restrooms in particular can be expensive to retrofit for ADA compliance, and care should be taken in allocating responsibility for ADA compliance between Landlord and Tenant.

3. Lender's Perspective

Lender wants to be assured that the Property is ADA compliant, so that the collateral value of the Property is maximized. Lender wants to make sure that as much of the future ADA compliance cost and risk as possible is shifted to Tenant. Lender may require an ADA compliance plan, if the Building or Premises do not currently comply with ADA.

C. COMPROMISES AND ALTERNATIVES

Costs can be shifted in any manner acceptable to parties. A Tenant may be more willing to pay ADA improvement costs if Tenant's share is limited to a fraction based on the Lease Term over the useful life of the renovations.

D. COMMENTS

Care should be taken not to allow this issue to be addressed by default through a "compliance with laws" clause that allocates the risk without considering the substantial cost and disruption this work can require. See Paragraph 25 for a discussion of compliance-with-laws issues.

E. TYPICAL PARAGRAPH

24. **Americans with Disabilities Act Compliance.**

(a) **Landlord represents, warrants and agrees that the Building shell structure, Building common areas accessible by Tenant's employees and invitees, and core conditions will conform upon completion, to all applicable legal requirements, including, without limitation, the requirements of Title III of the Americans with Disabilities Act ("ADA"). Landlord agrees to indemnify and hold Tenant harmless from any claims, losses, costs, damages, or other expenses (including, without limitation, rea-**

sonable attorneys' fees) arising from any breach of the foregoing warranty and covenants; provided, however, that nothing
herein shall require Landlord to indemnify Tenant for any noncompliance of the Premises with the ADA to the extent such
noncompliance results from acts or omissions of Tenant or
Tenant's breach of its obligations under this Paragraph.

(b) Tenant represents, warrants, and agrees that: (1) the placement
of Tenant's furniture, fixtures, and equipment within the
Premises and (2) all Tenant Improvements and "Alterations"
(both as that term is defined within the ADA and within this
Lease) to the Premises undertaken by Tenant will comply, to
the extent necessary, with the ADA. Further, in the event modifications are required to the Premises due to the nonconfor-
mity of the Premises to the requirements of the ADA regarding
Tenant's disabled employees or access by disabled members of
the public, including, without limitation, access standards relating to wheelchairs, doors, and entrances, Tenant shall promptly
comply with the requirements of the ADA with respect thereto.
Tenant agrees to indemnify and hold Landlord harmless from
any claims, losses, costs, damages, or other expenses (including,
without limitation, reasonable attorneys' fees) arising from any
breach of the foregoing warranty and covenants.

Compliance
with Laws

A. DESCRIPTION AND SCOPE

This paragraph seeks to allocate the risk and cost of compliance with laws and governmental mandates to the Tenant.

B. ANALYSIS

1. Landlord's Perspective

Landlord would like to allocate all of the compliance-with-laws risk relating to the Premises to Tenant, and this Paragraph does that. This is particularly true in industrial net lease situations. Most Landlords will reject any affirmative obligation or representation that the Property is in compliance with all laws, and instead suggest that Tenant rely on Landlord's covenant of quiet enjoyment. Landlord most likely believes that the Building is in compliance, but does not want to give Tenant the right to require Landlord to correct any nonconformities unless Landlord is so required to comply by a governmental authority. In addition, Landlord would prefer not to be responsible for costs or permits required as a result of Tenant's particular use of the Premises.

2. Tenant's Perspective

Tenant should take responsibility for its own use of the Premises but does not want to pay to bring Landlord's Building up to new standards. If a new law, regulation, or building code is enacted that requires a retrofit of the Building or Premises, Tenant wants to limit its costs to either noncapital expenditures or to an allocable share based on its Lease Term related to the useful life of the expenditures. See Compromises and Alternatives below for a Paragraph that favors Tenant.

3.   Lender's Perspective

Lender wants to make sure the Property is always in compliance with laws and would prefer risks and costs shifted to Tenant.

C.   COMPROMISES AND ALTERNATIVES

Tenant may request reciprocity and require that Landlord add the following paragraph:

> *Upon issuance of a final non-appealable government order, Landlord shall, at its own expense, promptly observe and comply with all present and future laws, ordinances, requirements, orders, directions, rules, and regulations of federal, state, county, and city governments and of all other governmental authorities having or claiming jurisdiction, directly or indirectly, over the Property (excluding the Premises) or appurtenances or any part thereof (including governmental rules and regulations, and such regulations or standards as are or may be promulgated under the Federal Occupational Safety and Health Act of 1970 or similar federal, state, or local requirements), whether the same are in force at the commencement of the Term or may in the future be passed, enacted, or directed. Without limiting the generality of the foregoing, Landlord shall also procure each and every permit, license, certificate, or other authorization now or hereafter required in connection with the lawful and proper use of the Property. Tenant shall pay all costs of complying with laws, ordinances, requirements, orders, directions, rules, and regulations relating to the Premises. Under no circumstances shall Landlord be considered to be in default under this Lease, nor shall Tenant have the right to terminate this Lease as a result of Landlord's failure to comply with the provisions of this Paragraph 25.*

D.   COMMENTS

Tenant should procure its own operating permits, such as food service or liquor licenses that are usually personal and transferable apart from the ownership of the real property.

All parties must be careful that costs of ADA and environmental compliance that may be substantial do not unintentionally get allocated by default under this paragraph.

See Paragraph 23 for Environmental Laws Compliance and Paragraph 24 for ADA compliance.

E. TYPICAL PARAGRAPH

25. Compliance with Laws. Tenant shall, at its own expense, promptly observe and comply with all present and future laws, ordinances, requirements, orders, directions, rules, and regulations of federal, state, county, and city governments and of all other governmental authorities having or claiming jurisdiction, directly or indirectly, over the Premises or any part thereof (including governmental rules and regulations, and such regulations or standards as are or may be promulgated under the Federal Occupational Safety and Health Act of 1970 or similar federal, state, or local requirements), whether the same are in force at the commencement of the Term or may in the future be passed, enacted, or directed. Without limiting the generality of the foregoing, Tenant shall also procure each and every permit, license, certificate, or other authorization now or hereafter required in connection with the lawful and proper use of the Premises.

PARAGRAPH 26

Diminution of Services

A. DESCRIPTION AND SCOPE

This Paragraph provides that Landlord is not liable to Tenant if Landlord fails to provide any service for certain reasons beyond its control or during repairs and that the Annual Base Rent and Additional Rent shall continue notwithstanding any interruption of services.

B. ANALYSIS

1. Landlord's Perspective

This Paragraph is intended to protect Landlord from liability and rent abatements for interruptions in services Landlord is obligated to provide.

2. Tenant's Perspective

Tenant will want to abate rent if essential services are interrupted for a specified period of time. Tenant may also want the bargaining mechanism of termination in order to get the services restored as soon as possible. These arguments have some merit because any service failure will cause a disruption in the Tenant's operations at the site, and a service disruption could cause substantial harm to the Tenant's business. A negotiation is likely over the period of time and the materiality of a failure of service in order to qualify for an abatement of rent. Landlord will argue that Tenant can obtain business interruption insurance to cover this risk. Tenant will counter that Tenant is already paying its pro rata share of Landlord's rent loss insurance as part of the operating expense load, and therefore Landlord should permit a rent abatement if services are not restored. If Landlord concedes the point, Landlord may require that rent abatement occur only if the Premises become untenantable due to a service failure.

3.   Lender's Perspective

Any abatement of rent and Tenant termination provisions may adversely affect the "mortgageability" of this Lease. Lender ordinarily would much rather limit Tenant's remedy to an action against Landlord for damages. However, abatement of rent and Lease termination for lengthy interruptions are fairly common and are generally acceptable to most Lenders.

C.   COMPROMISES AND ALTERNATIVES

Alternatives can include a time period after which Tenant may abate rent and a longer time period after which Tenant can terminate the Lease. However, in no event should Landlord be liable to Tenant for consequential damages relating to service interruptions.

D.   COMMENTS

Whether or not Tenant is permitted to abate rent or terminate the Lease in connection with an interruption in services will generally depend on the relative leverage of Landlord and Tenant in the Lease transaction.

E.   TYPICAL PARAGRAPH

26.   Diminution of Services. Landlord shall not be liable for the interruption, curtailment, stoppage, or suspension of services and utilities to be furnished by Landlord pursuant to this Lease when necessary by reason of accident or emergency or suspension of utility services or when necessary for repairs, alterations, replacements, or improvements desirable or necessary in the reasonable judgment of Landlord or for any cause beyond the control of Landlord, nor shall Landlord have any liability for damages sustained by Tenant resulting therefrom. In the event of any such interruption, curtailment, stoppage, or suspension, there shall be no diminution or abatement of Annual Base Rent, Additional Rent, or other charges due from Tenant to Landlord hereunder. Tenant's obligations hereunder shall not be affected or reduced, and Landlord shall have no responsibility or liability for any such interruption, curtailment, stoppage, or suspension; however, Landlord shall exercise reasonable diligence to restore any services or utilities so interrupted, curtailed, stopped, or suspended.

Subordination, Nondisturbance, and Attornment

A. DESCRIPTION AND SCOPE

This Paragraph provides that the Lease will be subordinate to any mortgage, deed of trust, or underlying ground lease. Such subordination is conditioned on the mortgagee's and ground lessor's agreement that the Lease will not be terminated and that, so long as Tenant is not in default, Tenant's possession will not be disturbed upon the foreclosure of a mortgage or the termination of a ground lease. Further, Tenant agrees to attorn to and recognize any successor to Landlord, and at the election of the mortgagee, the Lease can be made superior to the mortgage.

B. ANALYSIS

1. Landlord's Perspective

This provision assists Landlord in obtaining financing for the Project from a Lender who is likely to require that its mortgage be superior in priority to all other interests, including the interests of Tenant under the Lease.

2. Tenant's Perspective

Although Tenant agrees to subordinate its interest to that of Landlord's mortgagee, Tenant is protected from having its interest terminated by the foreclosure of a mortgage or by the termination of a ground lease that has priority over the Lease. In situations where the Lease is being executed at a time when mortgage financing on the Property is already in place, Tenant will be motivated to ask for a Subordination, Nondisturbance, and Attornment Agreement because without such a document, the Lease is automatically subordinate to any existing mortgage, and a foreclosure of such mortgage would permit the mortgage lender to terminate the Lease. If Landlord requests Tenant to sign a Subordination, Nondisturbance, and Attornment Agreement after the Lease has been executed for the benefit of a Lender involved in a refinancing of the Property, the execution of such Subordination, Nondisturbance, and Attornment Agreement will be for the benefit of Landlord and Landlord's new mortgage Lender and, unless required by the terms of the Lease, may be difficult to obtain from Tenant.

3.   Lender's Perspective

A Lender wants to be sure that the lien of its mortgage or deed of trust has priority over all Leases. Lender does not want to be bound by prior acts of Landlord. The Subordination, Nondisturbance, and Attornment Agreement serves two primary functions: (i) the rights of Tenants under Leases which are in default may be extinguished by the Lender's exercise of its rights under the mortgage or deed of trust, and (ii) upon foreclosure, Tenants under surviving leases agree to recognize Lender, or its purchaser or designee, as the successor to Landlord, without claim of offset or other damages due to prior acts of Landlord. Lender is assured of an uninterrupted source of income and avoids the assumption (by law or otherwise) of certain liabilities created by the prior Landlord. In some states foreclosure will extinguish the Lease, unless the Lease has an attornment clause or is made superior to the Mortgage. In certain circumstances it may be preferable under local foreclosure law to have the Lease superior to the mortgage in order to permit the Lease to survive the foreclosure. The Lender would prefer that the Lease survive foreclosure if the rent payable under the Lease is at or above market rent.

C.   COMPROMISES AND ALTERNATIVES

Tenant may request modification of the form of Subordination, Nondisturbance and Attornment Agreement in order to modify or reinstate certain Lease obligations for which Lender seeks exculpation. In particular, if Landlord is required to complete certain improvements to the Premises or the Property; or if Landlord is required to pay Tenant a tenant improvement allowance, Tenant will request that Lender remain responsible for these obligations and that the SNDA specifically reference the survival of these obligations.

D. COMMENTS

In some instances Landlord's mortgagee may desire to have a strong, credit lease be superior rather than subordinate to its mortgage so that there is no question as to whether the Lease would survive in any foreclosure. See the Introduction to this Lease Manual for a discussion of "Subordination," "Nondisturbance," and "Attornment" and Part 4 of this Lease Manual for forms of Subordination, Nondisturbance and Attornment Agreements.

E. TYPICAL PARAGRAPH

27. **Subordination, Nondisturbance, and Attornment. This Lease shall be subject and subordinate to the lien of any present or future mortgage or deed of trust on all or any part of the Property and to all modifications, consolidations, renewals, extensions, or replacements therefore, and to any present or future underlying lease; provided that the holder of any such mortgage or deed of trust or the landlord under any such underlying lease shall agree in the mortgage, deed of trust, lease, or otherwise that this Lease shall not be terminated or otherwise affected by the enforcement of any such mortgage, deed of trust, or underlying lease if at the time thereof Tenant is not in default under this Lease. Upon written request from Landlord, Tenant agrees to execute and deliver a Subordination, Nondisturbance, and Attornment Agreement in the form attached hereto as Exhibit ___ subordinating this Lease to the lien of any such mortgage, deed of trust, or lease. Tenant shall attorn to any foreclosing mortgagee, purchaser at a foreclosure sale, purchaser by deed in lieu of foreclosure, or landlord of any underlying lease. At the election of the holder of any mortgage or deed of trust, this Lease may be declared superior and prior in right to such mortgage or deed of trust.**

Signs; Building and Floor Directory

RISK RATING: 2

A. DESCRIPTION AND SCOPE

This Paragraph assures Tenant that Landlord will provide a directory in the main lobby of the Building. The Paragraph reserves to Landlord the right to change the name, address, and exterior signage of the Building.

B. ANALYSIS

1. Landlord's Perspective

By providing adequate directory information, Landlord can ensure that a Tenant's visitors and clients locate Tenant with a minimum of inconvenience. Landlord further ensures an orderly flow of traffic through the lobby and reduces visitors' requests for information. Landlord must have the ability to control both interior and exterior signage. In choosing a Building's name and signage, Landlord should be cognizant that certain Tenants may exclude the Building from consideration if the name of the Building or exterior signage depicts a competitor. Also, if exterior signage or name of Building rights are given to a major Tenant, and thereafter that Tenant either reduces its space via surrender options, assignment, or subletting, Landlord should reserve the right to change the name of the Building and revoke Tenant's exterior signage rights.

2. Tenant's Perspective

Tenant wants to have Tenant information prominently posted so that clients and visitors can locate Tenant with a minimum of inconvenience.

Tenant may request that the directory include the names of Tenant's principal departments, sections, employees, and agents. Tenant may also request that the elevator lobby on each floor contain a directory of tenants on that floor. If Tenant will be one of the largest Tenants in the Building, then this Paragraph becomes much more important, and Tenant will want to negotiate for exterior and lobby signage rights, and, perhaps, naming rights to the Building.

3. Lender's Perspective

Lender wants to ensure that the Landlord offers services consistent with those found in a first-class office building.

C. COMPROMISES AND ALTERNATIVES

Tenant may agree that based on the number of tenants per floor, a floor directory may not be necessary. If Tenant requests that all employees be listed on the Building directory, Landlord could negotiate that only a certain number of employees or employees above a certain title be listed.

D. COMMENTS

Some Landlords now place electronic information kiosks in the entrance to the building that can display Tenant's location and provide a list of Tenant's employees. If an electronic kiosk is available, then Tenant will want to list all employees.

E. TYPICAL PARAGRAPH

28. **Signs; Building and Floor Directory. Landlord shall provide and maintain in the lobby of the main entrance level of the Building a directory listing all tenants in the Building. The directory shall list each tenant's name and its location in the Building designated by floor or by such designation as the Landlord may deem appropriate.**

Tenant shall not have any right to signage on the exterior of the Building. Tenant may, with Landlord's prior approval of design, location, and format, place directional signage on the floor where Tenant is located.

Landlord shall have the right to change the name and address of the Building and any exterior signage.

PARAGRAPH **29**

Time Is of
the Essence

A. DESCRIPTION AND SCOPE

This Paragraph provides that "time is of the essence" and obligates both parties to perform their obligations under the Lease in a strictly timely manner.

B. ANALYSIS

1. Landlord's Perspective

This statement protects Landlord against untimely performance by Tenant of its obligations including payment of Annual Base Rent and Additional Rent. Landlord may object to the application of this clause as it relates to Landlord completion of Tenant Improvements or to the scheduled Commencement Date. Tenant may demand that the clause apply, as these are the areas of greatest concern to Tenant. Landlord may want to limit this Paragraph to Tenant's obligations under the Lease. If there are any renewal options, rights of first refusal, or purchase option under the Lease, Tenant will be held strictly to the precise dates in exercising such rights and options.

2. Tenant's Perspective

This statement may protect Tenant against the untimely completion of Tenant improvements, delivery of the Premises at a date later than the scheduled Commencement Date, and other untimely performance by Landlord. The existence of this Paragraph should cause Tenant to pay close attention to any renewal or extension rights of Tenant or any expansion options of Tenant under the Lease. Tenant may want to require that Landlord notify Tenant prior to the expiration of any such rights.

3.   Lender's Perspective

Lender generally wants to ensure that all obligations under the Lease, whether by Landlord or Tenant, are performed in a strictly timely manner.

C.   COMPROMISES AND ALTERNATIVES

Landlord should seek to except from the applicability of this Paragraph force majeure events relating to the completion of Tenant Improvements.

D.   COMMENTS

If "time is of the essence" is included in the Lease, mutually agreed-upon extensions on any time-defined provisions must be in writing and signed by all parties.

E.   TYPICAL PARAGRAPH

29.   Time Is of the Essence. Landlord and Tenant agree that, in fulfilling all terms and conditions of this Lease, time is of the essence.

PARAGRAPH **30**

Landlord's Work; Preparation of Premises

RISK RATING: 3

A. DESCRIPTION AND SCOPE

This Paragraph imposes an obligation upon Landlord to complete the Premises in accordance with plans and specifications and a Completion Schedule approved by Tenant. All costs in connection with such work in excess of the specified Tenant Allowance are the responsibility of Tenant.

B. ANALYSIS

1. Landlord's Perspective

Landlord is protected against excess costs that result from Tenant requesting improvements in excess of Building Standard or requiring change orders once construction has commenced. In addition, Landlord controls the construction process and the awarding of all contracts with subcontractors.

2. Tenant's Perspective

This Paragraph requires Landlord to construct the Premises in a manner suitable to Tenant. However, Tenant should be concerned as to whether the amount of Tenant Allowance will be sufficient to complete the Tenant Work. Tenant may want the ability to approve all construction contracts and subcontracts in order to control the cost of the Tenant Work. If Landlord determines that the cost of the work will exceed the Tenant Allowance, Landlord will likely request that Tenant pay such costs to Landlord prior to the application of the Tenant Allowance. Tenant will, of course, request that the Tenant Allowance be first applied to the construction costs and that

149

Tenant be billed for any excess costs as and when incurred. Should the cost of the work be less than the amount of the Tenant Allowance, then Tenant should request that the difference be credited against future rent payments due from Tenant, since the total amount of the Tenant Allowance has been factored into the amount of Annual Base Rent due under the Lease.

3. Lender's Perspective

Lender may not want to be responsible for paying the Allowance or completing the Tenant Work. Lender may specifically provide in the Subordination, Nondisturbance, and Attornment Agreement that Lender will not be responsible for these obligations.

C. COMPROMISES AND ALTERNATIVES

Landlord may complete the Tenant Work on a "turnkey" basis, meaning that all Tenant has to do is turn the key to the front door of the Premises and move in. If so, the following alternative Paragraph 30 may be used:

(a) *The provisions governing the planning, construction, and scope of work in connection with the build-out of the Premises are set forth below (together with the schedules referred to below, collectively, the "Tenant Work"). Landlord shall perform the Tenant Work at Landlord's sole cost and expense. Landlord and Tenant agree that the Tenant Work shall be performed in accordance with (i) the schedule of estimated completion attached hereto as Schedule ___ (the "Completion Schedule"); (ii) the plans and specifications attached hereto as Schedule ___ (the "Plans and Specifications"); and (iii) the estimated itemized budget attached hereto as Schedule ___ (the "Budget").*

(b) *Landlord shall be responsible for the construction and completion of the Tenant Work and for the payment of all amounts due and payable in connection therewith, all without cost or expense to Tenant except for Tenant's obligation to pay for all other improvements not set forth in the Plans and Specifications. The Tenant Work shall not include the cost of supplies and installation of phone, data, or telecommunication cabling and installation of Tenant's furniture. Landlord shall secure all licenses and permits necessary to perform the Tenant Work. Tenant shall secure all licenses and permits necessary to perform all work for which Tenant is responsible. No changes shall be made to the Plans and Specifications and the Completion Schedule without Landlord's and Tenant's prior written consent (such consent not to be unreasonably withheld), and any such changes requested by Tenant shall be at Tenant's sole cost and expense.*

(c) *Landlord and Tenant shall cooperate with each other and each other's contractors in scheduling and coordinating their respective work, to the end that all work for which either of them is responsible is performed on a timely basis in accordance with the Completion Schedule.*

D. COMMENTS

The amount of the Allowance must be filled in.

If the Tenant Work is performed by Tenant, and Landlord is disbursing the Allowance to Tenant for such Tenant Work, then a disbursement procedure with conditions should be included here. One of the conditions should be that Tenant obtains lien waivers from contractors and subcontractors for all prior disbursements. In addition, where the Tenant Work is performed by Tenant, the Commencement Date and Rent Commencement Date should be fixed at the execution of the Lease.

E. TYPICAL PARAGRAPH

30. **Landlord's Work; Preparation of Premises.**

(a) **Landlord shall provide Tenant with an allowance in an amount not to exceed the lesser of (a) the actual cost of the Tenant Work (as hereinafter defined), and (b) _____ and 00/100 Dollars ($_____.00) (the "Allowance") for tenant improvement work in the Premises, which tenant improvement work shall be approved by Landlord in Landlord's reasonable discretion (collectively, the "Tenant Work"). In addition to hard construction costs, the Allowance may be used for demolition fees, architect and design fees, contractor fees, engineering fees, and the cost of plans and permits in connection with the Tenant Work. Any portion of the Allowance not required to complete the Tenant Work in accordance with the final plans and specifications referred to below shall be the property of Landlord.**

(b) **Landlord may select the contractor and subcontractors (collectively, the "Contractors") that will perform the Tenant Work based on a competitive bid package approved by Tenant.**

(c) **Landlord and Tenant agree that the Tenant Work shall be performed in accordance with the schedule of estimated completion attached hereto as Schedule ___ (the "Completion Schedule"). Prior to the commencement of the Tenant Work, Landlord and Tenant shall use reasonable good faith efforts to agree on the final plans and specifications (the "Plans and Specifications") for the Tenant Work and the estimated budget and cost breakdown referred to in the Completion Schedule.**

Tenant agrees not to unreasonably withhold or delay its approval of such final Plans and Specifications, estimated budget, and cost breakdown, or any other items set forth in the Completion Schedule or elsewhere in this Paragraph 30.

(d) Landlord shall be responsible for the construction and completion of the Tenant Work and for the payment of all amounts due and payable in connection therewith up to the Allowance, all without cost or expense to Tenant except for Tenant's obligation to pay for all Tenant Work in excess of the Allowance and all Tenant Work not set forth in the original Plans and Specifications approved by Tenant. Landlord shall secure all licenses and permits necessary to perform the Tenant Work and for Tenant to occupy the Premises following completion of such Tenant Work. No changes shall be made to the Plans and Specifications and Completion Schedule without Landlord's and Tenant's prior written consent, and any such changes requested by Tenant shall be at Tenant's sole cost and expense.

PARAGRAPH **31**

Parking

A. DESCRIPTION AND SCOPE

This Paragraph establishes a fixed number of parking spaces for Tenant's use in the parking facility adjacent to the Building. Tenant is required to pay a reasonable parking charge for the use of such spaces.

B. ANALYSIS

1. Landlord's Perspective

Landlord generally allocates parking spaces in order to provide Tenant with its proportionate share of the available parking spaces based on the rentable square feet of the Premises. Landlord also wants to reserve a fixed number of parking spaces to be used by visitors or to be leased by Tenant at an additional cost. In some geographical areas, particularly downtown areas of large cities, Landlord may require that an additional parking charge be paid each month for each parking space.

2. Tenant's Perspective

Tenant may assign a certain number of employees to the Premises, in part, based on the availability of parking spaces. In the event that the required number of parking spaces exceeds Tenant's allocation, Tenant may need to make alternative parking arrangements, which may include leasing additional parking spaces at the Building and/or contracting with a third party. For most suburban locations the parking charge requirement should be deleted. Tenant may want to provide that Landlord does not overallocate parking to other Tenants of the Building so that the Parking Garage or Parking Lot does not become overparked. In addition, Tenant may want to specify a parking rate so that if Tenant exercises options for additional space, the number of parking spaces will be increased. Most parking rates are expressed as X number of spaces per 1000 square feet of rentable area. For example, Tenant may require 4 spaces per 1000 square feet of rentable area of the Premises. Tenant may also desire reserved spaces for certain executive employees of Tenant. In such case the location and cost of such exclusive reserved spaces should be specified.

3.   Lender's Perspective

Lender, as a potential owner of the Building, will want to confirm that there is parking available on-site for all Tenants and that parking fees may be collected at Landlord's discretion in appropriate locations.

C.   COMPROMISES AND ALTERNATIVES

Alternatives will depend largely upon the available supply of parking spaces and whether Tenant agrees to an additional charge for parking; however, this Paragraph should be included to establish a fixed number of parking spaces for each Tenant and to provide Landlord with the right to institute and to change parking fees.

D.   COMMENTS

Depending on whether the Building is located in a suburb or downtown (where paid parking is the norm), parking requirements vary considerably. Tenant's allocation of parking spaces should be shown on the diagram attached as Exhibit ___. In buildings with more than one tenant, or with one major tenant, Landlord must ensure that the number of spaces provided in each Tenant's Lease does not cumulatively total more spaces than are available. In addition, parking should be reserved for visitors.

E.   TYPICAL PARAGRAPH

31. Parking. Landlord hereby grants _____ (____) parking spaces (the "Parking Spaces") located in a paved parking facility adjacent to the Building, as shown on Exhibit ___ hereto, for Tenant's nonexclusive use. Tenant shall have the right to park in the Parking Spaces upon such terms and conditions, including the imposition of a reasonable parking charge, established by Landlord from time to time during the term of this Lease, including the following terms and conditions: no trucks, trailers, boats, oversize vehicles, vehicle storage, and no maintenance work shall be permitted within parking areas. Landlord shall have the

right to tow for violations, including parking in visitor spaces. Tenant will enforce any and all rules with its employees. Landlord shall have the right to establish parking verification programs including, but not limited to, the use of stickers. Landlord, at its sole election, may designate the types and locations of the Parking Spaces, and Landlord shall have the right, at Landlord's sole election, to change said types and locations from time to time; provided, however, such designation shall be uniformly applied and shall not unfairly favor any tenant in the Building. It is understood that Tenant or its employees shall not use those parking spaces reserved for other tenants in the Building.

(a) If requested by Landlord, Tenant shall, within ten (10) days of Landlord's request therefore, notify Landlord of the license plate number, year, make, and model of the automobiles entitled to use the Parking Spaces. If Landlord institutes such an identification procedure, Landlord may provide additional parking spaces for use by customers and invitees of Tenant on a daily basis at prevailing parking rates.

(b) The Parking Spaces and additional parking spaces are provided solely for the accommodation of Tenant, and although Landlord, without being obligated to do so, shall provide and maintain the parking facilities, Landlord assumes no responsibility or liability of any kind whatsoever from whatever cause with respect to the use thereof by Tenant or Tenant's agents, employees, representatives, customers, or invitees.

Notice (Memorandum) of Lease

RISK RATING: 4

A. DESCRIPTION AND SCOPE

In most jurisdictions, a lease or a short form of Lease (Notice or Memorandum of Lease) must be recorded in the land records prior to the Lease being enforceable against any party other than the Landlord or Tenant. This Paragraph provides for the execution and recording of such Notice of Lease.

B. ANALYSIS

1. Landlord's Perspective

Landlord will not want to pay for the cost of recording the Notice. Landlord may not want the Notice of Lease to contain any information other than the statutory minimums. Landlord may object to recording a Notice of Lease so as to avoid further encumbering the title of the Property. It will be difficult for Landlord to clean up title should an early termination of the Lease occur because of a Tenant default. Landlord may request that Tenant also execute a recordable Termination of Lease or Quit Claim Deed and put such document in escrow with Landlord's lawyer pursuant to an Escrow Agreement, which Escrow Agreement would permit Landlord to record the Termination Agreement or Quit Claim Deed upon expiration of the Lease Term or an early termination of the Lease.

2. Tenant's Perspective

Tenant will want to have the Lease recorded, as recordation puts the world on notice as to Tenant's interest in Premises. With a recorded notice, any

157

purchaser will take the Premises subject to Tenant's Lease. Tenant may ask for a clause prohibiting the Landlord from disclosing the contents of the Lease to a third party other than professional advisor, existing and potential Lenders, or ground lessors, without Tenant's prior written consent. In addition, recording a Notice of Lease will establish Tenant's priority relative to any future Lender, if the Lease does not contain an automatic subordination provision.

3. Lender's Perspective

Lender may object to having a Notice or Memorandum of Lease recorded, as this creates an encumbrance on the title. If the Notice or Memorandum of Lease is recorded before the mortgage, Lender will require a Subordination, Nondisturbance, and Attornment Agreement from Tenant.

C. COMPROMISES AND ALTERNATIVES

Landlord will resist any Tenant request to have the cost of recording placed on the Landlord.

D. COMMENTS

It is suggested that the Notice of Lease be executed at the same time as the Lease itself and recorded immediately. The Notice or Memorandum of Lease may also have to be modified to take into account any particular legal requirements of the state in which the Premises are located. See Part 4 of this Lease Manual for a form of Notice of Lease.

E. TYPICAL PARAGRAPH

32. Notice [Memorandum] of Lease. Neither Landlord nor Tenant shall record this Lease. Landlord and Tenant have agreed that within ninety (90) days after the execution of this Lease, Landlord shall, at Tenant's sole cost, execute and record an appropriate Notice of Lease in the form attached hereto as Exhibit ___, containing such information as shall be required by the appropriate state statutes, in the Land Records of the city or county, as may be appropriate, where the Property is located.

Estoppel Certificate

RISK RATING: 4

A. DESCRIPTION AND SCOPE

This Paragraph obligates Tenant to deliver an estoppel certificate to Landlord upon ten (10) days' prior written notice, setting forth certain facts with respect to the status of the Lease and the tenancy.

B. ANALYSIS

1. Landlord's Perspective

This provision is primarily an aid to Landlord in financing or selling the Property, since mortgage lenders and purchasers typically require estoppel certificates from Tenants to identify issues that may impact the cash flow generated by the Lease. The typical paragraph is limited "to the reasonable knowledge of Tenant." Many leases will omit this knowledge limitation.

2. Tenant's Perspective

Tenant does not want to waive its claims of offset against Annual Base Rent or Additional Rent by inadvertently failing to disclose such claims in the estoppel certificate. However, Tenant can specify in its certificate those ways, if any, in which Landlord is in default, and Landlord may be required by a Lender or a purchaser to cure the default before financing or sale.

3. Lender's Perspective

A Lender will require estoppel certificates from Tenants of the Project, because it provides Lender with assurances that there are no claims or issues that may impact the income generated by the Leases.

C.   COMPROMISES AND ALTERNATIVES

Major Tenants may request that Landlord provide Tenant with a similar estoppel certificate for Tenant's financing purposes. Tenant may also ask that the number of Landlord requests for estoppels be limited to not more than one or two per year.

D.   COMMENTS

Most Lenders request estoppel certificates in advance of closing on a mortgage loan. See Part 4 of this Lease Manual for forms of Tenant Estoppel Letters.

E.   TYPICAL PARAGRAPH

33.   **Estoppel Certificate.** Tenant shall, upon ten (10) days' prior written request of Landlord, execute, acknowledge, and deliver to Landlord or its designee, which may include any mortgagee or purchaser of the Property, a written statement stating, to the reasonable knowledge of Tenant as of the date made: (a) the date this Lease was executed; (b) the Commencement Date, the Rent Commencement Date, and the Expiration Date; (c) the amount of monthly installment Annual Base Rent and the date to which installment Annual Base Rent has been paid; (d) that this Lease is in full force and effect, that neither Landlord nor Tenant is in default under the Lease, and the Lease has not been assigned, modified, supplemented, or amended in any way (or specifying the date and terms of any agreement so affecting this Lease); (e) that this Lease represents the entire agreement between the parties as to this lease transaction (or identifying those other documents that, together with this Lease, form the entire agreement between the parties as to this lease transaction); (f) that all conditions under this Lease to be performed by Landlord have been satisfied (or specifying those conditions that Landlord has not satisfied); (g) that all required contributions by Landlord to Tenant on account of Tenant's improvements have been received (or specifying those required contributions which Landlord has not made); (h) that as of the date of said statement there are no existing defenses or offsets that Tenant has against the enforcement of this Lease by Landlord except as set out by Tenant; (i) that no Annual Base Rent has been paid for more than one (1) month in advance except as set out by Tenant; (j) that no security has been deposited with Landlord (or the amount of such deposit, if any); and (k) any other matter relating to the Lease that Landlord may request. Any such statement may be relied upon by a prospective purchaser or any mortgagee of Landlord's interest in the Property.

Force Majeure

RISK RATING: 3

A. DESCRIPTION AND SCOPE

This Paragraph excuses performance of Lease obligations (except for the payment of Annual Base Rent or Additional Rent) for 90 days, if performance is made impossible by events outside the control of the nonperforming party. Failure to perform during the 90-day period is not a default under the Lease.

B. ANALYSIS

1. Landlord's Perspective

This Paragraph protects Landlord against default under the Lease obligations when events beyond the control of Landlord make compliance impossible. Landlord will want to exclude from the applicability of this Paragraph, the payment of Annual Base Rent, Additional Rent, or any other amount due Landlord.

2. Tenant's Perspective

This Paragraph protects Tenant from being in default under the Lease if it is unable to comply with its Lease obligations (other than the obligations to pay Annual Base Rent, Additional Rent, or other amounts due Landlord) due to events beyond Tenant's control. Tenant may want to exclude from the provisions of this Paragraph, Landlord's obligation to complete any required tenant improvements and Landlord's work by the Commencement Date.

161

3.   Lender's Perspective

Lender will require that obligations requiring Tenant to pay money, such as the rental obligation and the obligation to pay property taxes and operating expenses, be excluded from this Paragraph since inclusion potentially obstructs Property cash flow available for debt service.

C.   COMPROMISES AND ALTERNATIVES

If Tenant is moving to the Premises from another location with a lease expiration date that cannot be extended, Tenant may require that Landlord's obligation to perform Tenant Improvements or other construction work at the Premises or pay a Tenant Allowance be excluded from this Paragraph. This will likely be resisted by Landlord, since construction delays are common, and Tenant Improvement work represents a substantial obligation of Landlord under the Lease. Tenant may request that Tenant's obligations to pay Annual Base Rent, Additional Rent, and other charges also be suspended due to events beyond its control (since Tenant's possession of the Premises is likely to be interrupted).

Landlord or Tenant may also want to delete the last sentence of the first grammatical paragraph of the Typical Paragraph that limits the Force Majeure period to 90 days, and instead replace such sentence with the following:

> *"The period of such excused performance shall continue for so long as Landlord or Tenant, as the case may be, is unable to perform due to impossibility of performance, and at such time as performance is again possible, Landlord or Tenant, as the case may be, shall thereafter diligently prosecute and complete performance."*

D.   COMMENTS

Obligations involving solely the payment of money by Tenant are often carved out of this Paragraph.

E.   TYPICAL PARAGRAPH

34.   Force Majeure. Whenever during the Term it becomes impossible for Landlord or Tenant to perform the obligations on either party's part to be performed as a result of war, civil riots, labor disputes, or strikes (other than those caused by the direct act or omission of Landlord or Tenant), or acts of God or the elements, then Landlord or Tenant shall be excused from such performance without penalty or other liability or a breach of or default under this Lease to the other party for the period of

time in which the event or events giving rise to the impossibility of performance shall exist. Notwithstanding anything to the contrary contained in this Paragraph 34, Landlord and Tenant agree that neither party shall be excused from the timely performance of its obligations under this Lease for a period of time greater than ninety (90) days.

Nothing in this Paragraph 34 shall be construed to relieve Tenant of Tenant's obligation to pay Annual Base Rent or Additional Rent or any other amount due Landlord as and when due pursuant to the terms of this Lease.

Holding Over

RISK RATING: 2

A. DESCRIPTION AND SCOPE

If Tenant continues in occupancy of the Premises on a month-to-month basis after the expiration of the Term, this Paragraph states that such occupancy shall be upon the same terms and conditions, except that monthly amount of Annual Base Rent will be a multiple of the last monthly rental payment of the Term.

B. ANALYSIS

1. Landlord's Perspective

Landlord may hold Tenant to the terms of the Lease during any holdover period, and Landlord may terminate Tenant's continued occupancy upon appropriate notice under state law. Landlord wants Tenant to be considered a Tenant at will or a Tenant at sufferance to facilitate eviction of Tenant if so needed. As a disincentive for Tenant to hold over, Tenant must pay an increase in the monthly amount of Annual Base Rent and Additional Rent for the holdover period. Landlord desires this, since Landlord may have already relet the Premises to a third party and may be liable to such third party if the Premises are not available.

2. Tenant's Perspective

This Paragraph protects Tenant by permitting a Tenant to hold over in a situation where its new premises are not available for occupancy upon the expiration of the Term. Tenant may want to condition the applicability of this Paragraph to nonconsensual holdovers by Tenant. Tenant may also want to add a provision that reserves to Tenant a specific right to hold over at the

end of the Lease Term for an additional period of time (three to six months
may be appropriate) in order to facilitate Tenant's move to a new location.

3. Lender's Perspective

This Paragraph protects Lender, since it ensures increased cash flow during
the holdover period and requires Tenant to comply with the terms and
provisions of the Lease upon which Lender relied in providing financing.

C. COMPROMISES AND ALTERNATIVES

Landlord may want to modify this provision to increase the percentage of
Annual Base Rent (e.g., 200%, 250%, 300%) to apply during the holdover
period if Tenant has not obtained Landlord's consent to the holdover.
Landlord may also want to add a provision that holds Tenant liable for any
costs, expenses, or damages incurred by Landlord as a result of Tenant's
holdover. For example, if Landlord has leased the space to a third party and
that lease contains either a penalty or damage clause for failure of Landlord
to deliver the Premises to the new tenant in a timely manner, Landlord will
want to hold Tenant liable for such penalties and/or damages.

D. COMMENTS

By permitting Tenant to hold over, Landlord impliedly assents to Tenant's
continued tenancy (at-will) thereby permitting Tenant to avoid liability to
Landlord or any other new third-party tenant claiming the right to occupy
the Premises. Landlord must account for Tenant's holdover rights before
entering into a Lease of the space with a new Tenant. Tenant's status during the holdover will vary from State to State. In some jurisdictions Tenant
may be considered a Tenant at will, in others a Tenant at sufferance or a
Tenant with a month-to-month occupancy. Local counsel should be consulted on this matter.

E. TYPICAL PARAGRAPH

**35. Holding Over. If Tenant shall hold over after the expiration of the
Term, its tenancy shall be on a month to-month basis and shall be subject to all of the terms, conditions, provisions, and obligations of this
Lease, except that the monthly Base Rent due and payable hereunder
shall be equal to [150%–200%] of the monthly amount of Annual Base
Rent and Additional Rent payable as of the last month of the Term. [Ten-
ant shall be considered a Tenant at will during any such holdover period.]**

Lawyer Expenses

RISK RATING: 3

A. DESCRIPTION AND SCOPE

This Paragraph provides for the awarding of reasonable attorneys' fees to the prevailing party in a lawsuit concerning a default under the Lease.

B. ANALYSIS

1. Landlord's Perspective

Landlord may want Tenant to pay Landlord's legal fees regardless of who prevails and regardless of whether or not Landlord actually institutes an action.

2. Tenant's Perspective

Tenant wants this provision to be mutual so that Landlord must pay Tenant's legal fees if Tenant prevails and Tenant must pay Landlord's legal fees if Landlord prevails. This Paragraph benefits Tenant as well as Landlord in that it encourages compliance with the terms of the Lease and promotes cooperative resolution of disputes. It also discourages frivolous litigation.

3. Lender's Perspective

Lender wants a mechanism promoting dispute resolution but would prefer the clause ran in favor of its borrower, the Landlord, rather than benefiting Tenant and Landlord mutually.

C. COMPROMISES AND ALTERNATIVES

If Landlord objects to Tenant's right to obtain attorneys' fees, or cannot accept a reciprocal arrangement on the payment of legal fees, Tenant may find it more beneficial to delete the Paragraph entirely than to attempt to negotiate any changes to Tenant's rights. This would be particularly true for Tenants that do not have significant credit or financial support.

D. COMMENTS

None.

E. TYPICAL PARAGRAPH

36.   Lawyer Expenses. If either party shall at any time be in default here-under, and if either party shall institute an action or summary proceeding against the offending party based upon such default, then the losing party will reimburse the prevailing party for the expense of attorneys' fees and disbursements thereby incurred by the prevailing party, so far as the same are reasonable in amount. In addition, if Tenant makes any requests of Landlord hereunder and Landlord consults with or seeks the advice of a lawyer in connection therewith, Tenant shall immediately reimburse Landlord for all reasonable attorneys' fees incurred by Landlord.

Partial Invalidity

A. DESCRIPTION AND SCOPE

In the event one clause of the Lease is held to be invalid or unenforceable, this Paragraph allows the remainder of the Lease to remain in effect and enforceable. This Paragraph negates a legal rule that would permit a court in some situations to declare that if one clause of a Lease is invalid, the entire Lease is invalid.

B. ANALYSIS

1. Landlord's Perspective

This Paragraph protects Landlord in that it permits the Lease from being invalidated as a result of one, perhaps minor, clause being held invalid. Landlord may request that if any clause, which Landlord deems essential to Landlord's interests, is held invalid, Landlord has the right to terminate the Lease. If requested, Tenant will give careful consideration to the provisions marked for such treatment.

2. Tenant's Perspective

This Paragraph similarly protects Tenant from determining that the whole Lease must fall if any one provision is deemed invalid or unenforceable. If Landlord is granted rights to terminate the Lease for material provisions of the Lease being declared invalid, Tenant should similarly obtain such rights.

3. Lender's Perspective

Lender is interested in keeping the Lease in force so that the rental income stream is not affected; therefore, the partial invalidity clause benefits Lender.

C. COMPROMISES AND ALTERNATIVES

Generally, it would be best not to modify this provision. Any modifications should be reviewed by legal counsel.

D. COMMENTS

This Paragraph is rarely the subject of negotiation.

E. TYPICAL PARAGRAPH

37. Partial Invalidity. If any provision of this Lease, or its application to any situation, shall be invalid or unenforceable to any extent, the remainder of this Lease, or the application thereof to situations other than that as to which it is invalid or unenforceable, shall not be affected thereby, and every provision of this Lease shall be valid and enforceable to the fullest extent permitted by law.

Notices

RISK RATING: 3

A. DESCRIPTION AND SCOPE

This Paragraph sets out the addresses and method of delivery for any notices or copies of notices required under the Lease.

B. ANALYSIS

1. Landlord's Perspective

This Paragraph protects against notices being sent to the incorrect address or without record of timely posting. Landlord wants to ensure that both Landlord and its designated representative receive copies of all notices. Landlord should refuse a request by Tenant that the notice is effective only upon receipt unless a clause is added stating that a notice shall be deemed to have been received upon attempted delivery so as to negate the situation where Tenant refuses to accept delivery.

2. Tenant's Perspective

Tenant desires that both it and its legal counsel receive copies of all notices.

3. Lender's Perspective

A Lender is concerned that adequate provision for notice be made so that it can give and receive appropriate notices in cases where the Lender has succeeded to the interests of Landlord under the Lease.

C. COMPROMISES AND ALTERNATIVES

An alternative would be to use a post office box number; the risk is that overnight delivery services usually will not deliver to post office boxes (U.S. overnight delivery will). Other alternatives include delivery via fax or email. The concern with both of these alternatives is verification of receipt. One alternative is to require that a confirming original hard copy of the fax or email be delivered overnight the next day, but that the notice is deemed received upon sending the fax or email.

D. COMMENTS

None.

E. TYPICAL PARAGRAPH

38. Notices. Any notice required or permitted under this Lease shall be given by notice in writing, sent by a private carrier of overnight mail or United States Certified Mail, Return Receipt Requested, postage prepaid and addressed as follows:

(a) If to Landlord, at the address shown in Paragraph 1, with a copy mailed to _____, to the Attention of _____; and

(b) If to Tenant, at the address shown in Paragraph 1, to the Attention of _____, with a copy mailed to _____.

Either Landlord or Tenant may at any time change the address(es) to which notice is to be sent, provided that the other party is notified of the change in writing. All notices shall be deemed effective (i) the day after being sent by a private carrier of overnight mail; or (ii) three (3) days after being sent by United States Certified Mail.

Successors and Assigns

A. DESCRIPTION AND SCOPE

This paragraph binds the heirs, executors, administrators, successors, and permitted assigns of Landlord and Tenant and requires that they perform their predecessor's obligations under the Lease.

B. ANALYSIS

1. Landlord's Perspective

This Paragraph protects Landlord from a claim that a transfer of Tenant's interest in the Lease has terminated Landlord's rights under the Lease against the original Tenant or that a permitted successor Tenant is not bound by the terms of the Lease.

2. Tenant's Perspective

This Paragraph similarly protects Tenant from a claim that a transfer of the Premises by Landlord has terminated Tenant's rights under the Lease or that a successor Landlord is not bound by the terms of the Lease.

3. Lender's Perspective

This Paragraph protects Lender by preventing the termination or impairment of rights and obligations resulting from an assignment of the Lease, which rights and obligations were relied upon by Lender in providing financing.

C. COMPROMISES AND ALTERNATIVES

None.

D. COMMENTS

Landlord will generally require that Tenant obtain Landlord's written consent to an assignment of Tenant's interest, while permitting Landlord to freely assign its interest in the Lease.

E. TYPICAL PARAGRAPH

39. Successors and Assigns. This Lease shall be binding upon and shall inure to the benefit of the parties hereto, their heirs, executors, administrators, successors, and permitted assigns.

No Partnership or Joint Venture

RISK RATING: 5

A. DESCRIPTION AND SCOPE

This Paragraph sets forth the statement that Landlord and Tenant are not associated as partners in any respect.

B. ANALYSIS

1. Landlord's Perspective

This statement will serve as evidence of an intent not to create any form of legal association between Landlord and Tenant. Such a statement is necessary to limit Landlord's liability for the acts of Tenant that are done in the course of Tenant's business.

2. Tenant's Perspective

Tenant will be equally concerned that it not bear responsibility for the acts of Landlord, and therefore, Tenant is unlikely to resist the inclusion of this Paragraph in the Lease.

3. Lender's Perspective

Lender has the same concerns as Landlord regarding this Paragraph. If Lender succeeds to Landlord's interest under the Lease, Lender will desire an affirmative statement in the Lease concerning the nonexistence of any legal association between Lender and Tenant.

C. COMPROMISES AND ALTERNATIVES

None.

D. COMMENTS

This clause occurs in many office and retail leases. It is probably most important in those retail leases requiring the payment of percentage rent since rent derived from a percentage rent clause may be viewed as giving Landlord a form of participation in Tenant's revenues. This clause should also be used with any other provisions that give Landlord some rights to exercise control over Tenant's operations. In such situations, it is advisable to include a clause in the Lease to indicate that the parties do not intend the establishment of a partnership or joint venture.

E. TYPICAL PARAGRAPH

40. No Partnership or Joint Venture. Landlord shall in no event be construed, held, or become in any way or for any purpose a partner, associate, or joint venturer of Tenant or any party associated with Tenant in the conduct of its business or otherwise.

Merger

A. DESCRIPTION AND SCOPE

This paragraph provides that only the terms and provisions of the written Lease (which can only be modified by a written amendment) and any Exhibits, Riders, or Addenda attached to it are binding on the parties.

B. ANALYSIS

1. Landlord's Perspective

This paragraph protects Landlord against any representations, statements made in negotiation, oral agreements, or extraneous agreements being construed as part of the Lease.

2. Tenant's Perspective

Tenant wants to ensure that its only obligations under the Lease are those specifically described in the Lease. Similarly, Tenant needs to be aware that all of Landlord's obligations need to be specifically described or else they will not be enforceable. Verbal understandings or agreements with the Landlord will not be upheld if they are not contained in the Lease.

3. Lender's Perspective

Lender is relying on the written Lease as being the entire Agreement between Landlord and Tenant. Therefore, for example, an oral agreement between Landlord and Tenant to reduce rent payments would not be valid. As a result Lender is assured that the relationship between its borrower/

Landlord and Tenant is clear. Lender will want to specify in the Subordination, Nondisturbance, and Attornment Agreement that any written amendment to the Lease is not valid without Lender's written consent.

C.   COMPROMISES AND ALTERNATIVES

None.

D.   COMMENTS

This Paragraph should not be controversial.

E.   TYPICAL PARAGRAPH

41.   Merger. This Lease and the Exhibits, Riders and/or Addenda, if any, attached hereto, set forth the entire agreement between the parties. Any prior conversations or writings are merged herein and extinguished. No subsequent amendment to this Lease shall be binding upon Landlord or Tenant unless reduced to writing and signed.

PARAGRAPH 42

Brokers

RISK RATING: 3

A. DESCRIPTION AND SCOPE

This Paragraph specifies the broker or brokers, if any, involved in negotiating the Lease and states that Landlord shall be responsible for any fees or commissions payable to the Broker. The Paragraph also provides an indemnification by Tenant for commissions owed to any brokers who are not named.

B. ANALYSIS

1. Landlord's Perspective

This Paragraph protects Landlord by requiring Tenant to identify all brokers with which Tenant has had any dealings regarding the Lease. The Paragraph further requires that Tenant indemnify Landlord in the event any unspecified brokers with whom Tenant has had dealings should make any claims after the execution of the Lease.

2. Tenant's Perspective

Generally, Tenants expect that Landlord will pay the cost of all brokers involved in the Lease transaction. Tenant knows that Landlord usually has a budget for broker fees and that the amount of these fees factor into the Annual Base Rent calculation that is offered by Landlord. Any broker retention letter or agreement entered into between Tenant and Tenant's broker or representative should indicate that the broker will look to Landlord for payment of the broker fees and should set a maximum amount or percentage of Annual Base Rent that Tenant's broker will seek to obtain from Landlord. It is then incumbent upon Tenant's broker to negotiate a satisfactory arrangement with Landlord that is within the parameters set by Tenant's retention letter or agreement with its broker. Tenant needs to be careful in its interaction with multiple brokers since Landlord will likely be unwilling to compensate more than a single Tenant broker. There should be no circumstances where there is more than one broker claiming to be the "procuring cause" of Tenant's new lease, unless an agreement exists among multiple brokers to share the fees.

3. Lender's Perspective

This Paragraph benefits Lender by specifying the responsibility of each party to pay the claims of named and unnamed brokers.

4. Broker's Perspective

A broker or tenant's representative will want to make sure they are named in this Paragraph. The Broker should also obtain the written compensation agreement from Landlord prior to Lease execution. Many states restrict enforceability of broker's commission to that specified in a written agreement.

C. COMPROMISES AND ALTERNATIVES

A prospective tenant might seek a reciprocal indemnity from Landlord under which Landlord would indemnify Tenant for claims made against Tenant by an unspecified broker whose dealings were initiated by Landlord.

D. COMMENTS

A modified version of this paragraph should be used even if no broker or tenant representative is involved. If a broker or tenant representative is not involved, both Landlord and Tenant will want a representation from the other party to that effect.

E. TYPICAL PARAGRAPH

42. **Brokers. Tenant warrants and represents it has not engaged or dealt with any realtor, broker, or agent in connection with the negotiation of this Lease, except for _____ and _____ (collectively, the "Broker"). Tenant shall indemnify and hold Landlord harmless from any cost, expense, or liability (including costs of suit and reasonable attorneys' fees) for any compensation, commission, or charges claimed by any realtor, broker, or agent with respect to this Lease and the negotiation thereof, other than a claim of the Broker or a claim based upon any agreement between such person and Landlord. Landlord shall pay any and all fees and commissions owed to the Broker in connection with this Lease.**

Late Payments

A. DESCRIPTION AND SCOPE

This Paragraph permits Landlord to impose a late charge on Tenant in the event Tenant fails to pay any installment of Annual Base Rent or Additional Rent on or prior to the fifth day of the month after which the same is due. The late charge is imposed at a rate that is the greater of five percent (5%) of the overdue amount or 18% interest on the overdue amount.

B. ANALYSIS

1. Landlord's Perspective

This Paragraph will encourage Tenant to make timely payments of any monies due Landlord under the Lease. If Tenant fails to make timely payments, Landlord will be in a position of having to make its mortgage payment on time without having obtained the rental income with which to make such payment and will therefore want a disincentive for Tenant not paying the rent in a timely manner.

2. Tenant's Perspective

Tenant will strive to assert its credit rating (if any) and its reliability in making rental payments. Tenant may attempt to delete this entire section or negotiate a reduction in the percentage amount for the late charge.

3. Lender's Perspective

Lender, which may have its loan affected by Tenant's late payments to Landlord, will want to be sure Tenant is timely paying any monies due Landlord, and that Landlord is protected from the additional costs associated with late payments to Lender. Landlord's promissory note with Lender will also likely contain a provision for late fees or default interest if Landlord fails to make a loan payment on time. Also, if Lender must assume ownership of the Premises, Lender will want to have the late charge available to Lender as a remedy for any late payment by Tenant.

C. COMPROMISES AND ALTERNATIVES

Different percentage amounts for subsection (i) may be agreed to by Landlord and Tenant. However, the late charge should be reasonably related to the costs that may be incurred by Landlord in dealing with a late rental payment. Most leases provide for 4% or 5%, but leases do exist with late charges ranging from 1% to 10%. The late charge should not be set so high as to be a "penalty," since penalties are generally not enforceable in most jurisdictions.

Landlord may insist that the late charge under the Lease be tied to any default interest and late charge for which Landlord may be liable for under its mortgage loan. Landlord may request both a flat percentage late charge of the amount due plus default interest from three to six percentage points above Landlord's mortgage interest rate.

Tenant should consult with its accountant or broker to determine what steps can be taken to assure Landlord's timely receipt of the rent payment following an initial late charge being incurred. Tenant may permit Landlord to make a direct withdrawal from Tenant's checking account to pay Annual Base Rent.

D. COMMENTS

Tenant's failure to make Annual Base Rent payments to Landlord on time can result in significant adverse financial consequences to both Tenant and Landlord.

E. TYPICAL PARAGRAPH

43. Late Payments. Tenant acknowledges that the late payment to Landlord of Annual Base Rent, Additional Rent, or any other sum due hereunder will cause Landlord to incur costs not contemplated under this Lease. Tenant further acknowledges that the exact amount of such costs are and will be extremely difficult to ascertain. Accordingly, if any Annual Base Rent, Additional Rent, or such other sum is not received by Landlord or Landlord's designated agent within five (5) days after it is due and payable, then Tenant shall pay to Landlord, in addition to all attorneys'

fees and costs incurred by Landlord in connection with Tenant's failure to pay such amount when due and payable, an amount equal to the greater of (i) a late charge equal to five percent (5%) of such overdue amount, or (ii) interest at eighteen percent (18%) per annum or the highest rate permitted by law of the amount due, whichever is less, from its due date until paid (the "Late Charge"). Landlord and Tenant agree that the Late Charge represents a fair and reasonable estimate of the costs Landlord will incur as the result of Tenant's late payment of any such amount. Landlord's acceptance of any Late Charge shall not constitute Landlord's waiver of Tenant's default with respect to such overdue amount or estop Landlord from exercising any of its rights or remedies under this Lease.

Condition of Premises

A. DESCRIPTION AND SCOPE

Alternative 1 (If Tenant Work will not be performed): Landlord has no obligation to complete Tenant improvements to the Premises. Tenant is deemed to have accepted the Premises in their "AS-IS" condition upon Tenant's occupancy.

Alternative 2 (If Tenant Work will be performed): This Paragraph dovetails with Paragraph 30—Landlord's Work; Preparation of the Premises. It gives Tenant (i) a short period of time (i.e., five days) to inspect the Tenant Work, and (ii) a right to delay the Commencement Date only if deviations in the Tenant Work would unreasonably interfere with Tenant's use and occupancy of the Premises.

B. ANALYSIS

1. Landlord's Perspective

Landlord wants (i) Tenant to acknowledge that Tenant has accepted the Premises in their "AS-IS" condition, or (ii) if Tenant Work is to be completed, to make the Commencement Date as certain as possible by limiting Tenant's right to postpone the Commencement Date only if material deviations in the Tenant Work would unreasonably interfere with Tenant's use and occupancy of the Premises. In a tight leasing market Landlord may be able to eliminate the five (5) days' "move-in" service after completion of the Tenant Improvement Work.

2. Tenant's Perspective

Tenant wants to be satisfied that the condition of the Premises is sufficient to permit Tenant to use and occupy the Premises in accordance with the permitted use of the Premises. Tenant also does not want to pay Annual Base Rent or Additional Rent until it can so use and occupy the Premises. If Tenant is planning an extensive move or if Tenant will be unable to complete its telecommunications and computer cabling or the installation of other Tenant fixtures until after Landlord's work is completed, then a request for a fifteen (15) day or thirty (30) day "move-in" period prior to the commencement of rent would not be uncommon. Tenant may also need time terminate its existing lease arrangements and coordinate a move to the new location.

3. Lender's Perspective

Lender may be making additional advances to Landlord under its mortgage loan based upon the occupancy and the commencement of rent payments by a new Tenant. Lender will generally be unwilling to make these additional advances until the Premises are substantially complete and Tenant has accepted the Premises. Lender will also want to understand where the economic burden for maintenance, repair, and restoration is placed. This burden will certainly have an impact on the economics of the Lease. In addition, Lender will likely be concerned that Landlord has sufficient economic resources to lease the Premises and complete the necessary Tenant improvements.

C. COMPROMISES AND ALTERNATIVES

The first alternative Paragraph 44 should be used if no Tenant Work will be performed by Landlord and no maintenance will be performed by Landlord during the Lease Term. This would usually occur only where Tenant leases the entire building. The second alternative Paragraph 44 should be used if Tenant Work will be performed by Landlord.

D. COMMENTS

None.

E. TYPICAL PARAGRAPH

44. Condition of Premises.

Alternative 1 (If no Tenant Work will be performed)
Tenant shall be deemed to have accepted the Premises as of the Commencement Date in their "AS-IS" condition. Tenant's taking possession of the Premises shall be conclusive evidence that the Premises were in good order, condition, and repair when Tenant took possession. No promise of Landlord to alter, remodel, repair, or improve the Premises or the Building and no representation, either expressed or implied, respecting any matter or thing relating to the Building or this Lease (including the condition of the Premises or the Building) have been made by Landlord to Tenant.

Alternative 2 (If Tenant Work will be performed)
Tenant shall be deemed to have accepted the Premises in their "AS-IS" condition as of the date five (5) days after Tenant receives from Landlord a certification that the Tenant Work has been substantially completed, unless during such five (5) day period Tenant inspects the Premises and notifies Landlord in writing of any material deviations or variations from the Plans and Specifications for the Tenant Work that would unreasonably interfere with Tenant's use and occupancy of the Premises. Tenant's acceptance of the Premises and the Commencement Date shall be postponed until such material deviations or variations are corrected. If, as a result of such inspection, Tenant discovers minor deviations or variations from the Plans and Specifications for the Tenant Work of a nature commonly found on a "punch list" (as that term is used in the construction industry), then Tenant shall promptly notify Landlord in writing of such deviations and variations. Such minor deviations and variations shall not postpone the Commencement Date or the obligation of Tenant to pay Annual Base Rent, Additional Rent, or any other sum due under this Lease.

Rules and Regulations

RATING: 2

A. DESCRIPTION AND SCOPE

These paragraphs set forth a sample of all the Rules and Regulations Tenant, its employees, and its visitors are to comply with under the Lease. Violation of the rules and regulations is a default under the Lease. An inclusion of Rules and Regulations further clarifies the relationship between Landlord and Tenant and prevents disputes as prohibited behavior is expressly set forth.

B. ANALYSIS

1. Landlord's Perspective

Landlord wants to prevent any activities that may damage the Premises or disturb other tenants. Landlord wants to retain as much control over the Premises as possible.

2. Tenant's Perspective

Tenant wants to avoid having to consult Landlord prior to taking any minor action or making any alteration. Tenant should be sure that no Rules or Regulations interfere with Tenant's expected uses since a breach of the rules is a default. Tenant may also want assurance that Rules will be the same for all tenants of the Building and will be enforced in a nondiscriminatory manner. Since landlords may include provisions in the Rules and Regulations that are in direct conflict with provisions of the Lease, in such case, Tenant should request the addition of the following sentence: "In the event of any conflict between the other provisions of the Lease and the Rules and Regulations, the other provisions of the Lease shall prevail." In addition, Tenant may want to alter this Paragraph to provide that the Rules and Regulations will not be amended without Tenant's consent or that Tenant will not be subject to any such amendments unless Tenant's consent thereto has been obtained. Landlord may resist this change since any change to the Rules and Regulations would have to be approved by all Tenants having such approval rights. A compromise might be that any rule changes that materially affect Tenant's rights under the Lease must be approved by Tenant.

3.   Lender's Perspective

By clarifying the Rules and Regulations of the Premises, Lender is assured that disruptions and disputes at the Property are minimized. The clarification of the relationship between Landlord and Tenant will protect Lender's potential interest in the Premises.

C.   COMPROMISES AND ALTERNATIVES

Provided the Rules and Regulations do not conflict with any other provision of the Lease, the Rules and Regulations can be adjusted on a case-by-case basis to fit the requirements of the Building. Most often the Rules and Regulations are attached as an Exhibit to the Lease.

D.   COMMENTS

Even if the Rules and Regulations are preprinted and attached as an Exhibit to the Lease, a careful reading of the Rules and Regulations is required to assure that there is no conflict with the remaining portion of the Lease.

E.   TYPICAL PARAGRAPH

45. Rules and Regulations. The following Rules and Regulations shall be and are hereby made a part of this Lease, and Tenant's employees and agents, or any other person permitted by Tenant to occupy or enter the Premises, will at all times abide by said Rules and Regulations, unless otherwise specified or provided for in the Lease:

  1. **The sidewalks, entries, passages, corridors, stairways, and elevators of the Building shall not be obstructed by Tenant, or**

Tenant's agents or employees, or used for any purpose other than ingress and egress to and from the Premises.

(a) Furniture, equipment, or supplies will be moved in or out of the Building only upon the elevators designated by Landlord and then only during such hours and in such manner as may be reasonably prescribed by Landlord. Tenant shall cause its movers to use only the loading facilities, common entrances, and elevators designated by Landlord. In the event Tenant's movers damage the elevators or any part of the Building, Tenant shall pay to Landlord the amount required to repair said damage.

(b) No safe or article, the weight of which may in the opinion of Landlord constitute a hazard or damage to the Building or the Building's equipment, shall be moved into the Premises without Landlord's approval, which approval shall not be unreasonably withheld, conditioned, or delayed.

(c) Safes and other equipment, the weight of which is not excessive, shall be moved into, from, or about the Building only during such hours and in such manner as shall be reasonably prescribed by Landlord, and Landlord and Tenant shall mutually agree to the location of such articles in the Premises.

2. Except as otherwise provided for in this Lease, no sign, advertisement, or notice shall be inscribed, painted, or affixed on any part of the inside or outside of the Building unless the color, size, style, and location are approved by Landlord. No furniture shall be placed in front of the Building or in any lobby or corridor without the prior written consent of Landlord. Landlord shall have the right to remove all nonpermitted signs and furniture without notice to Tenant.

3. Tenant shall not employ any person or persons other than the janitor or cleaning contractor of Landlord for the purpose of cleaning or taking care of the Premises without the prior written consent of Landlord. Except as otherwise provided in this Lease, Landlord shall not be responsible to Tenant for any loss of property from the Premises, however occurring. The janitor of the Building may at all times keep a passkey, and other agents of Landlord shall at all times be allowed admittance to the Premises in accordance with the provisions set forth in this Lease.

4. Water closets and other water fixtures shall not be used for any purpose other than that for which the same are intended, and

any damage resulting to the same from misuse on the part of Tenant or Tenant's agents or employees shall be paid for by Tenant. No person shall waste water by tying back or wedging the faucets or in any other manner.

5. No animals except seeing-eye dogs or other animals necessary to the functioning of disabled persons shall be allowed in the office, halls, corridors, and elevators of the building. No persons shall disturb the occupants of this or adjoining buildings or premises by the use of any radio, sound equipment, or musical instrument or by the making of loud or improper noises.

6. Bicycles or other vehicles, other than wheelchairs, shall not be permitted in the offices, halls, corridors, and elevators in the building, nor shall any obstruction of sidewalks or entrances of the Building by any such vehicles be permitted.

7. Tenant shall not allow anything to be placed on the outside of the Building, nor shall anything be thrown by Tenant or Tenant's agents or employees out of the windows or doors, or down the corridors, elevator shafts, or ventilating ducts or shafts of the Building. Tenant, except in case of fire or other emergency, shall not open any outside window.

8. No awnings shall be placed over any window.

9. Tenant shall not install or operate any steam or gas engine or boiler, or carry on any mechanical business, other than such mechanical business as normally is identified with general office use of the Premises. Explosives or other articles of an extra-hazardous nature shall not be brought into the Building.

10. Any painting or decorating as may be agreed to be done by and at the expense of Landlord shall be done during regular weekday working hours. Should Tenant desire such work on Saturdays, Sundays, holidays, or outside of regular working hours, Tenant shall pay for the extra cost thereof, if any.

11. Landlord may amend, modify, delete, or add new and additional rules and regulations to the use and care of the Property. Tenant shall comply with all such rules and regulations upon notice to Tenant from Landlord thereof. In the event of any breach of any rules and regulations herein set forth or any reasonable amendments, modifications, or additions thereto, Landlord shall have all remedies provided for in this Lease in the event of default by Tenant.

Insurance

A. DESCRIPTION AND SCOPE

The insurance provision is designed to protect the Landlord by requiring the Tenant to obtain $5 million of liability insurance on the Premises, and replacement value casualty insurance on the contents of and improvements to the Premises. Liability insurance protects the insured against liability due to injuries to persons or property of others at the Premises. Casualty insurance offers protection against damage to the Premises.

B. ANALYSIS

1. Landlord's Perspective

By requiring insurance, Landlord and Lender benefit by obtaining funds to repair the Premises in the event of damage so that the rental income stream can be maintained after a casualty. Because Landlord, Tenant, and Lender each have an insurable interest in the Property, Landlord and/or Lender will want to be named as insured parties under the Tenant's policy. The amount and type of coverage are often determined by relatively objective standards (for example, in accordance with a particular industry form) or subjectively (for example, "as Landlord may require").

Landlord wants to be sure that Tenant maintains adequate insurance to make Landlord whole in the event of damage to the Premises or a claim by a third party for damage suffered on the Premises. In particular, Landlord wants to be sure that the insurance company will have the financial capacity to make good on claims, that Landlord is notified in advance before any lapse of insurance coverage, and that Tenant's deductible is small. In addition, Landlord will want an undertaking by Tenant either not to engage in any activity that could raise the rates of Landlord's insurance premiums, or to reimburse Landlord for the cost of such additional premiums.

2.   Tenant's Perspective

Tenant wants to keep its insurance obligations consistent with its own needs. Furthermore, if Tenant leases more than one property, the insurance requirements of the Lease should conform with a possible blanket insurance policy carried by Tenant insuring other properties it leases. Coverage levels that are set at Landlord's discretion could lead to significantly increased premium costs for Tenant if the levels are increased. Tenant's casualty insurance obligations should be limited to the value of the improvements to the Premises plus the value of Tenant's property on the Premises. Tenant may request that Landlord's insurance policy cover any building Tenant Improvements since it will likely be more cost effective to insure the Tenant Improvements under Landlord's policy. Tenant's obligation would then be limited to insuring any special or above-Building-Standard Tenant Improvements. Tenant may also object that the deductible amount of $1,000 is too low, with $5,000, $10,000, or $25,000 being a more reasonable amount. Tenant may also object to the relatively high $5 million liability insurance coverage requirement and may suggest that $1 million or $2 million of coverage would be sufficient. Finally, for investment-rated credit Tenants, Tenant may want to request the right to self-insure all risks so long as Tenant maintains an investment-grade credit rating.

3.   Lender's Perspective

Lender wants to see that its security is adequately protected against damage or destruction. Therefore, Lender is less interested in the level of Tenant's liability coverage. Whenever possible, Lender will want a clause providing that the Tenant's insurance coverage will be set as Landlord's mortgagee shall require.

C.   COMPROMISES AND ALTERNATIVES

To avoid unduly burdensome insurance requirements, Tenant may require that any coverage levels set by Landlord or Landlord's mortgagee shall be reasonable.

D.   COMMENTS

This section relates to Paragraph 52, the Waiver of Subrogation paragraph.

E. TYPICAL PARAGRAPH

46. Insurance.

(a) Tenant shall maintain at its own cost and expense (i) insurance against fire and such other perils as may be included in the so-called special form fire and special extended coverage insurance on the leasehold improvements and Tenant's property in an amount adequate to cover their replacement cost; and (ii) comprehensive commercial general liability insurance on an occurrence basis with limits of liability in an amount not less than five million dollars ($5,000,000) combined single limit for each occurrence with respect to loss of life, bodily or personal injury, and damage to property. All such insurance shall be issued by insurers approved by Landlord (which approval shall not be unreasonably withheld) and authorized to do business in the State, shall name Landlord as additional insured, shall provide for a deductible not greater than $1,000 from any loss payable, and shall contain a provision whereby each insurer agrees not to cancel such insurance without 30 days' prior written notice to Landlord. On or before the Commencement Date, Tenant shall furnish Landlord with a certificate evidencing the aforesaid insurance coverage, and renewal certificates shall be furnished to Landlord at least 30 days prior to the expiration date of such insurance.

(b) If, during the term of this Lease, insurance premiums on any insurance policy carried by Landlord on the Building or the Premises are increased due to or resulting from Tenant's occupancy hereunder, Tenant shall pay to Landlord as Additional Rent the amount of such increase in insurance premiums. Any amount payable by Tenant hereunder shall be paid to Landlord within ten (10) days after notice to Tenant accompanied by the premium notice or other evidence of the amount due.

Limitations of Landlord's Liability

RISK RATING: 4

A. DESCRIPTION AND SCOPE

This provision limits the Landlord's liability to Tenant to the value of Landlord's interest in the Property where the Premises are located. It specifically excludes the assets of any individuals having an interest in Landlord as well of any other assets owned by Landlord.

B. ANALYSIS

1. Landlord's Perspective

Landlord wants to limit its potential liability to Tenant as much as possible. In particular, potential liability of individuals who control Landlord should be limited.

2. Tenant's Perspective

Tenant wants to have the largest possible pool of assets to pursue in the event it has a claim against Landlord. Tenant may therefore object to this paragraph entirely. This will particularly be the case if Landlord has little or no equity in the Property.

3. Lender's Perspective

Lender has an interest in seeing that the damages against Landlord are minimized since Landlord is Lender's borrower and Landlord's assets may provide additional security for Lender's loan.

C. COMPROMISES AND ALTERNATIVES

A prospective tenant who is in a strong negotiating position might seek to increase the assets that it might pursue upon Landlord's default by removing some of the restrictions noted in this Paragraph. Because many Landlords are single-purpose entities whose sole assets are often the property being leased, the practical effect of these efforts may be limited.

D. COMMENTS

Landlords with large holdings will want to include a clause similar to this.

E. TYPICAL PARAGRAPH

47. Limitations of Landlord's Liability. If Landlord becomes obligated to pay Tenant a money judgment arising out of any failure by Landlord to perform or observe any of the terms, covenants, conditions, or provisions to be performed or observed by Landlord hereunder, Tenant shall be limited for the satisfaction of said money judgment solely to Landlord's interest in the Building and Land or any proceeds arising from the sale thereof and no other property or assets of Landlord or the individual partners, members, directors, officers, or shareholders of Landlord shall be subject to levy, execution, or other enforcement procedure whatsoever for the satisfaction of said money judgment.

Transfer of Landlord's Interest

RISK RATING: 4

A. DESCRIPTION AND SCOPE

This Paragraph provides that both the obligations of and the benefits to Landlord that arise under this Lease can be transferred, and that only the person or entity in Landlord's position at a given time has the rights and responsibilities of Landlord.

B. ANALYSIS

1. Landlord's Perspective

This provision benefits Landlord since it will be relieved of further responsibility to the Tenant after Landlord sells the Property.

2. Tenant's Perspective

Tenant wants to be sure that any subsequent Landlord is required to fulfill the current Landlord's obligations. In addition, Tenant would like the original Landlord to remain liable after the transfer of the Lease for acts committed during the time that the then-Landlord was lessor of the Property. If there are outstanding obligations in the past of Landlord, such as a return of a security deposit, the payment of a Tenant Allowance, or the completion of Tenant Improvements, Tenant may want to condition the current Landlord's release of liability upon the new Landlord's assumption of and completion of the obligations and liabilities.

3. Lender's Perspective

Lender wants to be sure that whoever is in the position of Landlord is entitled to receive rent payments from Tenant in order to maintain the income stream of the Property.

C. COMPROMISES AND ALTERNATIVES

Although a Landlord is unlikely to want any impediments to its ability to sell or otherwise transfer the Lease and the Premises, a prospective Tenant might seek to use a similar rationale to negotiate less-restrictive terms in the Assignment and Subletting clause. For example, Tenant might request that Tenant should have no further liability under the Lease after an assignment to and assumption of Tenant's interest in the Lease by a creditworthy replacement Tenant. However, Tenant should expect resistance from both Landlord and Lender to such a provision.

D. COMMENTS

None.

E. TYPICAL PARAGRAPH

48. Transfer of Landlord's Interest. The term "Landlord" as used in this Lease, so far as covenants or agreements on the part of Landlord are concerned, shall be limited to mean and include only the owner or owners of Landlord's interest in this Lease at the time in question. Upon any transfer or transfers of such interest, Landlord herein named (and in case of any subsequent transfer, the then-transferor) shall thereafter be relieved of all liability for the performance of any covenants or agreements on the part of Landlord contained in this Lease.

Bankruptcy

RISK RATING: 4

A. DESCRIPTION AND SCOPE

This Paragraph describes the changes in the financial condition of Tenant or any guarantor of Tenant's obligations that constitute a default under the Lease, as well as Landlord's remedies with respect to such a default.

B. ANALYSIS

1. Landlord's Perspective

The automatic stay that arises under the Federal Bankruptcy Code upon the filing of a bankruptcy petition will prevent the Landlord from recovering possession or obtaining immediate satisfaction of a monetary award granted against the Tenant. However, all rents and other charges that accrue after filing of the petition become an administrative charge against the debtor's estate entitled to priority against all other unsecured claims, irrespective of whether the Lease is assumed or rejected. It should be noted that much of Paragraph 49 may not be enforceable under the current Bankruptcy Code. However, these provisions should remain in the event that during the Term the Bankruptcy Code is changed.

2. Tenant's Perspective

Tenant may not want a change in the financial condition of any Guarantor to constitute a default under the Lease, since Tenant is meeting its obligations.

3. Lender's Perspective

Same as Landlord's Perspective.

C. COMPROMISES AND ALTERNATIVES

The time period for failure to discharge an involuntary bankruptcy petition is generally negotiable.

D. COMMENTS

None.

E. TYPICAL PARAGRAPH

49. Bankruptcy. In the event that any of the following events occur, Landlord may terminate this Lease and pursue any and all remedies set forth in this Lease or available at law or in equity:

(a) Any sale of Tenant's interest in the Premises created by this Lease as a result of any bankruptcy, insolvency, execution, or similar legal process;

(b) Tenant or any guarantor of Tenant's obligations under this Lease (a "Guarantor") shall make an assignment for the benefit of its creditors or shall admit in writing the inability to pay its debts generally as they become due;

(c) Tenant or any Guarantor files or consents to the filing of any petition, or commences or consents to the commencement of, any proceeding, action, petition, or filing under the Federal Bankruptcy Code or any similar state or federal law now or hereafter in effect relating to bankruptcy, reorganization, or insolvency, or the arrangement or adjustment of debts (a "Bankruptcy Proceeding") with respect to Tenant or Guarantor;

(d) Any petition shall have been filed against Tenant or Guarantor in connection with a Bankruptcy Proceeding and the same is not withdrawn, dismissed, canceled, or terminated within sixty (60) days of such filing;

(e) Tenant or Guarantor is adjudicated bankrupt or insolvent or a petition for reorganization of Tenant or Guarantor is granted;

(f) A receiver, liquidator or trustee of Tenant or Guarantor or of any of the properties of Tenant or Guarantor shall be appointed and the same not be dismissed or terminated within sixty (60) days thereafter; or

(g) Tenant's interest under this Lease shall pass to another by operation of law or in any manner other than as may be permitted by Paragraph 11 of this Lease.

Security Deposit

RISK RATING: 4

A. DESCRIPTION AND SCOPE

This Paragraph sets forth Tenant's obligation to maintain a Security Deposit and Landlord's right to apply the Security Deposit in the event of a default under or breach of the Lease by Tenant. It also establishes the Landlord's duties with respect to the Security Deposit.

B. ANALYSIS

1. Landlord's Perspective

Landlord wants a source of funds to repair damage to the property or to offset nonpayment of rent by Tenant. Landlord, however, wants the option of enforcing other remedies it has against a defaulting Tenant and saving the Security Deposit for future application. Landlord also wants a Security Deposit to assure Tenant's performance of its obligations at the end of the Lease Term, including any restoration obligations of Tenant.

2. Tenant's Perspective

Tenant wants to ensure that the Security Deposit held by Landlord is not subject to claims by the Landlord's creditors, and that it will be returned to Tenant at expiration of the Lease Term. Requiring Landlord to segregate the Security Deposit from its other funds, to hold such funds in trust, and to pay interest on the Security Deposit demonstrates the parties' intent that Tenant retains title to the Security Deposit. Tenant may want Landlord to place the Security Deposit in an interest-bearing account with interest payable periodically or upon expiration of the Lease Term. Tenant may also want the option to substitute a letter of credit or a Certificate of Deposit for cash as the Security Deposit. For investment-grade credit Tenants, Tenant will likely request that this Paragraph be omitted from the Lease.

3. Lender's Perspective

Tenants have at times sought to protect the Security Deposit by making it a lien against the Property through a recording of the Lease or a Notice or Memorandum of Lease. If Landlord and Lender agree to such a provision, they will likely require that any such lien be automatically subordinate to any mortgage financing on the Property. Lender will also want to be sure it is not liable to return a Security Deposit unless actually received. Lender may want to require the escrow of security deposits so that they are available upon default under the Mortgage.

C. COMPROMISES AND ALTERNATIVES

Tenant may want Landlord to segregate the Security Deposit from Landlord's general funds so as to protect the funds from any bankruptcy proceeding against Landlord. Tenant may also want the funds to be placed in an interest-bearing account.

A Tenant may want the option to provide a letter of credit in lieu of cash. If a letter of credit is to be supplied, this Paragraph should provide that if the letter of credit expires before the end of the Term, Tenant must provide evidence of a renewal or a new letter of credit before the original letter of credit expiration date. Landlord should carefully review the terms of the letter of credit to ensure any conditions of drawing on it are acceptable; if the letter of credit requires a certificate of any kind, Landlord should ensure the terms of the certificate do not impose notice or other obligations on Landlord beyond those that would apply with a cash security deposit. Finally, the letter of credit should be transferable by its terms.

The security deposit might be phased out over time if Landlord has recouped the cost of Tenant Improvements, leasing commissions, or incentives, or if Tenant has established a solid history of default-free performance.

It may be acceptable for Landlord to accept a guaranty of the Lease by a third party in lieu of a cash security deposit.

D. COMMENTS

Information in this Paragraph pertaining to the rights and obligations concerning the Security Deposit should be as specific as possible to avoid questions when a default occurs and Landlord seeks to apply the Security Deposit.

E. TYPICAL PARAGRAPH

50. Security Deposit. Tenant has deposited $_____with Landlord (the "Security Deposit") as security for the full and faithful performance of every provision of this Lease to be performed by Tenant. If Tenant defaults with respect to any terms, covenants, and provisions to be performed and observed in this Lease as well as in all extensions and renewals thereof, including payment of the Annual Base Rent and Additional Rent, Landlord may, at Landlord's sole discretion, use, apply, or retain all or any part of the Security Deposit for the payment of any Annual Base Rent and Additional Rent, or to satisfy any mechanic's lien placed on the Property as a result of Tenant's acts, or to compensate Landlord for any other loss, cost, or damage that Landlord may suffer by reason of Tenant's default. Landlord's possession of the Security Deposit does not bar Landlord from enforcing any other rights, at law or equity, that Landlord may have against Tenant. If any portion of the Security Deposit is used or applied, Tenant shall, within five (5) days after written notice thereof, deposit cash with Landlord in an amount sufficient to restore the Security Deposit to its original amount, and Tenant's failure to do so shall be a default under this Lease. Landlord shall not, unless otherwise required by law, be required to keep the Security Deposit separate from its general funds, nor pay interest to Tenant. If Landlord is required to maintain the Security Deposit in an interest-bearing account, Landlord shall retain the maximum amount permitted under applicable law as a bookkeeping and administrative charge. If Tenant shall fully and faithfully perform every provision of this Lease to be performed by it, the Security Deposit or any balance thereof shall be returned to Tenant (or, at Landlord's option, to the last transferee of Tenant's interest hereunder) at the expiration of the Term and upon Tenant's vacation of the Premises. If Tenant exercises an option to extend or renew the term of this Lease the Security Deposit and the provisions of this Section shall be carried over to all extensions and renewals thereof. If the Building is sold, the Security Deposit may be transferred to the new owner, and this Section shall also apply to any subsequent transferee, and Landlord shall be discharged from further liability with respect thereto. The holder of a mortgage shall not be responsible for the return of or any application of the Security Deposit, whether or not it succeeds to the position of Landlord hereunder, unless such deposit shall have been received in hand.

Relocation
of Premises

A. DESCRIPTION AND SCOPE

This Paragraph gives Landlord the right to move Tenant to other space in the Building. Notwithstanding any relocation of Tenant, the Lease remains in full force and effect except for the recalculation of Annual Base Rent and Additional Rent for the substituted space. Landlord will be obligated to pay for Tenant's costs and expenses for such relocation.

B. ANALYSIS

1. Landlord's Perspective

Landlord wants to have the ability to relocate Tenant to (i) make the space available for a more desirable tenant, or (ii) to consolidate space in the Building for a potential Tenant that is a large user of space. This is particularly important for new Buildings or a Building that Landlord intends to expand. If Property is an office park where Landlord owns multiple Buildings, Landlord may also want to extend this relocation right to any Building owned by Landlord in the Office Park.

2. Tenant's Perspective

Tenant should be assured that it receives (i) comparable space (e.g., same views or floor level), or (ii) a reduction in rent. The expense of tenant improvement costs, moving, and decorating the new space should fall on the Landlord as should the cost of new stationery and business cards, if needed. Many Tenants will not agree to this provision since such a move will generally cause significant disruption to Tenant's business.

3.   Lender's Perspective

Landlord's quest for financing can be enhanced if Landlord has the ability to relocate Tenant, making the Premises available to a more desirable or "key tenant" that offers an economic anchor to the Building.

C.   COMPROMISES AND ALTERNATIVES

Tenant may want the ability to relinquish part of its space, or take additional space in connection with a relocation, depending on its needs. Tenant's right to more space, however, may be contingent on the additional space being available. A mechanism to determine the rent for the additional space must be included in such a provision.

D.   COMMENTS

Landlord's right to relocate Tenant, and the exercise of this right, have been held not to destroy the concept of exclusive possession and control of the Premises.

E.   TYPICAL PARAGRAPH

51.   Relocation of Premises. Tenant covenants and agrees that Landlord shall have the absolute and unqualified right upon at least thirty (30) days' written notice to Tenant to require Tenant move to other space in the Building. Such notice shall specify and designate the space to which Tenant shall be required to move. Notwithstanding said substitution of space, this Lease and all terms, provisions, covenants and conditions, contained herein shall remain and continue in full force and effect, except that Landlord shall recalculate the rent for the substituted space based upon the number of square feet in the substituted space and Annual Base Rent and Additional Rent shall be deemed amended to reflect said recalculation. Landlord shall move Tenant to the substituted space without cost or charge to the Tenant.

Waiver of Subrogation

A. DESCRIPTION AND SCOPE

This Paragraph provides for a mutual waiver of subrogation by Landlord and Tenant with respect to insurance claims. Subrogation is the right of the insurer to make a claim of the insured against a third person causing the damage. A mutual waiver of subrogation of the insured by Landlord and Tenant shifts the risk of damage back to the insurer.

B. ANALYSIS

1. Landlord's Perspective

Waiver of Tenant's insurer's right of subrogation against Landlord protects Landlord by shifting the responsibility for damage to the insurance company, which is in the business of assuming this risk for compensation. Failure to obtain such a waiver would mean that Landlord may be held responsible for insured damage caused by Landlord.

2. Tenant's Perspective

As stated above, obtaining a waiver of subrogation from Landlord's insurer protects Tenant by placing the risk of loss on the insurance company.

3. Lender's Perspective

Lender is concerned that each insurance policy for the Building contains a "mortgagee endorsement" clause insuring the Lender.

C. COMPROMISES AND ALTERNATIVES

In seeking to preclude subrogation and shift the risk back to the insurers, consideration may be given to insuring Landlord and Tenant on the same policy. Inclusion of Tenant makes Tenant an insured. An insurance company has no claim of subrogation against its own insured. Conversely, there is no right of subrogation against Landlord if Landlord is included as a named insured in Tenant's policy.

D. COMMENTS

Since insurance companies are paid to take the risk of such losses, it should not be able to shift such losses to party related to the transaction.

E. TYPICAL PARAGRAPH

52. Waiver of Subrogation. Landlord shall cause each insurance policy carried by it insuring the Premises against loss by fire or any of the casualties covered by its insurance to be written in such a manner so as to provide that the insurer waives all right of recovery by way of subrogation against Tenant in connection with any loss or damage covered by the policy. Tenant will cause each insurance policy carried by it insuring the Premises as well as the contents thereof, including trade fixtures and merchandise, against loss by fire or any of the casualties covered by its insurance to be written in a manner as is provided in [Insurance Section of Lease, See Paragraph 46 of this Manual] hereof and to provide that the insurer waives all right of recovery by way of subrogation against Landlord in connection with any loss or damage covered by the policy. Neither party hereto shall be liable to the other for any loss or damage caused by fire or any of the casualties covered by the insurance policies maintained by the other party. It is agreed that should either party fail to procure such waiver, it will pay to the other in liquidated damages all monies to which any insurer becomes entitled from the party for whose benefit such waiver was intended.

Alterations and Improvements to Premises

A. DESCRIPTION AND SCOPE

This Paragraph requires Tenant to obtain the prior written consent of Landlord in order to alter or add to or improve the Premises in any way. If Landlord consents to any alterations, additions, or improvements, then they will be at Tenant's sole expense and performed by Tenant unless Landlord elects to perform the approved alterations, additions, or improvements.

B. ANALYSIS

1. Landlord's Perspective

Landlord wants to ensure that all alterations, additions, and improvements requested by Tenant and approved by Landlord are at Tenant's sole cost and expense and comply with all laws, in particular, the ADA. Landlord will not want to rely on "boilerplate" provisions regarding Tenant's compliance with laws, but will likely insist on ADA compliance by Tenant. Landlord also wants control over alterations, additions, and improvements by Tenant. Not only does Landlord want Tenant to pay for the installation of all improvements, but also, Landlord will want to assess whether (i) Tenant will have the financial wherewithall to remove those improvements if so requested by Landlord at the end of the Term, and (ii) whether the improvements will adversely affect the appearance or structural integrity of the Building. If the requested improvements are significant, then Landlord may require a performance bond or guaranty for their completion. Landlord wants control over the construction process to assure integrity of the Building and its systems.

2.   Tenant's Perspective

Tenant desires flexibility under the Lease in altering the Premises during the Term in order to meet its needs. If alterations are approved by Landlord, Tenant will want control over the installation of the improvements to ensure their timely completion. Tenant will want to exclude minor alterations that do not affect the structure or systems of the Building from the provisions of this Paragraph.

3.   Lender's Perspective

See Landlord's Perspective above. In addition, Lender will not want to assume the obligations of Landlord to complete improvements that Landlord has agreed to perform.

C.   COMPROMISES AND ALTERNATIVES

Landlord may agree not to unreasonably withhold or delay its consent to Tenant's requests for alterations, additions, or improvements or may consent to nonstructural alterations in advance.

D.   COMMENTS

None.

E.   TYPICAL PARAGRAPH

53.   Alterations and Improvement to Premises.
   (a)   Tenant shall not make or allow to be made any alterations, additions, or improvements to or on the Premises without obtaining the prior written consent of Landlord. If Landlord consents to such alterations requested by Tenant and decides in Landlord's sole discretion to perform such alterations, then Tenant shall pay Landlord within ten (10) days of demand the cost therefore plus fifteen percent (15%) for Landlord's overhead and profit. Otherwise in order to induce Landlord to consent to Tenant's requested alterations, additions, or improvements, any such approved alterations, additions, or improvements, including wall covering, paneling, and built-in cabinet work, shall (i) be

made at Tenant's sole expense in accordance with plans and specifications approved in writing by Landlord by a licensed contractor in compliance with all applicable federal, state, and local laws, including, without limitation, the Americans with Disabilities Act; (ii) be completed in a good and workmanlike manner conforming in quality and design with the Premises existing as of the Commencement Date; (iii) not diminish the value of the Building or the Premises; (iv) upon completion become a part of the Property; (v) be surrendered with the Premises upon the expiration or sooner termination of this Lease unless removal is required by Landlord as hereinafter provided; and (vi) Tenant shall obtain for the benefit of Landlord a completion bond satisfactory to Landlord, and Tenant shall not permit any mechanic's liens to be placed on the Property in connection with any such work. Upon the expiration or sooner termination of this Lease, Tenant shall, upon written demand by Landlord at Tenant's sole expense, promptly and diligently remove any alterations, additions, or improvements, including any cabling, made by or on behalf of Tenant designated by Landlord to be removed, and repair any damage to the Property or portion thereof caused by such removal. Tenant shall remove all of its personal property and trade fixtures that can be removed without damage to the Property upon the expiration or sooner termination of this Lease, and shall pay Landlord for any damages to the same resulting from such removal. If Tenant fails to remove any such movable property, trade fixtures, alterations, additions, or improvements in accordance with this Section, then Landlord may, in accordance with the provisions of applicable statutes governing commercial landlord and tenant matters, remove and store the same without liability for loss thereof or damage thereto for the account of and at the sole expense of Tenant. If Tenant fails to pay the cost of storing any such property within thirty (30) days of demand therefore by Landlord, then Landlord may sell any or all of such property at one or more public or private sales without notice to Tenant and Landlord shall apply the proceeds of any such sale to the following costs in the following order: (1) the cost and expense of such sale, including reasonable attorneys' fees; (2) the payment of the costs or charges for storing any such property; (3) the payment of any sums which may then be or thereafter become due Landlord from Tenant under any of the terms hereof; and (4) the balance, if any, to Tenant.

(b) If Landlord gives its consent to the making of alterations by Tenant, all such work shall be done in accordance with such requirements and upon such conditions as Landlord, in its sole discretion, may impose. Any review or approval by Landlord of any plans or specifications with respect to any alteration is solely for Landlord's benefit, and without any representation or warranty whatsoever to Tenant with respect to the adequacy, correctness, or sufficiency thereof or otherwise.

(c) Tenant shall defend, indemnify and save harmless Landlord from and against any and all mechanic's and other liens and encumbrances filed by any person claiming through or under Tenant, including security interests in any materials, fixtures, equipment, or any other improvements or appurtenances installed in and constituting part of the Premises, and against all costs, expenses, and liabilities (including reasonable attorneys' fees) incurred in connection with any such lien or encumbrance or any action or proceeding brought thereon. Tenant at its expense shall procure the satisfaction or discharge of record of all such liens and encumbrances within twenty (20) days after the filing thereof.

(d) Unless Landlord demands removal of certain alterations, additions, or improvements in accordance with Paragraph 53(a) above, all alterations, additions, and improvements, including, without limitation, fixtures, equipment, and appurtenances attached to or built into the Premises, whether or not by or at the expense of Tenant, and any carpeting or other personal property in the Premises installed by Landlord or Tenant: (i) shall be and remain a part of the Premises; (ii) shall be deemed the property of Landlord; and (iii) shall not be removed by Tenant.

Right to Exhibit Premises

RISK RATING: 2

A. DESCRIPTION AND SCOPE

This Paragraph sets forth the rights of Landlord to enter into and show the Premises to existing and prospective Lenders and to purchasers and other interested parties. It also permits Landlord to effectively advertise the Premises by having the ability to exhibit the leased space to a prospective Tenant prior to an existing Tenant vacating.

B. ANALYSIS

1. Landlord's Perspective

Landlord wants the authority to enter the Premises to show the leased space in order to finance or sell the Property and to keep the Premises leased at all times.

2. Tenant's Perspective

Tenant desires protection against Landlord's unwarranted and unjustified intrusions onto the Premises. Tenant also desires protection against any damage or disruption to the Tenant's business or leased space during said intrusions. Tenant may want to condition Landlord's rights under the Paragraph to Landlord giving Tenant prior written notice of such inspections or that such inspections will not disrupt Tenant's business operations.

3. Lender's Perspective

Lender will want the right to inspect the Property and the Premises so as to determine that its collateral is in good condition. Lender would have the same concerns as Landlord as to the ability to keep the Premises leased at all times by effectively exhibiting the leased space.

C. COMPROMISES AND ALTERNATIVES

Landlord could use good-faith efforts to exhibit the Premises only during Tenant's normal business hours, provided Landlord minimizes any disruptions.

D. COMMENTS

None.

E. TYPICAL PARAGRAPH

54. Right to Exhibit Premises. Landlord reserves the right to enter the Premises and exhibit them (i) at any reasonable time to existing and prospective mortgagees, purchasers, vendors, insurance companies, ground lessors, ground lessees, and other interested parties; and (ii) at any time within ____ days prior to the expiration of the Term to prospective tenants.

Surrender of the Premises

A. DESCRIPTION AND SCOPE

This Paragraph sets forth a specific obligation of Tenant to surrender the Premises to Landlord in good condition on the Expiration Date. This Paragraph also serves to clarify the title of any abandoned property of Tenant.

B. ANALYSIS

1. Landlord's Perspective

Landlord wants to protect itself from having to restore or repair the Premises as each new Tenant gains possession. Landlord wants the authority to dispose of any of Tenant's abandoned property in order to minimize the time period that the Premises is not leased.

2. Tenant's Perspective

Tenant would like its obligations to be set forth precisely to protect Tenant against a claim for damages by Landlord. Tenant also should seek to have the condition of the Premises upon surrender remain "as is" so that Tenant does not have to restore or remove any alterations or additions made by Tenant during the Term.

3. Lender's Perspective

Lender will want to see that Tenant fulfills its obligation to restore the Premises and to surrender the Premises in "broom-clean condition," thereby minimizing the cost of repair or restoration to Landlord as well as minimizing the amount of time the Premises is not leased.

C. COMPROMISES AND ALTERNATIVES

Tenant may want to limit its restoration obligation to nonstructural or nonstandard alterations or may want to exclude those alterations and additions approved by Landlord.

D. COMMENTS

None.

E. TYPICAL PARAGRAPH

55. **Surrender of the Premises.**
   (a) **Tenant, on the Expiration Date (or earlier termination, if this Lease is terminated prior to the Expiration Date), shall peaceably surrender the Premises, including the leasehold improvements, in broom-clean condition, and Tenant shall, at the request of Landlord, restore the Premises and return the Premises to Landlord in as good condition as when Tenant took possession, except for: (i) reasonable wear and tear; (ii) loss by fire or other casualty; and (iii) loss by condemnation. Tenant shall, on Landlord's request, remove Tenant's property on or before the termination date and pay the cost of repairing all damage to the Premises or the Building caused by such removal.**
   (b) **If Tenant abandons or surrenders the Premises, or is dispossessed by process of law, or otherwise, any of Tenant's property (except money, securities, and other like valuables) left on the Premises shall be deemed abandoned; and, at Landlord's option, title shall pass to Landlord under this Lease as by a bill of sale, or, if Landlord elects to remove all or any part of such Tenant's property, the cost of such removal, including repairing any damage to the Premises or Building caused by such removal, shall be paid by Tenant within ten (10) days of Landlord's demand therefor; this obligation shall survive the termination of this Lease. On the Expiration Date (or such earlier termination), Tenant shall surrender to Landlord all keys to the Premises.**

Services and Utilities

A. DESCRIPTION AND SCOPE

This Paragraph is a listing of certain services that Landlord has agreed to provide Tenant, including HVAC, elevators, janitorial, water, and electricity. This Paragraph requires Tenant to pay for any excess usage of such services and exculpates Landlord from any liability to Tenant in connection with any interruptions of those services.

B. ANALYSIS

1. Landlord's Perspective

Landlord must be careful about covenanting to provide Tenant with heat, hot water, elevators, or other services without incorporating a "breakdown" or "diminution-of-services" clause in the Lease. Such a clause excuses Landlord from liability for damages in case of interruption of these services due to a necessity for repair, inspection, or causes beyond a Landlord's reasonable control. This clause usually does not provide for rent abatement during a period of such interruption. Landlord wants to make sure there are limits on watts per square foot that Tenant may use in electrical consumption so that system capacity is not exceeded. See Paragraph 34 for a discussion of Force Majeure.

2. Tenant's Perspective

To assure Tenant the right to such services, the list of services to be provided by Landlord should be comprehensive and detailed in its scope. Tenant may ask for a rent abatement or termination right if such cessation of services makes the Premises unusable for more than a specified number of days. If the Building has broadband internet access or fiber optic cable service, Tenant will want to specify these services as required services.

3.   Lender's Perspective

Any rent abatement or termination right during a cessation of services will not be perceived favorably by Lender, since Lender regards the Lease (and its rent payments) as important security for its mortgage. Any rent abatements will make it more difficult for Landlord to obtain financing for the Property.

C.   COMPROMISES AND ALTERNATIVES

If Landlord were able to rely on rental-interruption insurance, an abatement of rent would be considered after a specified number of days.

D.   COMMENTS

None.

E.   TYPICAL PARAGRAPH

56.   **Services and Utilities.**
   (i)   **Climate Control: Landlord shall provide climate control to the Premises during normal business hours as required in Landlord's reasonable judgment for the comfortable use and occupation of the Premises. If Tenant requires climate control at any other time, Landlord shall use reasonable efforts to furnish such service upon reasonable notice from Tenant, and Tenant shall pay Landlord's charges therefore on demand. The current charge (subject to change) for such overtime services is $____ per hour.**

   The performance by Landlord of its obligations under this Paragraph 56 is subject to Tenant's compliance with the conditions of occupancy and connected electrical load established by Landlord. Use of the Premises or any part thereof in a manner exceeding the heating, ventilating, or air-conditioning design conditions (including occupancy and connected electrical load in excess of _____ watts per rentable square foot), including rearrangement of partitioning that interferes with normal operation of the heating, ventilating, or air-conditioning in the Premises, or the use of computer or data-processing machines or other machines or equipment, may require changes in the

heating, ventilating, air-conditioning or plumbing systems or controls servicing the Premises or portions thereof, in order to provide comfortable occupancy. Any such required change shall be made by Landlord at Tenant's expense as alterations in accordance with the provisions of Paragraph 53 of this Lease, but only to the extent permitted and upon the conditions set forth in that Paragraph.

(ii) Elevator Service: If the Building is equipped with elevators, Landlord shall furnish elevator service during normal business hours to be used by Tenant in common with others. At least one elevator shall remain in service during all other hours. Landlord may designate a specific elevator for use as a service elevator.

(iii) Janitorial Services: Landlord shall make janitorial and cleaning services available to the Premises in accordance with the cleaning specifications described in Exhibit ___. Tenant shall pay to Landlord on demand the costs incurred by Landlord for (A) extra cleaning in the Premises required because of (1) misuse or neglect on the part of Tenant or Tenant's representatives; (2) the use of portions of the Premises for special purposes requiring greater or more difficult cleaning work than office areas; (3) interior glass partitions or unusual quantities of interior glass surfaces; and (4) nonbuilding-standard materials or finishes installed by Tenant or at its request; and (B) removal from the Premises of any refuse and rubbish of Tenant in excess of that ordinarily accumulated in general office occupancy or at times other than Landlord's standard cleaning times.

ALTERNATIVE PARAGRAPH:

(iii) [Tenant's Option to provide own janitorial services]: Tenant shall have the right at any time during the Term to

(a) contract independently with any cleaning contractor of Tenant's choice for the cleaning of all of the Premises; or

(b) utilize the services of Tenant's own employees for the cleaning of the Premises. Tenant shall give Landlord written notice of Tenant's election of either of said alternatives at least sixty (60) days in advance of effecting same. In the event that Tenant elects either alternative, then beginning with the effective date of the institution of said services by Tenant, (A) Building Operating Expenses shall be deemed to include only the cost of janitorial services for all of the Common Areas; (B) the Annual Base Rent and the amount of Building Operating Expenses for the Base Year shall be reduced by the amount specified in Paragraph 7, as equitably adjusted in accordance with Paragraph 7; and (C) the Operating Expense Payment payable by Tenant in accordance with the provisions of Paragraph 7 shall be reduced accordingly.

(iv) Water and Electricity: (A) Landlord shall make available domestic water in reasonable quantities to the Common Areas and to the Premises and cause electric service equivalent to the Watt Load to be supplied for lighting the Premises and for the operation of ordinary office equipment. "Ordinary office equipment" shall mean office equipment wired for 120-volt electric service and rated and using less than 6 amperes or 750 watts of electric current. (B) Landlord shall have the exclusive right to make any replacement of lamps, fluorescent tubes, and lamp ballast replacement periodically on a group basis in accordance with good management practice. (C) Tenant's use of electric energy in the Premises shall not at any time exceed ____ watts per rentable square foot and shall not exceed the capacity of any of the risers, piping, electrical conductors, and other equipment in or servicing the Premises. In order to ensure that such capacity is not exceeded and to avert any possible adverse effect upon the Building's electric system, Tenant shall not, without Landlord's prior written consent in each instance, connect appliances or heavy-duty equipment, other than ordinary office equipment, to the Building's electric system or make any alteration or addition to the Building's electric system. Should Landlord grant such consent, all additional risers, piping, and electrical conductors or other equipment therefore shall be provided by Landlord and the cost thereof shall be paid by Tenant within ten (10) days of Landlord's demand therefore. As a condition to granting such consent, Landlord may require Tenant to agree to an increase in Annual Base Rent by the expected cost to Landlord of such additional service, that is, the cost of the additional electric energy to be made available to Tenant based upon the estimated additional capacity of such additional risers, piping and electrical conductors or other equipment. If Landlord and Tenant cannot agree thereon, such cost shall be determined by an independent electrical engineer, to be selected by Landlord and whose fees shall be paid by Tenant.

(v) Landlord may install separate meters for the Premises to register the usage of all or any one of the utilities, and in such event Tenant shall pay for the cost of electricity usage as metered that is in excess of the Watt Load (or in the case of other utilities, the metered usage in excess of that usage reasonably anticipated by Landlord). Tenant shall reimburse Landlord for the cost of installation of meters if such usage exceeds the Watt Load (or such anticipated usage, as the case may be) by more than 10%. In any event, Landlord may require Tenant to reduce its consumption to the Watt Load or such anticipated usage.

(vi) Landlord does not warrant that any of the services referred to above, or any other services that Landlord may supply, will be free from interruption, and Tenant acknowledges that any one or more of such services may be suspended by reason of accident, repairs, inspections, alterations, or improvements necessary to be made, or by strikes or lockouts, or by reason of operation of law, or cause beyond the reasonable control of Landlord. Any interruption or discontinuance of service shall not be deemed an eviction or disturbance of Tenant's use and possession of the Premises, or any part thereof, nor render Landlord liable to Tenant for damages by abatement of Annual Base Rent, Additional Rent, or otherwise, nor relieve Tenant from performance of Tenant's obligations under this Lease. Landlord shall, however, exercise reasonable diligence to restore any service so interrupted.

Additional Services and Utilities

RISK RATING 3

A. DESCRIPTION AND SCOPE

This Paragraph gives Tenant the flexibility to have its Premises separately metered for electricity and, in that case, to have the cost of electricity supplied to other tenants of the Building carved out of the calculation of Building Operating Expenses. Within a specified number of days after Landlord's approval of Tenant's plans and budget, Landlord will be obligated to use its best efforts to substantially complete the work in Tenant's telephone and other designated equipment rooms. It also permits telephone company representatives and others to have access to the Premises prior to the Commencement Date to install equipment.

B. ANALYSIS

1. Landlord's Perspective

Paragraph 57(a) provides an alternative method of electricity metering if Tenant is dissatisfied with the one in place. Landlord will likely limit consent to Paragraph 57(a) to large Tenants with significant leverage. Landlord may object to separate metering if it would have an impact on the bulk rates that Landlord may be receiving from the utility company based on the size of the Building.

With respect to Paragraph 57(b), Landlord's obligation to commence the additional work is subject to its approval of Tenant's plans and budget. Landlord is only obligated to use reasonable and diligent efforts to complete the work within the designated time frame. If Landlord has completed its work as required, it is protected against Tenant's refusal to accept delivery of the Premises on a specified date. Landlord will want to dictate the completion date for the equipment rooms.

2.   Tenant's Perspective

This Paragraph protects Tenant against having to shoulder more than its fair share of the costs of electricity, a situation that could arise when other tenants of the Building are heavier consumers of electricity than is Tenant. Tenant is not protected against Landlord's failure to complete the work required within the specified time frame. It does assure that Landlord will use reasonable efforts to complete the same and assures that access to the Premises is guaranteed to install the equipment prior to the scheduled Commencement Date.

3.   Lender's Perspective

Lender has the same perspective as Landlord.

C.   COMPROMISES AND ALTERNATIVES

Landlord might have a reason for not wanting separate meters installed in its building even if the installation were at Tenant's cost. In such event, Tenant might have to make a business judgment as to whether the present or potential future tenant mix in the Building could result in an unfair burden on Tenant in the area of reimbursement of costs for electrical consumption.

Tenant may request that the telephone and equipment rooms be completed by a specific date. If Landlord is certain that the work can be completed within the specified time period, Landlord may agree to affirmatively obligate itself to do so, subject to any force majeure.

Tenant may request that other utilities be separately metered, and if so, the following language may be useful:

Tenant shall have the right on a space-available basis, subject to Landlord's prior written approval, to have such other utilities introduced into the Premises as Tenant might reasonably require in the Premises, at Tenant's sole cost and expense, and Tenant shall pay the cost of such other utilities directly to the utility companies providing the same

D.   COMMENTS

Landlord will not want to use this Paragraph if separate metering affects Landlord's bulk rates received from the utility company or if Landlord places a surcharge on electric company billing.

E. TYPICAL PARAGRAPH

57. Additional Services and Utilities.

(a) Electricity: Upon notice to Landlord at any time during the Term, Tenant may elect to have Tenant's electricity consumption in the Premises separately metered, subject to the availability of separate metering by the electric utility company. In the case of such separate metering of Tenant's electricity consumption: (i) Tenant shall pay the cost of such metering and shall pay the cost of Tenant's electricity consumption directly to the electric utility company; (ii) Building Operating Expenses for electricity shall be deemed to include only the cost of electricity consumption for the Common Areas; (iii) the Annual Base Rent and the amount of Building Operating Expenses for the Base Year shall be reduced accordingly by Landlord; (iv) the Operating Expense Payment payable by Tenant to Landlord shall be reduced accordingly; and (v) Tenant's electrical consumption shall in no event exceed ___ watts per rentable square foot.

(b) Telephone Equipment and Data Service Installations: Within _____ (___) days after Landlord's approval of Tenant's plans and the expense budget [subject to Tenant's Improvement Allowance, if any], Landlord will use all reasonable and diligent efforts to complete Landlord's work relative to Tenant's telephone and other designated equipment rooms and have such portion of the Premises ready for occupancy. For purposes of this Paragraph 57(b), "complete" and "ready for occupancy" shall be deemed to mean that Landlord's work (e.g., installation as required of telephone and data conduit, HVAC ductwork and equipment, ceiling tile, electrical outlets and wiring, partitions, doors and door hardware, and floor covering, etc.) in such rooms has been substantially completed. Landlord will permit telephone company representatives and other agents and contractors hired by Tenant to enter the Building and Premises during such time for the purpose of installing Tenant's telephone equipment and other designated services to be installed by Tenant, and Landlord will provide facilities and working conditions reasonably satisfactory for the telephone company and said agents and contractors to accommodate their installations so that Tenant may occupy the Premises on the scheduled Commencement Date.

Mechanic's Liens

RISK RATING: 3

A. DESCRIPTION AND SCOPE

This Paragraph obligates Tenant to either (i) discharge or (ii) bond to the satisfaction of Landlord, any mechanic's or materialmen's liens filed against the Premises. If not, Landlord has the right to do the same and charge Tenant as Additional Rent or subtract it from any amounts owed to Tenant by Landlord.

B. ANALYSIS

1. Landlord's Perspective

Depending upon the State where the Premises are located, Landlord may or may not be liable for the cost of work done for the benefit of Tenant. In any event Landlord has a vested interest, particularly if Landlord has mortgaged the Property as collateral to Lender, in seeing that the liens are satisfied and discharged.

2. Tenant's Perspective

Tenant's obligation to remove the lien could be troublesome particularly if Tenant questions the amount for which the lien was filed, or disputes that the work conformed to the requirements of the contract. Tenant may not be able to remove or bond the lien within 10 days. A more reasonable period of time to deal with the lien is 30 days.

3. Lender's Perspective

Lender is particularly concerned if a mechanic's lien is placed on the Property that constitutes its collateral. It also may be deemed a default under

Lender's loan documents if Landlord does not remove the liens within a specified period of time.

C. COMPROMISES AND ALTERNATIVES

Tenant may want to increase the time period given to Tenant to remove the lien. The Lease may also require that, as a condition for work or installation to commence, a completion bond must be provided by Tenant.

D. COMMENTS

If the lien is bonded, Landlord must make sure that it is written by a reputable company that has a sufficient net worth to protect Landlord against potential losses.

E. TYPICAL PARAGRAPH

58. **Mechanic's Liens. In the event any mechanic's or materialmen's lien shall at any time be filed against the Premises allegedly by reason of work, labor, services, or materials performed or furnished to Tenant or to anyone holding the Premises through or under Tenant for work or materials performed or used with respect to the Premises, Tenant shall within ten (10) days cause the same to be discharged of record or bonded to the satisfaction of Landlord. If Tenant shall fail to cause such lien forthwith to be so discharged or bonded after being notified of the filing thereof, then, in addition to any other right or remedy of Landlord, Landlord may discharge the same by paying the amount claimed to be due, and the amount so paid by Landlord and all costs and expenses, including reasonable attorneys' fees incurred by Landlord in procuring the discharge of such lien, shall be due and payable by Tenant to Landlord as Additional Rent on the first day of the next following month, or may, at Landlord's election, be subtracted from any sums owing to Tenant by Landlord.**

Arbitration

RISK RATING: 4

A. DESCRIPTION AND SCOPE

This provision establishes arbitration before the American Arbitration Association as the methodology by which binding adjustments to lease terms (for example, amount of renewal rent and market-rate rent adjustments) can be made during the Term of the Lease.

B. ANALYSIS

1. Landlord's Perspective

Arbitration frequently results in "splitting the difference," which can erode the expectations of a Landlord relying on the language in a Lease. Generally, arbitration will be favored by the weaker party that cannot afford costs of protracted litigation; a stronger party may want to take its chances in court.

Landlord may not object to arbitration, but a Landlord with confidence in its lease documents may prefer to refer disputes to a court that will enforce commercial contracts according to their terms so that a Tenant will be inclined to settle rather than pursue expensive litigation.

2. Tenant's Perspective

Tenant wants to ensure that disputes can be decided in an efficient and fair manner, and that the arbitrator's decision will be binding. Tenants are usually more interested in arbitration since it can soften the hard edges of application of commercial contract law.

3. Lender's Perspective

See Landlord's Perspective above.

C. COMPROMISES AND ALTERNATIVES

It is also common to provide for two arbitrators, and only in case of a disagreement between the two, for a third. However, this could place decisive power in the third, which may not be intended. This can be avoided by providing that two arbitrators would determine, for example, the increase in rent. In case of disagreement, a third arbitrator would make the determination. If the third arbitrator's determination were lower than the lower of the first two arbitrators, the lower of the first two would govern; and if the third arbitrator's determination were higher than the higher of the first two, the higher of the first two would govern. It is occasionally provided that if the two arbitrators disagree, a third arbitrator will be authorized to decide only which determination of the first two arbitrators will govern. This is intended to encourage the first two arbitrators to give realistic appraisals rather than to act as advocates for either Landlord or Tenant. The same result can be achieved by discarding the outlying estimate before averaging, if, for example, it differs from the mean by greater than 10%.

Another form of arbitration currently in use is "Baseball Arbitration." In Baseball Arbitration, a single arbitrator is used, and the arbitrator has the choice only to select either the Landlord's version or the Tenant's version and is not permitted to "split the difference." This works particularly well where there is a disagreement as to "market rent" in a renewal option.

D. COMMENTS

The parties should ensure that the types of disputes that will be subject to arbitration are clearly spelled out in the appropriate sections of the Lease.

E. TYPICAL PARAGRAPH

59. Arbitration. In any case in which it is provided by the terms of this Lease that any matter shall be determined by arbitration, such arbitration shall be conducted in accordance with the rules then used by the American Arbitration Association, before three arbitrators: one chosen by Landlord, one by Tenant, and one by the arbitrators thus chosen, and judgment upon the award rendered shall be fixed and binding upon all parties and may be entered in any court having jurisdiction thereof. Landlord and Tenant shall each be entitled to present evidence and argument to the arbitrators and to any appraiser.

PARAGRAPH 60

Governing Law

RISK RATING: 3

A. DESCRIPTION AND SCOPE

This Paragraph sets forth the applicable law that will control construction and the enforceability of the terms of the Lease and the rights, remedies, and duties of the parties thereto.

B. ANALYSIS

1. Landlord's Perspective

Landlord wants to establish the controlling law so it can evaluate, at the inception and throughout the term of the Lease, the enforceability of the Lease's terms and its rights and remedies.

2. Tenant's Perspective

Tenant shares same concerns as Landlord.

3. Lender's Perspective

Lender's interest would be served by the laws of a jurisdiction that favors the rights of secured parties and imposes the least restrictions on the enforcement of Lender's rights under its mortgage.

C. COMPROMISES AND ALTERNATIVES

If Landlord is unable to prevail as to its choice of governing law, it should include specific provisions in the terms of the Lease that grant it rights not otherwise granted by the controlling law. Alternatively it could seek a waiver by Tenant, where permitted by the applicable jurisdiction, of Tenant rights that are adverse to Landlord's interests.

D. COMMENTS

Careful drafting of specific lease provisions can mitigate the effect of rights and remedies granted to Tenant by controlling law. Since leases are contracts affecting land, they will be construed in accordance with local law absent provisions to the contrary. Consumer-protection aspects of local lease law may not be waivable directly or by choice of law of another jurisdiction.

E. TYPICAL PARAGRAPH

60.   Governing Law. This Lease and the rights and obligations of Landlord and Tenant hereunder shall be governed by and construed in accordance with the laws of the jurisdiction in which the Premises are located.

Floor-Load Limitations

RISK RATING: 3

A. DESCRIPTION AND SCOPE

This Paragraph establishes limits on the Tenant's physical use of the Premises so that the design floor-load limits of the Building will not be exceeded.

B. ANALYSIS

1. Landlord's Perspective

Landlord is concerned about the type and extent of office equipment and fixtures Tenant proposes to install since it may adversely affect the structural integrity of the Building. Landlord also wants to approve the installation and placement of Tenant's machinery and electrical equipment so that it can consider the effects on electrical capacity, noise levels, other tenants, and the marketability of the Property.

2. Tenant's Perspective

Tenant wants to ensure that its contemplated use of the Premises is within the Property's stated structural capacity and can be conducted without additional cost and without interruption or requirement for subsequent consent.

3. Lender's Perspective

Lender wants to ensure that the structural integrity of the Property and the value of its security are protected, and that adjacent tenants have no cause to complain as a result of Tenant's operations.

C.   COMPROMISES AND ALTERNATIVES

Landlord might agree to share with Tenant the cost of strengthening and reinforcing the Premises where the modifications enhance the long-term value of the Property and improve its marketability. Alternatively, Landlord could allow Tenant to pay for the cost of any alterations over the remainder of the Lease Term rather than in one lump sum.

D.   COMMENTS

Landlord should take care in making representations concerning the Premises, and ensure that breach of such representations should not be a default permitting termination or self-help by Tenant to correct the breach.

E.   TYPICAL PARAGRAPH

61.   Floor-Load Limitations. Landlord represents that the floor space of the Premises will carry __ pounds per square foot of floor live load uniformly distributed. Tenant shall not place a load upon any floor of the Premises that exceeds __ pounds floor load per square-foot area that such floor was designed to carry. Landlord reserves the right to prescribe the weight and position of all business machines, mechanical equipment, and fixtures that shall be placed so as to distribute the weight. If Tenant shall desire a floor load in excess of __ pounds floor load per square foot for which the floor and any portion of the Premises is designed, to the extent such excess is allowed by law, upon submission to Landlord of plans showing the location of and the desired floor live load for the area in question, Landlord, in its sole discretion, may strengthen and reinforce the same, at Tenant's sole expense, so as to carry the live load desired. Business machines and mechanical equipment used by Tenant that cause vibration or noise that may be transmitted to the Building or to any leased space to such a degree as to be reasonably objectionable to Landlord or to any tenants in the Building shall be placed and maintained by Tenant, at its expense, in settings of cork, rubber, or spring-type vibration eliminators sufficient to reduce such vibration or noise to an unobjectionable level.

Tenant shall not move any safe, heavy machinery, heavy equipment, freight, bulky matter, or fixtures into, within, or out of the Premises without Landlord's prior written consent. If moving of such business machines, mechanical equipment, files, and/or fixtures require special handling, Tenant agrees to employ only persons holding a Master Rigger's License to do said work, and that all work in connection therewith shall comply with applicable laws and regulations. Any such moving

shall be at the sole risk and hazard of Tenant, and Tenant will exonerate, indemnify, and save Landlord harmless against and from any liability, loss, injury, claim, or suit resulting directly from such moving. Tenant shall schedule such moving at such times as Landlord shall require for the convenience of the normal operations of the Building.

Name of Building

RISK RATING: 2

A. DESCRIPTION AND SCOPE

This Paragraph establishes that Landlord has the unilateral right to change the name of the Building and exterior signage of the Building.

B. ANALYSIS

1. Landlord's Perspective

Landlord wants the option of renaming the Building to enhance the Building's image, and, it is hoped, its marketability, and as a mechanism for attracting an anchor Tenant by agreeing to name the Building after that Tenant.

2. Tenant's Perspective

Tenant wants to avoid confusion on the part of its customers and clients as to its business address. Additionally, to the extent that Tenant may have incorporated the Building name into its stationery and promotional materials, Tenant may incur expenses if the name is changed. Larger Tenants will also be concerned about Landlord changing the name of the Building to a name that reflects one of Tenant's competitors. Tenant may want to request that this process be modified so that Tenant receives at least 30 days' prior written notice of any name change.

3. Lender's Perspective

Lender is most likely indifferent to a name change provision unless it adversely affects the value of the Property. If a new name has marketing appeal and can be trademark-protected, Lender will want to be sure it has rights to use that name if it takes over Property.

C. COMPROMISES AND ALTERNATIVES

Landlord may agree to compensate Tenant for any costs involved in changing stationery and other materials that mention the previous Building name. Landlord might also agree to run newspaper advertisements announcing the change of name and/or share Tenant's cost incurred notifying its customers and clients.

D. COMMENTS

If a Landlord agrees to name the Building after a large anchor tenant, it should retain the right in the Lease to change the name if that Tenant fails to occupy the anticipated amount of leasable space in the Building.

See Paragraph 28 for additional discussion regarding name of Building and signage.

E. TYPICAL PARAGRAPH

62. Name of Building. Landlord reserves the right at any time after the execution of this Lease to name or change the name of the Building or the exterior signs to be affixed to the Building or located on the Property.

Right of First Refusal/Offer to Lease Additional Space

RISK RATING: 4

A. DESCRIPTION AND SCOPE

This Paragraph sets forth the terms of Tenant's right of first refusal or right of first offer. Option A provides that Tenant shall have the preferential right to accept or refuse Landlord's offer to lease additional space that has been offered to a proposed tenant. Option B provides that Tenant shall have the first opportunity to submit to Landlord its offer for lease of the additional space.

B. ANALYSIS

1. Landlord's Perspective

Landlord and prospective tenants do not want to expend time and money to negotiate potential lease terms only to have Tenant exercise its right of first refusal with respect to such terms. Landlord would prefer to grant a right of first offer, because if Tenant fails to exercise the same within the allotted time, Landlord may proceed to lease the additional space to any prospective tenant. Landlord must be careful to survey other Tenants' Lease options to avoid conflicts with other Lease terms. Landlord wants to limit the space for which Tenant has the right of first refusal/offer because Landlord wants to have the ability to lease space to others. Landlord therefore wants to designate specific space, rather than the entire Building. For example, Landlord might designate space on a certain floor or floors or in a certain elevator bank, for which Tenant has the right of first refusal/offer. If Tenant has the right to lease space contiguous to the Premises, Landlord should make sure that "contiguous" is narrowly defined in the Lease. To avoid confusion, an exhibit that shows the space subject to the right of first refusal/offer is often attached to the Lease. In addition, the Tenant Work or Tenant Improvement Allowance in connection with Right of First Refusal/First Offer Space should be addressed as should any increase in the Security Deposit and any allocated parking spaces.

2. Tenant's Perspective

Tenant wants the flexibility to expand to meet its future needs. Tenant would prefer to have the right to refuse (rather than present) an offer to lease. Tenant may also request longer time periods to respond to Landlord's notice. Tenant will also be concerned if Landlord does not complete a lease transaction or materially modifies the terms of a lease transaction that is the subject of a right of first refusal. In such case, Tenant will again want a right of first refusal before Landlord proceeds with a lease transaction with a third party. With respect to the right of first offer, Tenant will want to require that the Landlord again offer the space to Tenant if Landlord intends to offer the space to a third party at a rent that is less than that offered to Tenant or on terms materially more advantageous than those offered to Tenant. With respect to the financial statement requirement contained in the right of first refusal, Tenant will want to limit Landlord's ability to reject Tenant's financial condition to those situations where there has been a material adverse decline in Tenant's financial condition since the inception of the original Lease Term.

3. Lender's Perspective

Lender wants the period within which the option may be exercised to be limited. For the reasons stated above, Lender also would prefer a right of first offer.

C. COMPROMISES AND ALTERNATIVES

Tenant may object to the requirement that Landlord approve Tenant's financial condition. However, Landlord must be able to confirm Tenant's ability to meet its obligations with respect to the additional space.

D. COMMENTS

None.

E. TYPICAL PARAGRAPH

63. Right of First Refusal/Offer to Lease Additional Space.

Option A: Right of First Refusal
Provided that Tenant is not in default under this Lease beyond any
applicable cure period, Tenant shall have a right of first refusal to lease
_____ square feet of space on the _____ floor of the Building as such additional space is shown in on the attached Exhibit ___,
subject to the following terms and conditions:

    (a) Prior to Landlord entering into a lease for all or any part of the
additional space with a third party, Landlord shall first offer in
writing such space for lease to Tenant on the same terms and
conditions quoted to such third party.

    (b) Within three (3) business days after Tenant receives said offer
from Landlord, Tenant shall either accept or reject such offer
by written notice to Landlord. Failure by Tenant to deliver to
Landlord a written acceptance thereof within such period shall
be deemed a rejection by Tenant of such offer.

    (c) If Tenant rejects or is deemed to have rejected said offer, this
right of first refusal shall be deemed to have terminated and
Landlord shall thereafter be entitled to lease all or any portion
of said additional space to such third party; provided, that said
right of first refusal shall remain in effect if Landlord does not
consummate a lease with the third party.

    (d) If Tenant accepts said offer in accordance with the provisions
hereof, Landlord and Tenant shall thereupon execute an
amendment to this Lease adding the additional space to this
Lease in accordance with the provisions of subparagraph (a)
above. If Tenant fails to execute said amendment within ten
(10) days after Landlord furnishes same to Tenant, the acceptance of Landlord's offer shall be deemed to have been rejected
by Tenant and thereupon the provisions of subparagraph (c)
above shall apply. If Tenant rejects Landlord's offer, or if Tenant
is deemed to have rejected such offer, Tenant's right of first
refusal to lease the additional space in the Building shall immediately terminate and shall be of no further force or effect.

    (e) Prior to Landlord's execution of the Lease amendment, Tenant
shall furnish to Landlord current financial statements of Tenant prepared by a certified public accountant prepared in
accordance with generally accepted accounting principles. As a
condition of Landlord's adding the additional space to the

Lease, Landlord shall have the right to approve the financial condition of Tenant. If the Landlord does not approve the financial condition of Tenant, Tenant's right of first refusal shall terminate and shall immediately be of no further force or effect.

Option B: Right of First Offer

Provided that Tenant is not in default of its obligations under this Lease, during the Term hereof, Tenant shall have the right of first offer to lease _____ square feet of additional space on the _____ floor of the Building.

Landlord shall give Tenant written notice of the availability of any of said additional office space and Landlord's good-faith estimate of the market net effective rent at which such space will be offered. Tenant shall have ten (10) business days from the receipt of Landlord's notice to notify Landlord in writing whether it will lease the space at the rent specified in Landlord's notice. In the event Tenant declines the offer to lease additional space or fails to notify Landlord within said ten (10) business days, Tenant's right of first offer with respect to that space shall be null and void and of no further force and effect, and Landlord shall be free to lease such space to any person or entity upon any terms and for any purpose. However, after such space has been leased by Landlord to another person or entity, if any of such space should again become available, Tenant shall again have the right of first offer to lease with respect thereto in accordance with the terms and conditions hereof.

Option to Lease Additional Space

RISK RATING: 4

A. DESCRIPTION AND SCOPE

This Paragraph provides Tenant with the option to increase the area of the Premises.

B. ANALYSIS

1. Landlord's Perspective

This Paragraph protects Landlord against Tenant outgrowing the Premises and seeking to terminate the Lease in favor of a lease in a building better suited to its spatial needs. If Landlord has previously granted other tenants options for additional space, Landlord must be careful when choosing the potential additional space to accommodate the rights of other tenants. Landlord also wants the rental and other terms applicable to the lease of such space to be specifically identified. Options to Lease Additional Space have many of the same concerns and problems as Rights of First Refusal. See Landlord's Perspective in Paragraph 63 for a more complete discussion of these issues.

2. Tenant's Perspective

This Paragraph provides Tenant with some flexibility against the possibility that it will outgrow the Premises during the Term. Tenant may want to specify the condition of the additional space and any Tenant Improvement Allowance that Tenant is to receive. Tenant would prefer to fix the rent for the Additional Space, rather than pay a market rent. If parking spaces are allocated, Tenant will want a proportional increase in the number of allocated parking spaces. For larger Tenants a series of expansion options with sequential exercise windows may be appropriate.

3.   Lender's Perspective

A Lender wants the terms of the option to be clearly defined, and the time for the exercise of such option to be limited, so that Lender may analyze the present and potential income generated by the Project.

C.   COMPROMISES AND ALTERNATIVES

This provision is negotiated on an individual-deal basis, depending upon Tenant's projected need for additional space and its desire to maintain flexibility, and Landlord's ability to accommodate Tenant's projected needs.

D.   COMMENTS

This Paragraph should set forth all of the terms of Tenant's option to lease additional space. Landlord wants the "window period" during which the option may be exercised to be limited so that Landlord has the flexibility to lease such space to other tenants.

E.   TYPICAL PARAGRAPH

64.   Option to Lease Additional Space. Provided that Tenant is not in default of its obligations under this Lease, Tenant shall have the option (the "Option") during the period commencing on _____, 2_ _ _ and ending on _____, 2_ _ _ (the "Option Period") to lease _____ rentable square feet of additional space on the _____ floor of the Building as more particularly described in Exhibit ___ hereto (the "Option Space"). The Annual Base Rent for the Option Space shall be $_____ payable in monthly installments of $_____ per month. The term of the Option Space shall be coterminous with the Term of the original Premises and shall end on the Expiration Date of the Lease, provided that to the extent this Lease permits Tenant to extend the Term, then the term of the Option Space shall also be extended.

  Tenant must exercise the Option, if at all, by delivering written notice to Landlord of Tenant's exercise of the Option during the Option Period. Time shall be of the essence with respect to Tenant's exercise of the Option. Should Tenant exercise the Option, then the Option Space shall become part of the Premises and Annual Base Rent on the Option

Space shall commence on _____, 2_ _ _ . Tenant shall accept the Option Space in an "as-is" "where-is" condition, and Landlord shall have no obligation to improve the Option Space.

Option to Renew

RISK RATING: 3

A. DESCRIPTION AND SCOPE

This Paragraph sets forth Tenant's right to renew the Lease at a rental rate equal to the greater of the Annual Base Rent that Tenant is then paying or the fair-market rental value of the Premises as determined by Landlord.

B. ANALYSIS

1. Landlord's Perspective

Depending on Landlord's perspective regarding long-term market rental rates, Landlord may or may not agree to a renewal option. The rent that Tenant is willing to pay during the renewal term, if not fixed, should be a market rate. If such an option is included in the Lease, Landlord will require that Tenant exercise its right to renew by a specific date (at least 6 months and possibly 12 months) so that Landlord may find other tenants should Tenant elect not to renew. Renewal rights shift the power to Tenant to control space in the Building over time.

2. Tenant's Perspective

The concept of an option to renew protects Tenant against being burdened with long-term commitments to space that it no longer requires or is unsuitable, while providing the flexibility to remain for a long period in space that is still needed and remains acceptable. If the rental for the option period is fixed, the provision also protects Tenant against the risks of an uncertain rent in the future. If a market rate rent is used, Tenant will want to participate in the selection of the market rate and/or an appraiser or use arbitration rather than having Landlord determine the market rental rate. See Paragraph 59 for discussion of Arbitration. In addition, Tenant may want the right to revoke the option to renew if it is not satisfied with the market rate. Tenant may also desire to specify a Tenant Improvement Allowance. Tenant may also want to pay only a percentage of a market rent rate (e.g., 90%) to reflect the lower cost to Landlord of the renewal (e.g., no broker's fees, no down time, and lower Tenant Allowances). Tenant may also want several sequential options to renew, for example, three 5-year renewal options.

3.   Lender's Perspective

A Lender wants the ability to evaluate the income generated by the Lease during the Renewal Term.

C.   COMPROMISES AND ALTERNATIVES

If Landlord is unwilling to grant an option to renew, Tenant may propose that it be given a right of first refusal or right of first offer in the event that Landlord elects to re-let the Premises. This alternative gives both Landlord and Tenant the opportunity to assess current market rental rates.

D.   COMMENTS

The parties should be aware that lease provisions that state that the parties will agree to negotiate renewal terms in good faith may be deemed unenforceable in many states. Thus, a well-drafted renewal option clause should identify specifically all pertinent terms, including the rent to be paid during the extended Term.

E.   TYPICAL PARAGRAPH

65.   Option to Renew. Provided Tenant is not in default under this Lease beyond any applicable cure period, Tenant may, at its option, renew this Lease for a period of _____ years at the greater of the then–Annual Base Rent being paid by Tenant or the fair-market rental value of the Premises as determined by Landlord and otherwise upon the same terms and conditions contained herein, by giving notice to Landlord of its intention to renew at least 12 months prior to the expiration of the Lease Term. Tenant shall have no other rights to extend or renew the Term of this Lease.

Storage Space

RISK RATING: 1

A. DESCRIPTION AND SCOPE

This Paragraph sets out the agreement of Tenant to lease Storage Space from Landlord and the agreement of Landlord to lease Storage Space to Tenant during the Term. This Paragraph describes the location and square footage of the Storage Space and provides that Tenant will accept the Storage Space in its "as-is" condition. The monthly rent for the Storage Space is due on the first business day of every month during the Term.

B. ANALYSIS

1. Landlord's Perspective

Landlord is concerned with having a clear and accurate description of the Storage Space. Landlord is also concerned with having a clear and accurate statement of the rent for the Storage Space, stating exactly when each installment of rent is due. The provision of this Paragraph providing that Tenant takes the Storage Space in its "as-is" condition protects the Landlord from having to install shelving or otherwise prepare the storage space for use as a storage area.

2. Tenant's Perspective

Tenant is concerned with having a clear and accurate description of the Storage Space for space planning purposes. Tenant is also concerned with having a clear and accurate statement of the rent to be charged for the Storage Space, stating exactly when each installment of rent is due.

3.   Lender's Perspective

Lender is concerned with preserving the cash flow generated by the Property that is, in part, produced through lease of Storage Space. This is the operative paragraph that binds Landlord and Tenant to the lease of Storage Space.

C.   COMPROMISES AND ALTERNATIVES

The rent and improvements to the Storage Space are subject to negotiation.

D.   COMMENTS

The location of the Storage Space should be attached as an Exhibit.

E.   TYPICAL PARAGRAPH

66.   Storage Space. In addition to the Premises, Tenant agrees to lease from Landlord, and Landlord agrees to lease to Tenant during the Term, approximately _____ rentable square feet of Storage Space (the "Storage Space") on the _____ floor. Tenant accepts the Storage Space in its "as-is" condition. The Storage Space shall be located as shown on Exhibit _____ attached hereto. The monthly rent for the Storage Space shall be _____ ($____.__) computed as one-twelfth (1/12th) of the product of _____ ($____.__) multiplied by the total rentable square footage of the Storage Space. The monthly rent for the Storage Space shall be due on the first business day of each month during the Term.

PARAGRAPH **67**

Miscellaneous

RISK RATING: 1

A. DESCRIPTION AND SCOPE

This Paragraph contains provisions that aid in the interpretation of the
Lease and therefore minimize disputes between Landlord and Tenant.

B. ANALYSIS

1. Landlord's Perspective

This Paragraph protects Landlord against unreasonable interpretations of
the Lease by a court and prevents the Lease provisions from being inter-
preted against the Landlord as drafter.

2. Tenant's Perspective

This Paragraph protects Tenant from unreasonable interpretations by a
court.

3. Lender's Perspective

Lender will want to ensure a clear interpretation of the Lease to minimize
disputes between Tenant and Landlord and thereby enhancing the success
of leasing on the Property.

C. COMPROMISES AND ALTERNATIVES

This Paragraph can be adjusted on a case-by-case basis to fit the requirements of Landlord and Tenant.

D. COMMENTS

None.

E. TYPICAL PARAGRAPH

67. Miscellaneous.
    (a) The captions appearing within the body of this Lease have been inserted as a matter of convenience and for reference only and in no way define, limit, or enlarge the scope of meaning of this Lease or any provision of this Lease.
    (b) This Lease may be executed in several counterparts, all of which constitute one and the same instrument.
    (c) The language of this Lease shall be construed according to its normal and usual meaning and not strictly for or against either Landlord or Tenant. It is the intention of the parties to this Lease that the rule of construction that allows a court to construe a document more strictly against its author shall not govern the interpretation of this Lease.
    (d) As used in this Lease, the terms "include" and "including" shall be construed as if followed by the phrase "without limitation."

PART 2

Description and Analysis of Retail Lease Paragraphs

Operating Covenant; Store Hours

RISK RATING: 4

A. DESCRIPTION AND SCOPE

Operating covenants obligate Tenant to remain open for business during certain hours and operate in a manner that will maximize gross sales. Thus, Landlord will want Tenant to agree to "continuously and uninterruptedly" operate its business and will seek to require hours of operation customary for similar businesses in the area (or, in the case of a shopping center or mall, to the hours maintained by the major department stores). Landlord is concerned that Tenant will go out of business or move to a new location ("go dark") but continue paying Landlord Annual Base Rent under the Lease.

In a shopping center, Tenant's duty to conduct an active business is important to Landlord not only because of the percentage rent derived from Tenant's business, but also because of the effect of Tenant's operations on the entire center—particularly where the Tenant is an anchor Tenant. Operating covenants may also be in other agreements, such as a reciprocal easement agreement, operating agreement, or supplemental agreement.

To enforce operating covenants, the specific remedy of "recapture" is often used. If there is a "closure" and Landlord declares a "recapture," Tenant must surrender the Premises and the Lease is terminated. Typically, "closure" includes such occurrences as closing of business for seven consecutive days; removal by Tenant of substantially all of its inventory from the Premises; or failure to operate during 75% of the hours per day customary in Tenant's business. Tenant will seek a right to cure after notification of its breach of such standards. In giving Landlord the option to terminate the Lease and thus to seek a tenant more willing or able to remain in business, the clause provides greater protection for Landlord than a suit for damages or injunctive relief.

B. ANALYSIS

1. Landlord's Perspective

This Paragraph is very important to Landlord because it will allow Landlord some ability to maximize rent based on a percentage of sales and because it affects all other tenants in Landlord's shopping center and their respective sales, since each tenant relies on the other tenants to bring traffic to the center. In addition to requiring Tenant to remain open for business, Landlord wants Tenant to maximize its business. For example, Landlord would like to require Tenant to keep the Premises adequately stocked with merchandise and trade fixtures to service its customers. Landlord may require that Tenant obtain and maintain at all times all necessary or desirable licenses and the highest available ratings from all applicable governmental agencies. Landlord also may seek to secure rights of review or approval of standards for Tenant's employees, the sales area, lighting, display, layout, pricing, and advertising, and may seek to require that Tenant participate in merchant's associations and merchandising events.

2. Tenant's Perspective

Tenant would like to minimize Landlord's control over its business and, in particular, would like to specify circumstances in which Tenant will have the right to close temporarily for reasons such as the taking of inventory, force majeure, severe weather, and vacation of the Premises at the end of the Lease term. Tenant also may want the right to close permanently if certain other anchor tenants close. Anchor Tenants may also limit the operating covenant to a period of time; for example, the first five years of the Lease Term.

3. Lender's Perspective

Lender will have interests similar to its borrower, the Landlord.

C. COMPROMISES AND ALTERNATIVES

The specifics of store hours and operating covenants can be negotiated; but if Tenant is a tenant at a shopping center and has a percentage rent arrangement, then Landlord will want Tenant to agree to remaining open for business for specified times during the Lease Term as it is standard in those situations.

Landlord sometimes will request that Tenant agree to "use its best efforts to maximize Tenant's gross sales," if Landlord does not wish solely to rely upon the Tenant's motivation to make a profit (sometimes a tenant can actually make more profit by reducing sales). Alternatively, Tenant may be required to use "due diligence" to achieve a certain percentage rent.

Tenant may require that it need not operate for more hours than one or more of the major tenants.

D. COMMENTS

None.

E. TYPICAL PARAGRAPH

1. **Operating Covenant; Store Hours. Tenant shall at all times during the term hereof (a) conduct its business in the entire Premises; (b) remain open for business from 10:00 A.M. to 9:00 P.M., Monday through Saturday, and from 12:00 noon to 5:00 P.M. on Sunday (if permitted by law) during the term hereof excepting Christmas Day and Thanksgiving Day, which days the Retail Complex shall be closed. Said minimum operating hours may be modified by Landlord upon ten (10) days' written notice to Tenant. Tenant's failure to keep the Premises open for business as aforesaid shall be conclusively deemed for any and all purposes to be a violation or breach of a condition, covenant, or obligation of this Lease that cannot afterward be cured or performed; (c) adequately staff its store with sufficient employees to handle the maximum business and carry sufficient stock of merchandise of such size, character, and quality to accomplish the same; (d) maintain displays of merchandise in the display windows, if any; (e) keep the Premises and interior portions of windows, doors, and all other glass or plate glass fixtures in a neat, clean, sanitary, and safe condition; (f) warehouse, store, or stock only such goods, wares, and merchandise as Tenant intends to offer for sale at retail; (g) if the Premises contain a mezzanine, the use thereof for storage purposes or sales purposes shall be subject to Landlord's written approval; (h) except for mezzanine space, use for office or other non-selling purposes only such space as is reasonably required for Tenant's business, but in no event shall the space used for such purposes exceed five percent (5%) of the square foot area of the Premises; (i) neither solicit business nor distribute advertising matter in the common areas;**

(j) not place any weight upon the floors which shall exceed _____
pounds per square foot of floor space covered; (k) not change the advertising name of the business operated in the Premises without the written permission of Landlord; and (l) use the insignia or other identifying mark of the Retail Complex designated by Landlord in Tenant's advertising, whether printed or visual, and make reference to the name of the Retail Complex in each instance of audio advertising.

PARAGRAPH 2

Radius Restriction

RISK RATING: 4

A. DESCRIPTION AND SCOPE

"Radius" restrictions affect competition not only within the Property controlled by Landlord, but also within a geographic area surrounding the Premises. Such restrictions prevent Tenant from opening additional locations and thus diluting gross sales at the Premises.

B. ANALYSIS

1. Landlord's Perspective

Landlord would like to impose radius restrictions on Tenant if Tenant pays percentage rent. Landlord also would like to ensure that Landlord could enforce such restrictions; enforcement is often effected through a clause that grants Landlord the option to include the Gross Sales from a competing business in Tenant's Gross Sales for the purpose of computing Percentage Rent. Such provision is usually easier to enforce than a clause requiring Landlord to get an injunction to force Tenant to close a competing store.

2. Tenant's Perspective

If Tenant wishes to open another store in the area, then Tenant will resist any restriction on its right to do so. If Tenant is already operating another store within the restricted area, then Tenant must get an exception for currently operating businesses. Tenant also may wish to decrease the restricted area (e.g., 1 or 2 miles).

3. Lender's Perspective

Lender's interest is similar to that of Landlord in that Lender wants Tenant to maximize percentage rent by not opening competing stores that might dilute Gross Sales.

C. COMPROMISES AND ALTERNATIVES

The actual area (how many miles) of the radius restriction can be negotiated, but the radius restriction may not be unreasonable under the facts and circumstances, or else it may be deemed anticompetitive and unenforceable. In addition, the restriction may be softened somewhat to provide that Tenant cannot operate another business within the restricted area without the prior written consent of Landlord. The provision also can be changed from unilateral to mutual so that both Landlord and Tenant are subject to parallel restrictions.

D. COMMENTS

None.

E. TYPICAL PARAGRAPH

2.   Radius Restriction. In recognition of the fact that this Lease provides for Percentage Rent based upon the sales made by Tenant in or from the Premises, Tenant covenants and agrees that, for the period commencing with the execution of this Lease and continuing for the full term of this Lease, neither Tenant nor any parent, subsidiary, or affiliate of Tenant, nor any principal partner, member, or majority shareholder of Tenant, nor any Guarantor of this Lease, shall operate, either directly or indirectly, another store (including a department or concession in another store) of a similar kind (other than stores, departments, or concessions presently being operated by it or them) within a reasonable area of the Premises, without the prior written consent of Landlord. Tenant acknowledges that the area within a circle having as its center the Premises and having a radius of ten (10) miles is a reasonable area for this purpose. In addition to any other remedy otherwise available to Landlord for breach of this covenant, it is specifically agreed that Landlord may, at Landlord's election, require that any and all sales made in and from any such other store be included in the computation of the Percentage Rent due hereunder with the same force and effect as though such sales had actually been made in or from the Premises.

Signage

RISK RATING: 3

A. DESCRIPTION AND SCOPE

This Paragraph requires Tenant, at Tenant's expense, to install signs on the Property that comply with Landlord's Sign Criteria, and all applicable laws, codes, and zoning requirements. It also places the burden on Tenant to install, maintain, and remove each approved sign.

B. ANALYSIS

1. Landlord's Perspective

This Paragraph protects Landlord from having to install, maintain, or remove signs. Landlord retains control, however, over the size, style, and type of sign that may be placed on the Property. Landlord is interested in a uniform look to the Shopping Center and therefore requires that all signs conform to Landlord's Sign Criteria.

2. Tenant's Perspective

Tenant wants as few restrictions on signage and advertisement as possible. Tenant may want the right to place special "sale" signs in or on the Premises that are visible from the exterior of the Premises.

3. Lender's Perspective

Lender wants to ensure that the Property maintains an appeal to the public so that the collateral value of its Property will be enhanced. Although Lender realizes that signs are necessary to the operation of a business, it may want assurances as to the size and type of signs so that first-class standards are maintained so as to preserve the value of its collateral.

C. COMPROMISES AND ALTERNATIVES

Landlord will want Tenant to agree to signage that is appropriate in the prevailing environment, provided that Landlord's criteria for signage do not prohibit a size, style, or location that is essential to Tenant's business.

D. COMMENTS

None.

E. TYPICAL PARAGRAPH

3.   Signage. Tenant shall, at Tenant's sole expense, install identification signs of a size, material, and design as Landlord, in its sole discretion, shall deem appropriate. All signs shall conform to Landlord's published Sign Criteria. Such signs shall be installed at a place designated by Landlord and shall be in compliance with and conform to all applicable laws, including zoning and code requirements, of the city or town where the Property is located. Except as provided above, Tenant shall not place or suffer to be placed or maintain any sign, awning, or canopy in, upon, or outside the Premises or on the Building or within a half-mile of the Building. Tenant shall not place in the display windows any sign, decoration, lettering, or advertising matter of any kind without first obtaining Landlord's written approval and consent in each instance. Tenant shall maintain all of such signs and other installations, in good condition and repair, and Tenant shall remove all of such signs and installations upon termination of this Lease. Landlord is under no obligation to place or maintain any such sign or to remove any such sign at the termination of this Lease.

Percentage Rent

A. DESCRIPTION AND SCOPE

This Paragraph requires that Tenant commence making Percentage Rent payments after its Gross Sales for the applicable lease year exceeds Minimum Gross Sales. The Minimum Gross Sales amount, sometimes referred to as the "break point," is generally calculated by taking the amount of Annual Base Rent and dividing that amount by the decimal equivalent of the percentage specified in the Percentage Rent calculation. For example, if 48,000 square feet were being leased at $5.00 per square foot, and the applicable percentage was 1%, then Minimum Gross Sales would be calculated as follows:

$$[48,000 \times \$5.00] \div .01$$
$$= 240,000 \div .01$$
$$= \$24,000,000$$

An alternative method of calculating payments of Percentage Rent during the Lease year is to require Tenant to make Percentage Rent payments each month during the Lease year based upon Gross Sales in such month in excess of one-twelfth of Minimum Gross Sales. This method is not preferred by Tenants with seasonal sales. In the example set forth above, the retail tenant would be required to pay Percentage Rent in any month where Gross Sales exceeded $2 million. If, for example, a retail tenant had sales of $1 million in each of January, February, and March, and then for its Easter Spring Sales Event had $3 million of gross sales in April, this retail Tenant would be required to pay Percentage Rent of $10,000 in April, even though its total Gross Sales of $6 million in January through April did not exceed 4/12 of Minimum Gross Sales, e.g., $8 million. Paragraph 4 also provides Landlord with the right to review Tenant's books to confirm the calculation of Percentage Rent.

B. ANALYSIS

1. Landlord's Perspective

A typical Lease provision requires that Tenant commence paying Percentage Rent after its aggregate Gross Sales for the year exceed Minimum Gross Sales. Landlord may prefer to have estimated payments made throughout the course of the year. In many retail situations, Tenant will refuse to make estimated payments based upon the seasonality of its sales. Landlord may want to add a clause to Paragraph 4 that states that the under-reporting of Gross Sales by Tenant of greater than 5% in any one year or the under-reporting of Gross Sales by greater than 3% in any two consecutive years shall constitute an Event of Default under the Lease.

2. Tenant's Perspective

Tenant may request that one lump-sum payment of Percentage Rent be made at the end of each Lease year. Tenant also may try to exclude internet sales, mail-order sales, or other unique sales that, arguably, are not originated or generated at or from the Premises. Tenant is unlikely to agree to make estimated payments of Percentage Rent if doing so would require Tenant to pay those estimates out-of-pocket.

3. Lender's Perspective

Lender's primary concern is having a sufficient historical basis upon which to underwrite for Percentage Rent, if a substantial amount of Percentage Rent is to be relied upon in the debt service coverage ratio calculation. Also, Lender is likely to focus on Landlord's right to audit and whether under-reporting of Gross Sales gives rise to a default under the Lease.

C. COMPROMISES AND ALTERNATIVES

If Tenant is unlikely to exceed Minimum Gross Sales prior to the holiday shopping season, Landlord may consider allowing Tenant to pay all Percentage Rent at the end of each calendar year. The margin of error that triggers Tenant's obligation to pay Landlord's audit expenses is also likely to be negotiated.

D. COMMENTS

None.

E. TYPICAL PARAGRAPH

4.   Percentage Rent. In addition to Annual Base Rent, Tenant shall pay to Landlord Percentage Rent (as hereinafter defined). For purposes of this Paragraph 4, Percentage Rent shall mean the product of (a) the amount by which actual Gross Sales (as hereinafter defined [See Paragraph 5]) exceed Minimum Gross Sales (as hereinafter defined), multiplied by (b) _____%. As used herein, "Minimum Gross Sales" shall mean $_____. Within ten (10) days after the end of each calendar month during the term of this Lease, Tenant shall provide Landlord with a written statement, certified by an officer of Tenant to be correct, showing the total Gross Sales during the preceding calendar month. Within ten (10) days following the close of the calendar month in which Gross Sales for the Lease Year to date exceed the Minimum Gross Sales, Tenant shall pay to Landlord Percentage Rent based upon the amount of such excess. With ten (10) days following the close of each calendar month thereafter during such Lease Year, Tenant shall pay to Landlord Percentage Rent computed on total Gross Sales made during each such calendar month. Within thirty (30) days following the end of each Lease Year, Tenant shall provide Landlord with a written statement, certified by an independent certified public accountant, showing the calculation of Gross Sales on a month-by-month basis, for the immediately preceding Lease Year. If not previously paid in full, the balance of all Percentage Rent shall be paid to Landlord within thirty (30) days following the end of each Lease Year.

Tenant shall maintain at the Premises complete and accurate books and records of Gross Sales for each Lease Year. Such books and records shall be kept in accordance with generally accepted accounting principles, and shall include, without limitation, the following: (i) detailed original records of any exclusions or deductions from Gross Sales; (ii) sales tax records; and (iii) such other records as would customarily be examined by an independent accountant pursuant to generally accepted auditing standards in performing an audit of Tenant's sales. Such books and records shall be made available to Landlord and its representatives for the purpose of determining the accuracy of the statements of Gross Sales submitted by Tenant. Landlord may photocopy all or any portion of such books and records. If Landlord's examination of such books and records discloses that Gross Sales as reported by Tenant are less than ninety-seven percent (97%) of the actual Gross Sales as determined by Landlord based upon said review, then Tenant shall pay to Landlord all costs and expenses incurred by Landlord in connection with such examination by Landlord and its representatives, and Tenant shall pay

Landlord any additional Percentage Rent due and owing based upon the actual Gross Sales as determined by Landlord. Such sums shall be due and payable immediately and shall bear interest at ten percent (10%) per annum.

Gross Sales Definition

RISK RATING: 4

A. DESCRIPTION AND SCOPE

This Paragraph describes the items to be included in Gross Sales in order to determine Percentage Rent. The description of the items included in Gross Sales is very broad because it is often impossible to predict all methods by which Tenant may generate revenue from its use of the Premises.

B. ANALYSIS

1. Landlord's Perspective

Landlord's objective is to describe the items included in Gross Sales in the broadest possible manner.

2. Tenant's Perspective

Tenant would like to exclude as many items as possible from Gross Sales. For example, mail order sales, internet sales, or sales to employees "at cost" may be points of negotiation.

3. Lender's Perspective

If Lender is relying on Percentage Rent to pay its debt service, then Lender will have the same perspective as Landlord.

C. COMPROMISES AND ALTERNATIVES

Exclusions from Gross Sales should be considered thoroughly by Landlord and Tenant.

D. COMMENTS

None.

E. TYPICAL PARAGRAPH

5.   Gross Sales Definition. For purposes of calculating Percentage Rent, the term "Gross Sales" shall mean the actual sales prices and revenue from all goods, wares, and merchandise sold, leased, licensed, or delivered and the actual charges for all services performed by Tenant or by any subtenant, licensee, or concessionaire in, at, from, or arising out of the use of the Premises, whether for wholesale, retail, cash, credit, or otherwise, without reserve or deduction for the inability or failure to collect. Gross Sales shall include, without limitation, sales and services (a) where the orders therefore originate in, at, from, or arise out of the use of the Premises, whether delivery or performance of such sales or services is made from the Premises or from some other place, including but not limited to internet sales where delivery or performance of such sales is made from the Premises; (b) made or performed by mail, courier services, internet, computer, telephone, telegraph, or telecopy orders; (c) made or performed by means of mechanical or other vending devices on the Premises; (d) that Tenant or any subtenant, licensee, concessionaire, or other person in the ordinary and customary course of its business, would credit or attribute to its operations at the Premises or any part thereof; (e) of gift certificates; and (f) resulting from electronic funds transfers. A deposit shall be included in Gross Sales for the month in which such deposit is made, provided that if such deposit is later refunded, the amount of such refund may be deducted from Gross Sales for the month in which such refund is made. Each installment or credit sale shall be treated as a sale for the full purchase price of the sale item or service in the month during which such sale or service is made or performed, as the case may be, irrespective of the time when Tenant receives payment therefore. No franchise or capital stock tax and no income or similar tax based on income or profits shall be deducted from Gross Sales.

The following items shall be excluded from Gross Sales: (i) any exchange of merchandise between stores of Tenant if such exchange were made solely for the convenient operation of Tenant's business and not for the purpose of consummating a sale made in, at, or from the Premises, or depriving Landlord of the benefit of a sale that would otherwise be made in, at or from the Premises; (ii) returns to shippers or manufacturers; (iii) cash or credit refunds to customers on transactions (not to exceed the actual selling price of the item returned) otherwise included in Gross Sales; (iv) sales of trade fixtures, machinery, and equipment used in connection with Tenant's business; (v) amounts separately charged and collected from customers and paid directly by Tenant to any governmental unit or agency for any sales or excise tax; and (vi) the amount of any discount on sales to employees.

PARAGRAPH **6**

Tenant's Records

A. DESCRIPTION AND SCOPE

This Paragraph permits Landlord to review the books and records of Tenant to verify Tenant's calculation of Percentage Rent. Landlord may hire an independent certified public accountant to assist Landlord. If Tenant underestimated Percentage Rent by more than 3% or fails to deliver an annual certified statement of Gross Sales, then Tenant shall pay the fees and costs of such accountant.

B. ANALYSIS

1. Landlord's Perspective

Landlord wants to verify the accuracy of Percentage Rent. This Paragraph provides Tenant with incentive to keep and maintain accurate books, and to carry out its business in a professional manner.

If Percentage Rent is based on Tenant's Gross Sales, then Landlord will need access to Tenant's books and records to confirm Tenant's sales receipts.

2. Tenant's Perspective

Tenant may assert that Tenant's calculations of Percentage Rent will be accurate and do not need to be reviewed. Tenant may request that a provision be included in the Lease that would ensure that the records be kept confidential. Tenant may also request that reports be submitted quarterly rather than monthly, as monthly reports would be too burdensome.

3. Lender's Perspective

If Lender is depending on Percentage Rent to pay debt service under its loan to Landlord, then Lender will have the same perspective as Landlord.

C. COMPROMISES AND ALTERNATIVES

Depending on creditworthiness of Tenant, quarterly or even annual reports, rather than monthly reports, may be acceptable to Landlord. The 3% discrepancy percentage set forth in subparagraph (b) may be negotiated. Language with respect to confidentiality may be included.

D. COMMENTS

If the Lease provides for the payment of Percentage Rent, then Landlord will need to review and audit Tenant's books and reports.

E. TYPICAL PARAGRAPH

6. Tenant's Records.
    (a) For the purpose of permitting Landlord to verify Percentage Rent, or other sums due Landlord under this Lease that are based on Gross Sales, Tenant shall keep and preserve for at least four (4) years, and during the term of this Lease shall keep at the Premises, original or duplicate books and records that shall conform to generally accepted accounting practices and that shall disclose all information required to determine Percentage Rent. Such information shall show inventories, receipts of merchandise, expenditures for advertising, and Gross Sales for the year or fraction thereof, including, without limitation, cash register tapes from sealed, continuous total cash registers or permanent electronic records that shall be used to record all sales, serially numbered; mail, internet, and telephone order records; computer records; settlement report sheets of transactions with sublessees, concessionaires, and licensees; records showing that merchandise returned by customers was purchased by such customers; records of merchandise taken out on approval; bank deposit records; reports and returns for income; occupation, sales, and use taxes reflecting Gross Sales; and such other supporting data as independent accountants normally require to audit Gross Sales.
    (b) After prior notice to Tenant, Landlord or any mortgagee of the Premises or their respective agents and accountants, may dur-

ing business hours examine or audit such books and records. If any such examination or audit discloses Percentage Rent in excess of the amount theretofore paid by Tenant for any period, then Tenant shall promptly pay on demand such excess. If such excess is greater than three percent (3%) of the Percentage Rent payable for the applicable Lease Year, then Tenant shall promptly pay on demand to Landlord, Landlord's cost of such examination and audit plus interest thereon as Additional Rent, such interest payable from the date such Additional Rent should have been paid hereunder, at an annual rate equal to the least of (i) eighteen percent (18%); (ii) four percent (4%) above the Prime Rate for the [name of bank]; and (iii) the highest interest rate allowed by law.

(c) Tenant agrees to deliver to Landlord: (i) within fifteen (15) days after the close of each calendar month during the term of this Lease, a written report signed and certified by Tenant or by an authorized officer of Tenant, showing in each instance a complete and accurate statement of Gross Sales made in the preceding calendar month; and (ii) within thirty (30) days after the close of each Lease Year and after the expiration or earlier termination of this Lease, a complete and accurate statement of Gross Sales for the preceding Lease Year or partial Lease Year signed and certified by Tenant or an authorized officer of Tenant. If Tenant fails to deliver such certified statement to Landlord within such thirty (30) day period, then Landlord may hire an independent certified public accountant to examine such books and records to determine the amount of Gross Sales for such Lease Year, and Tenant shall promptly pay to Landlord as Additional Rent the cost of such examination.

Common Area Maintenance and Operation

A. DESCRIPTION AND SCOPE

This Paragraph requires that Tenant pay its proportionate share of Landlord's expenses incurred in connection with the maintenance and operation of the Common Areas. This Paragraph gains importance in a regional or super-regional shopping mall where Landlord provides significant amenities and incurs significant Common Area expenses. The ratio that establishes Tenant's Proportionate Share is described in words rather than using a fixed percentage to allow for changes in the ratio resulting from a change in the size of the Premises or a change in the size of the Retail Complex.

B. ANALYSIS

1. Landlord's Perspective

Landlord's objective is to be reimbursed in full for all Common Area Maintenance and Operating Expenses incurred in connection with the Retail Complex as soon as possible. The broad "including, without limitation" nature of the items included in Common Area Maintenance and Operating Expenses is designed to meet this objective. However, Landlord assumes the risk of vacancies in the Retail Complex that result in Landlord collecting less than 100% of such expenses. Landlord may have difficulty billing each Tenant on the first of each month for the Common Area

Maintenance and Operating Expenses incurred by Landlord in the immediately preceding month. If so, Paragraph 7 should be revised to provide for billing later in the month or for a 30-day lag so that Tenant is required to make payment on the first of each month for Landlord's expenses incurred in the month prior to the immediately preceding month. If Landlord is to be reimbursed for 100% of the Common Area Maintenance and Operating Expenses in connection with a Retail Complex that is partially vacant, then the definition of "Tenant's Proportionate Share" should be changed so that the ratio, expressed or a percentage, is the rentable square feet of the Premises over that leased area of the Building.

2. Tenant's Perspective

Tenant would rather pay for expenses actually incurred rather than estimated expenses. Tenant will seek assurances that all Common Area Maintenance and Operating Expenses are reasonable and necessary, and accordingly, request the right to review and audit Landlord's books and records in order to verify such expenses. Tenant also may request that payment of its share of Common Area Maintenance and Operating Expenses be spread evenly across all twelve months of each Lease year. Tenant may also want to exclude capital expenditure and depreciation.

3. Lender's Perspective

The enforceability of this paragraph is likely to be Lender's primary concern because Lender will want to be sure that Landlord is entitled to the payments described. Landlord must be able to separately account for its maintenance and operating expenses for the Common Areas versus the remainder of the Property.

C. COMPROMISES AND ALTERNATIVES

If Tenant requests billings based on actual expenses incurred, to avoid the logistical problems of billing for actual expenses incurred in the immediately proceeding month, Landlord may consider basing the current monthly payments upon the prior year's actual expenses incurred for Common Area Maintenance and Operating Expenses. Another alternative is to base the current monthly payment upon Landlord's "reasonable" estimate of expenses for the current year. Either of these alternatives would require that the Lease provide for a reconciliation mechanism at the end of each Lease Year. Following any such reconciliation, either Landlord will credit Tenant for any overpayments or Tenant will pay Landlord any shortage for the preceding year.

D. COMMENTS

Some Leases provide that Landlord's standard of care for the maintenance and operation of the Common Areas is to maintain the Common Areas in substantially the same condition as at the commencement of the Lease. In a multitenant building or project, this standard is troublesome for a Landlord because it creates different standards for each Tenant based upon the Commencement Date of its Lease.

E. TYPICAL PARAGRAPH

7.   **Common Area Maintenance and Operation.** In addition to Annual Base Rent, Tenant shall pay to Landlord, as Additional Rent, Tenant's Proportionate Share of Landlord's annual total costs and expenses incurred (including appropriate reserves) in operating, managing, equipping, insuring, lighting, correcting, repairing, replacing, heating, ventilating, cooling, and maintaining the Common Areas ("Common Area Maintenance and Operating Expenses"). For each calendar year Landlord shall estimate the annual Common Area Maintenance and Operating Expenses, and Tenant shall pay 1/12 of said estimated amount each month as Additional Rent. Such Additional Rent shall be payable by Tenant on the first day of each month, together with the monthly installment of Annual Base Rent, for the immediately preceding calendar month. At the end of each calendar year Landlord shall reconcile actual and estimated Common Area Maintenance and Operating Expenses, and Tenant shall within ten (10) days of Landlord's statement pay to Landlord any amount due Landlord because of any underpayment, or Landlord shall credit against any future Additional Rent the amount of any overpayment by Tenant.

For the purpose of this Paragraph 7:

(i) "Tenant's Proportionate Share" shall mean the ratio, expressed as a percentage, of the rentable square feet in the Premises, to the entire rentable area in the Building, which is _____ rentable square feet. The numerator of Tenant's Proportionate Share shall be adjusted if the rentable square foot area of the Premises changes pursuant to the provisions of this Lease, and the denominator of Tenant's Proportionate Share shall be adjusted if the rentable square foot area of the Building changes.

(ii) "Common Areas" shall mean those areas within the Property, including the Building's entrances, public lobbies, doors, windows, hallways, corridors, main elevators, freight elevators, loading docks, walkways, plazas, accessways, lavatories, roads, drives, public and fire stairways, sidewalks, exterior ramps, the parking facilities, and other areas not leased or held for lease within or contiguous to or serving the Property, but that are necessary or desirable for Tenant's full use and enjoyment of the Premises.

For purposes of this Paragraph 7, Common Area Maintenance and Operating Expenses shall include, without limitation, all costs and expenses incurred by Landlord in connection with: maintaining and repairing the Common Areas in the condition and status as Landlord deems consistent with a retail center of the nature and character of the Retail Complex; security and fire protection; cleaning and removing of rubbish, dirt, debris, snow, and ice; planting, replanting, and replacing flowers and landscaping, the care and maintenance of artwork, all water and sewer charges; all premiums for liability and property damage, fire, extended coverage, malicious mischief, vandalism, and workmen's compensation and employer's liability; and all other casualty or risk insurance obtained by Landlord in connection with the Retail Complex; all wages, unemployment taxes, social security taxes, special assessments, impositions, and surcharges; real estate and personal property taxes attributable to the Common Areas; supplies for the Common Areas; utility services; and maintaining lighting fixtures (including the costs of lightbulbs and electric current), depreciation of equipment, machinery and facilities, rents paid for the leasing of equipment and financing charges under any installment purchase of equipment, machinery, and facilities used in connection with the operation and maintenance of the Common Areas, and such other costs as Landlord may reasonably determine are required for the proper maintenance of the Common Areas.

PARAGRAPH 8

Promotional Funds

A. DESCRIPTION AND SCOPE

This Paragraph establishes Tenant's obligation to participate in advertising and promotional programs conducted by Landlord and to contribute funds to Landlord for advertising and promotional purposes related to the Retail Complex.

B. ANALYSIS

1. Landlord's Perspective

Landlord wants to ensure that a certain level and quality of advertising and promotional activities are conducted so as to increase sales volume at the Premises and the Retail Complex and in turn increase the Percentage Rent it collects from all Tenants. Accordingly, Landlord wants Tenant to share advertising and promotion costs since Tenant benefits from such expenditures.

2. Tenant's Perspective

Tenant wants to limit the amount it will pay into the Promotional Fund and the number of additional promotional activities in which it must join.

3. Lender's Perspective

Lender wants to ensure that sufficient promotional and advertising activities are conducted so as to maintain the value of its collateral. To the extent that Landlord, as borrower, has assigned the rents of the Retail Complex to Lender, Lender is interested in mechanisms that increase the Percentage Rent paid by Tenants.

C. COMPROMISES AND ALTERNATIVES

An alternative to the Promotional Fund is a merchant's association (See Paragraph 11 of this Manual) that includes most or all of the Tenants of the Retail Complex and Landlord and makes decisions concerning promotional and advertising activities. Landlords generally prefer a Promotional Fund since it is completely controlled by Landlord. Alternatively, Landlord could appoint a committee consisting of Landlord's representative and representatives from certain Tenants to review Promotional Fund expenditures and to establish Tenants' contribution to such fund. Depending on Landlord's bargaining position, it may agree to cap the amount paid by Tenants into the Promotional Fund in any given year.

Tenant may condition its payment into the Promotional Fund on the payment into the fund by a specified percentage of the other tenants of the Retail Complex. If Landlord agrees to this, Paragraph 8 should state that payments to the Promotional Fund must be made by Tenant so long as the other Tenants of the Retail Complex are required by the terms of their leases to make payments.

The bracketed provision in Paragraph 8 can be deleted when signing a lease for an existing shopping center.

D. COMMENTS

Landlord should be precise when describing the amount and calculation of Tenant's contribution to the Promotional Fund and Tenant's obligation to pay into the Promotional Fund.

E. TYPICAL PARAGRAPH

8.   **Promotional Funds. Tenant will, during the term of this Lease, to the fullest extent possible, participate in all coordinated advertising and promotion programs outlined by Landlord from time to time that, in Landlord's sole judgment, will benefit the Premises from time to time (the "Promotional Fund"). Tenant agrees to pay a minimum amount of _____ Dollars ($___) per month (calculated on the basis of ___ cents per rentable square foot per year of the total rentable square feet of the Premises) as Tenant's contribution to the Promotional Fund (the "Minimum Amount"), subject, however, to annual adjustments by a percentage equal to the percentage of increase or decrease from the Base Period (as hereinafter defined) of the United States Department of Labor Bureau of Labor Statistics Consumer Price Index for Urban Wage Earners and Clerical Workers (All Cities) 1982–84 =100 for that particular**

year. For the purpose of this Paragraph 8, the term "Base Period" shall mean the date on which such Index is published, which is closest to the Commencement Date. Notwithstanding any decrease in such Index, the amount payable by Tenant shall, at no time, be less than the Minimum Amount. [Tenant also agrees to pay, in addition to the foregoing, an initial assessment in the amount of _____ Dollars ($_____) (calculated on the basis of _____ (_____) cents per rentable square foot of the total rentable square feet of the Premises) for the purpose of defraying the advertising, promotion, and public relations expenses to be incurred (or to reimburse Landlord for advancing such expenses) in connection with the grand opening promotion of the retail complex. Such initial assessment shall be paid by Tenant within ten (10) days following Tenant's receipt from Landlord of a bill therefore.] If the Premises are expanded to the extent of at least _____ rentable square feet (at any time and from time to time), then Tenant shall make an additional contribution to the Promotional Fund, as Additional Rent, in connection with such expansion in an amount equal to _____ percent (____%) of the annual promotional charge payable under this Paragraph. Such contribution shall be made within ten (10) days after receipt of a bill therefore by Tenant. Tenant agrees to advertise in any and all special newspaper sections, tabloids, or other advertisements required by Landlord and agrees to cooperate and participate with Landlord in all special sales and promotions. The failure of any other tenant of the Retail Complex to contribute to the Promotional Fund shall in no way release Tenant from Tenant's obligations under this Paragraph. Landlord agrees to contribute not less than __ (__%) percent of the total amount of funds paid by the tenants of the Retail Complex with respect to the Promotional Fund. Nothing contained in this Lease shall obligate or require Landlord to expend more for the cost of Promotional Fund activities during any Lease Year than Landlord collects during such period from the tenants of the Retail Complex in the form of contributions to the Promotional Fund as adjusted by the Landlord's contribution. Landlord, at its option, may elect to contribute all or part of the services of a promotion director or secretary, or provide reasonable office space and equipment in lieu of Landlord's cash contribution to the Promotional Fund. The promotion director shall be under the exclusive control and supervision of Landlord, and Landlord shall have the sole right and exclusive authority to employ and discharge such promotion director. In addition to the foregoing, Tenant shall join and remain a member in good standing in a local merchant's association in the event such an association is formed for the betterment of retail business in the area in which the Premises are located.

Advertising

RISK RATING: 3

A. DESCRIPTION AND SCOPE

This Paragraph requires that Tenant participate in at least six (6) joint advertising events per year, and that Tenant spend at least 1% of the Gross Sales on Advertising.

B. ANALYSIS

1. Landlord's Perspective

Landlord wants to ensure the commercial viability of Tenant and the Retail Complex. Creating and enforcing advertising requirements helps to ensure a steady cash flow to Tenant and the timely payment of Annual Base Rent, Additional Rent, and Percentage Rent by Tenant.

2. Tenant's Perspective

Tenant wants to control the funds allocated to advertising. However, Tenant realizes that if all tenants in the Retail Complex are required to meet certain advertising obligations, the overall success and profitability of all businesses in the Retail Complex should increase.

3. Lender's Perspective

Lender, like Landlord, is concerned with the overall profitability of businesses in the Retail Complex since this profitability will directly affect Landlord's ability to pay debt service.

C.   COMPROMISES AND ALTERNATIVES

Tenant may choose to participate in the Merchants' Association or conduct its own advertising, but not both.

D.   COMMENTS

Tenants that are franchisees of large franchise-based retail organizations may be required under their franchise agreements to participate in local or national advertising campaigns. Those Tenants may object to additional advertising requirements and the payment into a Promotional Fund.

E.   TYPICAL PARAGRAPH

9.   **Advertising. In addition to any Merchants' Association assessments payable under this Lease, Tenant shall participate in at least six (6) major print, radio, or television joint-advertising events per year sponsored and coordinated by the Merchants' Association.**

Tenant shall be required to spend annually at least one percent (1%) of its Gross Sales on advertising its business at the Premises. To the extent that Tenant does not spend such amount, Tenant shall pay to the Merchants' Association as an additional assessment the difference between one percent (1%) of Gross Sales and the actual amount spent on such advertising.

PARAGRAPH **10**

Parking Requirements

RISK RATING: 3

A. DESCRIPTION AND SCOPE

This Paragraph establishes a fixed number of parking spaces (usually based on the number of rentable square feet of the Premises) provided for Tenant's use and reserves to Landlord the right to designate the location of the parking spaces.

B. ANALYSIS

1. Landlord's Perspective

Landlord wants to reserve a fixed number of parking spaces to be used by customers for the Retail Complex. In some geographical areas, particularly downtown areas of large cities, Landlord may require that an additional parking charge be paid each month for each of the Parking Spaces.

2. Tenant's Perspective

Tenant may assign a certain number of employees to the Premises, in part, based on the availability of parking spaces for these employees. Tenant generally will not be obliged to pay a parking fee for the Parking Spaces in a Retail Complex, and Tenant may negotiate to delete subparagraph (c). If Tenant is a major tenant, then Tenant may require that Landlord obtain Tenant's approval prior to establishing any parking fee for the Parking Spaces. In addition, Tenant may want Landlord to covenant to provide a certain number of parking spaces for customers at all times. This covenant may be expressed as ___ spaces per 1,000 square feet of gross leasable area.

287

3. Lender's Perspective

Lender wants to confirm that there is sufficient parking available on-site for all Tenants and their customers, and that the amount of parking conforms to zoning requirements.

C. COMPROMISES AND ALTERNATIVES

Alternatives will depend largely upon the available supply of parking spaces and whether Tenant is a major tenant of the Retail Complex.

D. COMMENTS

The Parking Spaces should be shown clearly on an attached Exhibit.

Local ordinances should be consulted to determine Landlord's rights, as owner of a private parking lot, to enforce rules and regulations with respect to the parking areas.

E. TYPICAL PARAGRAPH

10. Parking Requirements.
    (a) Landlord hereby grants to Tenant and its employees the right to use _____ (_____) parking spaces in such areas of the Retail Complex, as shown on Exhibit __ attached hereto (the "Parking Spaces"). Landlord, at its sole election, may relocate the Parking Spaces within the Retail Complex from time to time; provided, however, such designation shall be uniformly applied and shall not unfairly favor any tenant in the Retail Complex.
    (b) Tenant shall, within ten (10) days of Landlord's request therefore, notify Landlord of the license plate numbers, years, makes, and models of the automobiles of Tenant's employees entitled to use the Parking Spaces. It is understood that Tenant or its employees shall not use those parking spaces reserved for other tenants or for the retail customers of the Retail Complex. If Tenant or its employees fail to park their cars in the Parking Spaces, then Landlord shall have the right, after giving notice to Tenant, to charge Tenant, as additional rent, Ten Dollars ($10.00) per day per car parked in any parking areas other than the Parking Spaces.
    (c) Landlord reserves the right to charge Tenant a parking fee for each of the Parking Spaces, which fee shall be payable monthly in advance with monthly installments of Annual Base Rent.

(d) The Parking Spaces are provided solely for the accommodation of Tenant, and Landlord assumes no responsibility or liability of any kind whatsoever from whatever cause with respect to the use thereof by Tenant or Tenant's agents, representatives, customers, or invitees.

Merchants' Association

RISK RATING: 3

A. DESCRIPTION AND SCOPE

This Paragraph creates a Merchants' Association to provide for general advertising of all Tenants' businesses. The advertising is funded by assessment paid by Tenants.

B. ANALYSIS

1. Landlord's Perspective

A Merchants' Association provides an organized and consistent scheme of advertising for the Retail Complex.

2. Tenant's Perspective

Although Tenants also will benefit from a Merchant's Association, most Tenants prefer not to be locked into a flat-fee payment arrangement for association assessments since these arrangements limit business flexibility. Tenant may want to condition its obligations under this Paragraph upon at least 70% of all other Tenants joining the Merchants' Association.

3. Lender's Perspective

A Lender, like Landlord, favors the establishment of a Merchants' Association to promote the Retail Complex and thereby enhance its value as collateral.

C. COMPROMISES AND ALTERNATIVES

As an alternative to setting Merchants' Association assessments in the Lease, the determination could be left to the members of the Merchants'

Association. While adding flexibility, this option limits Landlord's control over advertising. Another alternative is to simply require contributions by Tenant to a promotional fund.

D. COMMENTS
None.

E. TYPICAL PARAGRAPH:
11. Merchants' Association. Tenant agrees to maintain its membership in the merchants' association formed for the purpose of creating and maintaining a fund for the general promotion and welfare of the Retail Complex (the "Merchants' Association"). Tenant agrees to be bound by the Articles of Incorporation and By-Laws of the Merchants' Association, copies of which are available for Tenant's inspection at Landlord's office. Tenant agrees to pay to the Merchants' Association an annual assessment as determined by the Merchants' Association. Tenant shall pay to the Merchants' Association all such assessments within ten (10) days after receipt of a statement therefore. Tenant shall pay a prorated amount of the first and last annual assessment if the Commencement Date does not coincide with the first day of the annual assessment period.

Notwithstanding anything to the contrary that may be contained in this Lease, or in any Articles of Incorporation or By-Laws of the Merchants' Association, Tenant agrees that Landlord may in its sole discretion elect to provide the Merchants' Association with any or all of the following, and Tenant expressly authorizes the Merchants' Association to reimburse Landlord for providing the same:

(a) The services of an advertising/marketing director selected by Landlord to carry out the advertising promotions and marketing of the Retail Complex.

(b) Such reasonable space as may be necessary to carry out the functions of the advertising/marketing director.

(c) Such office equipment as may be deemed necessary by Landlord to service fully the function of the advertising/marketing director.

Landlord may appoint the Merchants' Association as its agent for the collection of the Merchants' Association assessments.

Exclusives

RISK RATING: 4

A. DESCRIPTION AND SCOPE

This Paragraph grants to Tenant the exclusive right to engage in a certain line of business at the Retail Complex, and restricts Landlord's right to rent space at the Retail Complex to any tenant who operates a business in competition with Tenant.

B. ANALYSIS

1. Landlord's Perspective

Before granting an exclusive, Landlord must examine all of the other Leases with respect to the Retail Complex to determine whether other Tenants are prohibited from engaging in the business granted pursuant to the exclusive. If other Leases provide that Tenants may use their Premises for "any lawful use," then Landlord will not be able to abide by the exclusive granted to Tenant. One solution is to draft the exclusive so that it is subject to the rights of existing Tenants, and perhaps any future Anchor Tenants, but obligates Landlord to enter into new Leases that do not violate the exclusive granted to Tenant. Landlords are generally reluctant to grant exclusives and will generally want to exclude department stores and other anchor tenants from the exclusive.

2. Tenant's Perspective

Exclusives are most commonly sought and obtained by anchor Tenants. Before antitrust challenges to such clauses, which largely voided such efforts by large Tenants, these clauses often gave important Tenants the right to review and approve all other Leases affecting the Retail Complex, thus preventing Landlord from leasing space in the Retail Complex to competitors.

3.   Lender's Perspective

Lender should review all Leases to make sure that exclusive rights do not overlap (i.e., the same exclusive is granted to more than one Tenant) or violate state and federal antitrust laws. The loan documents should provide that a default by Landlord under such clause would constitute a default under the loan documents.

C.   COMPROMISES AND ALTERNATIVES

Exclusives can be very broad (e.g., an exclusive right to sell food and beverages) or very narrow (e.g., an exclusive right to operate a take-out pizza restaurant). The broad "food and beverages" clause, favored by Tenant, would preclude Landlord from renting space to a grocery store, gas station with food vending machines, ice cream shop, and other similar businesses. Such other businesses, however, may not compete with and may actually enhance Tenant's pizza business. The narrow clause, favored by Landlord, would allow uses that are not directly competitive with Tenant. There is usually a way to determine the scope of the restriction so as to prohibit Landlord's renting to most of Tenant's true competitors, thus benefiting both Landlord and Tenant by keeping Tenant's sales high. In addition, the parties may want to provide for exceptions to an otherwise rather broad restriction on Landlord.

D.   COMMENTS

Exclusive clauses are normally upheld, but are not favored. Any ambiguity in an exclusive will be construed against its restriction. Clauses restraining competition have been subject to attack on antitrust grounds in state and federal courts and through action by the Federal Trade Commission.

E.   TYPICAL PARAGRAPH

12.   **Exclusives. Landlord shall not during the term of this Lease enter into any leases with respect to the Retail Complex with any other person, corporation, limited liability company, partnership, or entity that allows the tenant under such lease to use any portion of the Retail Complex for the display and sale of any, or any combination, of the following items: [list prohibited items].**

Property Taxes

RISK RATING: 4

A. DESCRIPTION AND SCOPE

Option A requires that Tenant pay a proportionate share of real estate taxes for the Property based on dividing the rentable square feet of the Premises by the rentable square feet of the entire Building and multiplying this ratio by the real estate taxes payable by Landlord for the entire Retail Complex. Option B requires that Tenant pay its proportionate share of any increase in real estate taxes for the Retail Complex over real estate taxes for the Retail Complex due for the Base Tax Year.

B. ANALYSIS

1. Landlord's Perspective

Option A is a straight pass-through of the cost of real estate taxes from Landlord to Tenant. If Landlord underestimates Property Taxes for any lease year, then Tenant must pay any shortfall at the end of each Lease year. Option B, on the other hand, permits Landlord to recoup from Tenant only a proportionate share of any increase in real estate taxes. Like Option A, Option B also requires Tenant to pay to Landlord the amount by which actual real estate tax liability exceeds the estimate of tax liability provided by Landlord to Tenant at the beginning of each Lease Year.

While Option B protects Landlord from increases in Property Taxes, careful attention should be given by Landlord to ensure that Annual Base Rent during the first year of the Lease accounts for Property Taxes allocable to the Premises for that year.

2. Tenant's Perspective

Tenant will require that Landlord not be reimbursed more than 100% of the Property Taxes. Tenant should verify the accurateness of the rentable square feet of the Premises and the Building. Tenant will favor a "gross-up" clause in Option B, because it protects Tenant from increases in Property Taxes due to increased tenant occupancy.

3. Lender's Perspective

Lender wants to ensure that tenants of the Retail Complex are obligated to pay 100% of Property Taxes. To the extent the Retail Complex is 100% leased, either Option A or Option B accomplishes that objective.

C. COMPROMISES AND ALTERNATIVES

Tenant may request annual or semiannual payments rather than monthly payments of Property Taxes. Landlord may object to this if there is any doubt that Tenant may not have sufficient funds to pay its share of Property Taxes when due. Landlord and Lender will want to ensure that the Lease does not afford Tenant the right to avoid its obligation to pay its Share of Property Taxes by contesting the tax. If the Property is in the process of construction, Landlord may wish to consider whether increased assessments resulting from the completion of the improvements should be included as part of Tenant's Share of Property Taxes, whether or not the improvements benefit Tenant.

D. COMMENTS

None.

E. TYPICAL PARAGRAPH

Option A (Net Lease)

13. **Property Taxes.**
     (a) **For the purposes of this Paragraph 13:**
          (i)   **Lease Year shall mean each full twelve (12) calendar months commencing on _____, during the term of this Lease, as the same may be extended.**
          (ii) **Property Taxes shall mean the aggregate amount of any form of assessment, license, fee, rent tax, levy, penalty (if a result of Tenant's delinquency), or tax (other than income, estate, succession, inheritance, transfer, or franchise taxes), imposed by any authority having the direct or indirect**

power to tax, including, without limitation, any city, county, state, or federal government or other district or division thereof, on the Building or any part thereof, and the Retail Complex, or any other legal or equitable interest of Landlord in the same for each Lease Year, excluding penalty fees or charges incurred as a result of Landlord's failure to pay Property Taxes in a timely manner, any taxes or assessments charged or levied against Landlord that are not directly incurred as a result of the operation of the Retail Complex, and any real estate taxes directly payable by Tenant or any other tenant of the Building.

(iii) Property Taxes Allocable to the Premises shall mean the amount of Property Taxes payable by Landlord for each Lease Year multiplied by a fraction, the numerator of which is the total rentable square feet of the Premises, and the denominator of which is the total rentable square feet of the Building. Such numerator and denominator are subject to change if the rentable square feet of the Premises or the Building change.

(b) Prior to the commencement of each Lease Year, Landlord shall provide Tenant with a written estimate of Property Taxes Allocable to the Premises for such Lease Year. The amount estimated for Property Taxes Allocable to the Property shall be payable by Tenant as Additional Rent to Landlord in twelve (12) equal monthly installments for each month during such Lease Year. If the term of this Lease does not commence on the first day of a Lease Year and/or end on the last day of a Lease Year, then Property Taxes Allocable to the Premises shall be prorated based on the number of days after the Commencement Date for the first Lease Year and the number of days after the last day of the term of this Lease for the last Lease Year.

(c) Within ninety (90) days after the close of each Lease Year, Landlord shall deliver to Tenant a written statement setting forth actual Property Taxes Allocable to the Premises for such Lease Year. If actual Property Taxes Allocable to the Premises are greater than the estimated Property Taxes Allocable to the Premises, then Tenant shall pay such increase to Landlord within thirty (30) days after receipt of such statement by Tenant. If actual Property Taxes Allocable to the Premises are less than estimated Property Taxes Allocable to the Premises, Landlord shall credit such decrease against the next installment of Annual Base Rent payable by Tenant.

(d) Tenant shall pay, prior to delinquency, all personal property taxes payable with respect to all property of Tenant located in the Premises or at the Retail Complex and shall provide promptly to Landlord, upon request of Landlord, written proof of such payment.

(e) If this Lease commences on a day other than the first day or terminates on a day other than the last day of a Lease Year, then Property Taxes Allocable to the Premises shall be prorated accordingly. Any amount payable by Landlord to Tenant or Tenant to Landlord with respect to any partial Lease Year shall be payable within thirty (30) days after delivery by Landlord to Tenant of the statement of actual Property Taxes Allocable to the Premises for such Lease Year. This Paragraph 13(e) shall survive the expiration or earlier termination of this Lease.

Option B (Base Year Lease)

13. Property Taxes.
    (a) For the purposes of this Paragraph 13:
        (i) Lease Year shall mean each full twelve (12) calendar months commencing on _____, during the term of this Lease, as the same may be extended.
        (ii) Property Taxes shall mean the aggregate amount of any form of assessment, license, fee, rent tax, levy, penalty (if a result of Tenant's delinquency), or tax (other than income, estate, succession, inheritance, transfer, or franchise taxes), imposed by any authority having the direct or indirect power to tax, including, without limitation, any city, county, state, or federal government or other district or division thereof, on the Building or any part thereof, and the Retail Complex, or any other legal or equitable interest of Landlord in the same for each Lease Year, excluding penalty fees or charges incurred as a result of Landlord's failure to pay Property Taxes in a timely manner, any taxes or assessments charged or levied against Landlord that are not directly incurred as a result of the operation of the Building, and any real estate taxes directly payable by Tenant or any other tenant of the Building.
        (iii) Base Tax Year shall mean the first Lease Year.
        (iv) Property Taxes Allocable to the Premises shall mean the amount of Property Taxes payable by Landlord for each Lease Year multiplied by a fraction, the numerator of which is the total rentable square feet of the Premises, and

the denominator of which is the total rentable square feet of the Building. Such numerator and denominator are subject to change if the rentable square feet of the Premises or the Building change.

(v) Base Property Taxes shall mean Property Taxes Allocable to the Premises for the Base Tax Year.

(b) Prior to the commencement of each Lease Year (except the Base Tax Year), Landlord shall provide Tenant with a written estimate of Property Taxes Allocable to the Premises for such Lease Year. The amount, if any, by which such estimate exceeds Base Property Taxes shall be "Tenant's Share of Property Taxes," payable by Tenant as Additional Rent to Landlord in twelve (12) equal monthly installments for each month during such Lease Year. If the term of this Lease does not commence on the first day of a Lease Year and/or end on the last day of a Lease Year, then Property Taxes Allocable to the Premises shall be prorated based on the number of days after the Commencement Date for the first Lease Year and the number of days after the last day of the term of this Lease for the last Lease Year.

(c) Within ninety (90) days after the close of each Lease Year, Landlord shall deliver to Tenant a written statement setting forth actual Property Taxes Allocable to the Premises for such Lease Year. If actual Property Taxes Allocable are greater than or less than the estimate of Property Taxes for such Lease Year, then Tenant shall pay such increase to Landlord within thirty (30) days after receipt of such statement by Tenant, or Landlord shall credit such decrease against the next installment of Additional Rent payable by Tenant.

(d) Tenant shall pay, prior to delinquency, all personal property taxes payable with respect to all property of Tenant located in the Premises or at the Retail Complex and shall provide promptly to Landlord, upon request of Landlord, written proof of such payment.

(e) If this Lease commences on a day other than the first day or terminates on a day other than the last day of a Lease Year, then Tenant's Share of Property Taxes shall be prorated accordingly. Any amount payable by Landlord to Tenant or Tenant to Landlord with respect to any partial Lease Year shall be payable within thirty (30) days after delivery by Landlord to Tenant of the statement of actual Property Taxes Allocable to the Premises for such Lease Year. This Paragraph 13(e) shall survive the expiration or earlier termination of this Lease.

Remodeling Requirement

RISK RATING: 3

A. DESCRIPTION AND SCOPE

This Paragraph requires that Tenant make certain renovations to the Premises during the Term of the Lease to maintain the appearance and up-to-date look of the Premises. This Paragraph also provides a standard for the quality of the work and requires that Tenant obtain a performance bond for the work.

B. ANALYSIS

1. Landlord's Perspective

During the Term of the Lease, the Premises may deteriorate due to age and wear and tear. Unremedied, physical deterioration of the Premises may reduce the value of the Retail Complex and lessen its appeal to other tenants and the general public. This Paragraph places the burden on Tenant to maintain and upgrade the physical appearance of the Premises. Landlord may require more-frequent remodeling than is provided for in the Typical Paragraph. For example, Landlord may require remodeling every five years. The Typical Paragraph anticipates that a Lease Term of at least fifteen years will be used.

2. Tenant's Perspective

Tenant may object to the additional expense of renovating the Premises. Tenant may require a short time limit for Landlord to review the plans.

3.   Lender's Perspective

Lender has the same perspective as Landlord.

C.   COMPROMISES AND ALTERNATIVES

Landlord may require that Landlord perform the renovation work and charge Tenant for all costs. If Landlord performs the work, then it will control the quality of the work being performed.

D.   COMMENTS

Before commencing the work, Landlord and Tenant should carefully review the work to be performed and the quality of the materials to be used.

E.   TYPICAL PARAGRAPH

14. **Remodeling Requirement.** In consideration of the significant length of the Term of this Lease, Tenant agrees to commence the remodeling of its exterior storefront and the interior of the Premises consistent with Tenant's latest store design concept at any time during the period beginning on the eighth (8th) anniversary of the Commencement Date and ending on the eleventh (11th) anniversary of the Commencement Date, and complete such remodeling within twelve (12) months of commencing the same. Tenant agrees to submit to Landlord at least six (6) months prior to commencing such remodeling plans and specifications covering Tenant's work for Landlord's approval, which approval is within the sole and absolute discretion of Landlord. In the event that such work shall not have been completed in accordance with said plans and specifications within the time periods herein specified, this Lease shall, at Landlord's option, automatically terminate as of the eleventh (11th) anniversary of the Commencement Date, and the Premises shall be surrendered in accordance with the provisions of this Lease. All of Tenant's work shall be performed in a good and workmanlike manner and shall be performed using materials equal to or better in quality and class than materials originally used to construct the improvements at the Premises. Tenant shall not commence such work without first delivering to Landlord, at its sole cost and expense, (i) a policy or policies of comprehensive liability and property damage insurance covering Tenant's work, naming Landlord as additional insured, and being in amounts and with insurers acceptable to Landlord; and

(ii) a payment and performance bond in the amount of one and one-half (1.5) times the estimated cost of the improvements, additions, or alterations to be made at the Premises, in a form and issued by a surety company acceptable to Landlord in its sole and absolute discretion.

Storage and Office Use

A. DESCRIPTION AND SCOPE

This Paragraph sets forth the amount of space that a retail Tenant may use for office and storage space.

B. ANALYSIS

1. Landlord's Perspective

Landlord wants to maximize the retail space of the Premises in order to maximize Gross Sales and Percentage Rent. The storage and office space of the Premises should be minimized.

2. Tenant's Perspective

Tenant wants to ensure that it has adequate room to store inventory and supplies and run business operations requiring office facilities. Tenant also wants to maximize sales, and therefore, is unlikely to overuse retail space for storage and office functions unless Tenant is having financial difficulties that result in operating losses.

3. Lender's Perspective

Lender has the same perspective as Landlord.

C. COMPROMISES AND ALTERNATIVES

If extensive storage or business operations are required to run Tenant's business, then these operations may be located outside of the Premises, thereby maximizing productive use of retail space.

D. COMMENTS

The percentage of space required for storage and office use will depend on the type of retail operation in which Tenant engages.

E. TYPICAL PARAGRAPH

15. Storage and Office Use. Tenant agrees that it shall use not more than ten percent (10%) of the rentable square feet of the Premises for short-term storage and office purposes.

Landlord's Right to Make Changes

A. DESCRIPTION AND SCOPE

This Paragraph gives Landlord the right to alter the Building and the Retail Complex.

B. ANALYSIS

1. Landlord's Perspective

It is important for Landlord to consider Tenant's views with respect to alterations of the Building and the Retail Complex to avoid problems that may arise in the future where Tenant disagrees with Landlord's plan of alteration. The success of the Retail Complex may depend upon Landlord's making appropriate modifications to the Retail Complex to attract and retain good tenants. If the Premises are a part of a partially completed Retail Complex that will be completed in several phases, then it is crucial to state Tenant's consent to such future construction.

2. Tenant's Perspective

Tenant generally will favor alterations that improve the character and quality of the Retail Complex, unless the alterations adversely affect the operation of its retail business. Any alterations that might block the visibility of Tenant's Premises (e.g., a kiosk) will be opposed by Tenant. Tenant will similarly oppose development of outparcels that block visibility of the Retail Complex or the Premises.

3. Lender's Perspective

A construction Lender will be concerned that Tenant not interfere with the completion of all phases of the Retail Complex. Lender will not want to be required to make future alterations to the Premises or any other portion of the Retail Complex if Lender succeeds to Landlord's interest under the Lease.

C. COMPROMISES AND ALTERNATIVES

If Tenant adamantly objects to alterations that will interfere with the visibility of the Premises, such alterations could be limited to locations described in an Exhibit to the Lease.

D. COMMENTS

If the Building or the Retail Complex is not yet complete, then it is important for Landlord to retain the right to modify the plans for the Building in which the Premises will be located without Tenant's consent, especially in situations where cost concerns necessitate building plan modifications.

E. TYPICAL PARAGRAPH

16. **Landlord's Right to Make Changes. Landlord hereby reserves the right at any time and from time to time (a) to make or permit changes to or revisions in its plan for, the Building or the Retail Complex, including, without limitation, additions to, subtractions from, rearrangements of, alterations of, modifications of, or supplements to the Building areas, grounds, walkways, parking areas, driveways, or other Common Areas, plants, street furniture (including, without limitation, fountains, benches, chairs, banners, lighting, and sculpture), kiosks, and other structures; (b) to construct other buildings or improvements in the Retail Complex and to make alterations or additions thereto and to build additional stories on any such building or buildings; (c) to make or permit changes or revisions in the Building or the Retail Complex, including, without limitation, additions thereto, and to convey portions of the Complex to others for the purpose of constructing thereon other buildings or improvements; and (d) change routes of ingress and egress and take such other action affecting the Premises and the Retail Complex as Landlord may deem necessary to implement the terms of this Paragraph 16.**

Painting and Displays by Tenant

RISK RATING: 2

A. DESCRIPTION AND SCOPE

This Paragraph allows Landlord to control the external appearance of the Premises by requiring Tenant to obtain written permission from Landlord before painting or decorating the exterior of the Premises and to maintain window displays at all times. It restricts Tenant's discretion over the physical appearance of the Premises by requiring that the interior of the Premises be appropriate for an upscale retail establishment.

B. ANALYSIS

1. Landlord's Perspective

Landlord wants each store in the Retail Complex to have a high-quality appearance and in some cases a uniform storefront design. Landlord will not want to have any store fail to maintain suitable window displays, as that can promote an abandoned or run-down atmosphere.

2. Tenant's Perspective

Tenant wants greater discretion over the physical appearance of the Premises. Tenant may want to have an unusual exterior facade so as to attract business.

3. Lender's Perspective

Lender has the same perspective as Landlord.

C. COMPROMISES AND ALTERNATIVES

Landlord may allow Tenant some discretion in choosing the external appearance of the Premises provided Tenant complies with Landlord's storefront design criteria. Landlord will want Tenant to provide to Landlord any proposal for the external appearance of the Premises for Landlord's approval. Any proposal will likely not be accepted if it would detract from other stores or the Retail Complex as a whole.

D. COMMENTS

None.

E. TYPICAL PARAGRAPH

17. **Painting and Displays by Tenant. Tenant shall not paint or decorate any part of the exterior of the Premises, or any part of the interior of the Premises visible from the exterior thereof, without first obtaining Landlord's written approval. Subject to the preceding sentence, Tenant shall install and maintain at all times displays of merchandise in the display windows (if any) of the Premises. Tenant shall maintain the general appearance of the interior of the Premises, including, without limitation, the displays, merchandise, and fixtures therein, in a neat, clean, and orderly appearance consistent with that found in an upscale retail establishment.**

PARAGRAPH 18

Use of Common Areas

RISK RATING: 3

A. DESCRIPTION AND SCOPE

This Paragraph covers some of the same concepts set forth in Paragraphs 10 and 16. It allows Landlord a range of flexibility in the operation of the Common Areas. Landlord may establish reasonable rules and regulations regarding the use of the Common Areas. Landlord may change the location and arrangement of the parking facilities and other Common Areas. Tenant's employees are prohibited from parking in areas other than the area designated by Landlord for Tenant parking. To facilitate Landlord's enforcement of the parking area designation, Tenant must provide to Landlord a list of the license numbers assigned to Tenant and Tenant's employees' cars. Landlord may charge Tenant, as Additional Rent, Ten Dollars ($10.00) per day for each car parked in violation of the parking area designation. Landlord has no obligation to designate any parking facilities for use by Tenant or Tenant's employees.

B. ANALYSIS

1. Landlord's Perspective

Landlord desires flexibility in the operation and maintenance of the Common Areas. Landlord may also want to prevent Tenant and its employees from occupying the parking facilities located closest to the Building. This Paragraph prohibits Tenant from parking in areas other than those designated for Tenant's use. Landlord's remedy for Tenant's violation is to charge Tenant Additional Rent in the amount of $10 per day for each car parked in violation of the parking area designation.

2. Tenant's Perspective

Tenant is concerned with providing adequate access to the Premises and parking for employees and customers. Tenant may insist that specific spaces or a specific number of spaces be reserved for use by Tenant's employees and customers.

3. Lender's Perspective

Lender has the same perspective as Landlord.

C. COMPROMISES AND ALTERNATIVES

The $10 per day Additional Rent may be modified, or it may not become effective until a certain minimum number of violations have occurred.

D. COMMENTS

None.

E. TYPICAL PARAGRAPH

18. **Use of Common Areas.**
   (a) **The Common Areas shall at all times be subject to the exclusive control and management of Landlord. Landlord may (i) establish reasonable rules and regulations with respect to the Common Areas, (ii) change the areas, locations and arrangement of the parking facilities and other Common Areas, (iii) restrict employee parking in the Common Areas, (iv) construct surface or elevated parking facilities in the Common Areas; (v) establish and change the level of parking facilities in the Common Areas; (vi) enforce parking charges (by operation of meters or otherwise) at rates to be determined from time to time by Landlord; (vii) close all or any portion of such parking facilities or other Common Areas to prevent a dedication thereof or the accrual of any rights to any person or to the public therein; (viii) close temporarily any or all portions of the parking facilities or Common Areas; (ix) discourage noncustomer parking in the Common Areas; and (x) do and perform such other acts in and to the Common Areas and the improvements therein as, in the exercise of good business judgment, Landlord shall determine to be advisable.**
   (b) **Tenant and its employees shall park their cars only in the areas designated for that purpose by Landlord. Landlord shall not be**

obligated to provide a designated parking area for Tenant and its employees. At the request of Landlord, Tenant shall within five (5) days after the Commencement Date furnish to Landlord the automobile license numbers assigned to the cars used by Tenant's employees and shall thereafter notify Landlord within five (5) days after any changes to such license numbers. If Tenant or its employees fail to park their cars in the designated areas, after giving notice to Tenant, Landlord shall have the right to charge Tenant, as Additional Rent, Ten Dollars ($10.00) per day per car parked in any parking areas other than those designated. Tenant shall notify its employees of this policy.

PART 3

Description and Analysis of Industrial/Warehouse Lease Paragraphs

Net Lease

RISK RATING: 4

A. DESCRIPTION AND SCOPE

This Paragraph incorporates the "net lease" concept for a single-tenant building, whereby Tenant pays all utilities, Real Estate Taxes, and Building Operating Expenses on the entire Property.

B. ANALYSIS

1. Landlord's Perspective

Generally, this Paragraph protects Landlord from having to absorb any of the costs relating to the maintenance and operation of the Property, including the Building and the Premises. It is intended that this be a "triple net" or "absolutely net" Lease, meaning that the Tenant pays all (i) real estate taxes; (ii) insurance premiums; and (iii) costs of utilities, repairs, and maintenance of the Property. Thus, the net cash flow before debt service should equal the Annual Base Rent payable under the Lease. With respect to the payment of Building Operating Expenses or Real Estate Taxes, Landlord will insist that any free-rent period not be applicable to such payments and therefore require that Tenant begin making such payments on the Commencement Date rather than on the Rent Commencement Date.

2. Tenant's Perspective

Tenant may object to the definition of Building Operating Expenses and request that certain items such as specific anticipated capital improvements or structural maintenance be excluded from the definition of Building Operating Expenses. Tenant may want to include a provision that permits Tenant to contest any increases in Real Estate Taxes. Although

Landlord may agree to permit Tenant to contest the assessment of Real Estate Taxes, Landlord and/or Lender may insist that Tenant post a bond or deposit with Landlord certain funds pending Tenant's appeal of such Real Estate Taxes. If this is not a bondable net lease, Tenant will also want payments of Building Operating Expenses and Real Estate Taxes to abate in the event of damage or destruction of the Property or a condemnation that causes the Premises to become untenantable.

3. Lender's Perspective

Lender's primary concern is that if Lender is underwriting the Lease as a true net lease, then there must be no termination or offset rights on the part of Tenant, and there must be no maintenance exclusions, otherwise Lender will have to adjust its calculation of net cash flow available for debt service.

C. COMPROMISES AND ALTERNATIVES

Depending upon the length of the Lease Term, certain structural maintenance and capital replacements may be excluded from Tenant's obligations (e.g. roof replacement, exterior wall repairs, underground utilities, etc.).

D. COMMENTS

The definition of Real Estate Taxes and Building Operating Expenses is likely to be one of the most negotiated provisions of this Lease. A clear understanding of the ramifications of any changes is imperative.

E. TYPICAL PARAGRAPH

1. **Net Lease.**
    (a) **The Annual Base Rent shall be absolutely net to Landlord so that this Lease shall yield, net to Landlord, the Annual Base Rent specified. All additional costs, expenses, and obligations of every kind and nature relating to the Premises that may accrue or become due during the Term shall be paid by Tenant, including, without limitation, all utilities and other services consumed or otherwise utilized by Tenant in the operation of its business at the Premises, all Real Estate Taxes (as hereinafter defined), and all Building Operating Expenses (as hereinafter defined). Tenant shall indemnify and hold harmless Landlord from and against the same and all costs and expenses incurred by Landlord in connection therewith, including attorneys' fees.**

(b) For purposes of this Paragraph 1:
  (i) Real Estate Taxes shall mean all taxes, assessments, levies, and other charges, general and special, ordinary and extraordinary, foreseen and unforeseen, of any kind and nature whatsoever, that shall or may be during the Term assessed, levied, charged, confirmed, or imposed upon or become payable out of or become a lien on the Property, but shall not include any municipal, state, or federal capital levy, estate, succession, inheritance, transfer, sales, use, or franchise taxes, or any income, profits, or revenue tax, assessment or charge imposed upon the rent received as such by Landlord under this Lease; provided, however, that if at any time during the Term, the present method of real estate taxation or assessment shall be so changed that there shall be substituted for the whole or any part of such taxes, assessments, levies, impositions, or charges, now or hereafter levied, assessed, or imposed on real estate and improvements, a capital tax or other tax imposed on the rents or income received by Landlord from the Property or the rents or income reserved herein, or any part thereof, then all such capital taxes or other taxes shall, to the extent that they are so substituted, be deemed to be included within the term "Real Estate Taxes," but only to the extent that such taxes would be payable if the Property were the only property of Landlord subject to such capital taxes and other taxes.
  (ii) Building Operating Expenses shall mean the total expenses for the operation, maintenance, repair, and replacement of the Building and Common Areas that are incurred during the Term hereof, including without limitation, janitorial services, structural and nonstructural maintenance, fire and extended coverage, rental interruption and liability insurance, and water, electricity, gas, and other fuels and utilities.
(c) Tenant's obligations hereunder shall survive the expiration or early termination of the Lease and all such payments shall be prorated to reflect the actual Term of this Lease.

Maintenance and Repair of Building and Grounds

A. DESCRIPTION AND SCOPE

This Paragraph is intended for a long-term triple-net Lease and establishes Tenant's responsibility to make all repairs, restoration, and replacements that may be necessary at the Premises during the Term. Landlord is responsible only for the roof and exterior walls during the last ____ years of the Term. If Tenant must make repairs or replacements, the cost of which will be in excess of $_____, Tenant is required to submit plans to Landlord and obtain Landlord's approval.

B. ANALYSIS

1. Landlord's Perspective

Since this is a triple-net lease, Landlord does not want to be responsible for any repairs or replacements at the Premises. However, Landlord will want to be aware of and approve significant repairs undertaken by Tenant at the Premises that could affect value or future use of this Building by another Tenant.

2. Tenant's Perspective

Tenant will not want to be responsible during the entire Term for structural repairs set forth in subparagraph (b), and may delete any reference to a limitation on Landlord's responsibility for such repairs. Tenant may also attempt to delete the reference to painting the Premises, or lengthen the time between required paintings. Tenant may want the same right to repair as provided to Landlord by subparagraph (d).

3. Lender's Perspective

Lender will want to confirm that responsibility for repair, replacement, and restoration of the mortgaged property has been established by the parties to protect Lender's potential interest in the Premises. Lender will also want assurance that Landlord will not incur additional, unexpected costs with respect to the Premises that could jeopardize Landlord's ability to pay debt service.

C. COMPROMISES AND ALTERNATIVES

If the Building is a single-tenant building, Landlord will want Tenant responsible for repairs and replacements to the fullest extent possible.

However, if the Term is less than ten (10) years or if the Premises are part of a multitenant Building, Landlord may retain responsibility for repair and replacement of the exterior and structural portions of Premises, repairing and maintaining the paved areas and entrances and exits to the Property, and for painting the exterior of the Building.

If Tenant is provided the same right to repair the Premises on behalf of Landlord as is provided Landlord in subparagraph (d), Lender will likely object if Tenant is given the right to set-off this expense against rent payments due under the Lease, or is given the right to secure the claim by a lien against the Property.

D. COMMENTS

None.

E. TYPICAL PARAGRAPH

2.   **Maintenance and Repair of Building and Grounds.**

(a) **During the Term, Tenant at its sole cost and expense shall take good care of the Premises, keep the same in good order and condition and, whether or not caused by Tenant's own act or omission, make all necessary repairs and replacements thereto, interior and exterior, structural, except as specified in subparagraph (b) hereof, nonstructural, ordinary and extraordinary, foreseen and unforeseen, including, without limiting the generality of the foregoing, all plumbing, electrical, lighting, and mechanical** facilities and equipment within the Premises; underground utility and sewer pipes outside the exterior walls of the Premises; fixtures, bulbs, tubes, ballasts, interior walls, ceilings, windows, doors, signs, plate glass; all truck loading areas adjacent to the Premises and utilized by Tenant; the pavement area surrounding the Premises; all access and egress areas; and other areas included within the Premises. Tenant shall paint the paintable areas of the interior and exterior of the Premises every seven (7) years during the Term. All such repairs, replacements, and restorations shall be made by Tenant in compliance with all applicable governmental regulations in effect during the Term, and shall be made in a manner and with materials equal to or better than the existing quality of the construction and materials of the Premises. Tenant shall also be responsible for removing ice, snow, and debris from the walks, drives, and the pavement area (including access and egress thereto), curbs and other common areas, and shall maintain said walks, drives, pavement area, curbs and other common areas.

(b) During the last _____ (____) years of the Term, Landlord shall be responsible for necessary repairs and replacement of the roof and exterior structural walls (except for windows) of the Premises, the Building footings and foundation, the floor slab and other structural supports of the Building, except if necessitated by the negligence, willful act, or breach of lease by Tenant, its employees, agents, or invitees, in which event Tenant shall be responsible for repair or replacement as necessary. Landlord shall be under no obligation to inspect the Premises, and Tenant shall promptly report in writing to Landlord any defective condition in or about the Premises known to it that Landlord is required to repair hereunder. If Tenant fails to report to Landlord any such defective condition, then Tenant shall be responsible to Landlord for all liability incurred by Landlord caused directly or indirectly by such condition.

(c) Tenant shall submit plans and specifications to Landlord and shall obtain Landlord's prior written approval of each repair or replacement costing in excess of $_____, which approval shall not be unreasonably withheld or delayed.

(d) If Tenant fails to make any necessary repairs, replacements, or restorations to the Premises, Landlord, at its option, but without any obligation to do so, may enter upon the Premises, after five (5) days' prior written notice to Tenant (or with no prior written notice, in the case of an emergency), and put the same in good order, condition, and repair or otherwise perform Tenant's obligations hereunder, and the cost thereof, upon notice to Tenant, shall become due and payable as Additional Rent to Landlord, to be paid with Tenant's next rental installment.

(e) To the extent legally possible, Landlord shall assign to Tenant the benefit of any warranties or guaranties or both, from manufacturers, vendors, suppliers, contractors, or subcontractors whose products or services are incorporated into the Premises or the Building.

PARAGRAPH 3

Casualty and Liability Insurance

RISK RATING: 3

A. DESCRIPTION AND SCOPE

Lease insurance requirements are intended to protect Landlord from expenses resulting from damage to the Building and Premises, and liability from injuries to third parties that occur at the Property. In the Industrial and Warehouse context, where leased Premises are more likely to be free-standing structures and no other tenants are located on the Property, Tenant may be required to obtain casualty insurance to insure the value of the entire Building, rather than just the contents of and improvements to the Premises. Similarly, Tenant's liability insurance would have to cover grounds on which the Building sits.

B. ANALYSIS

1. Landlord's Perspective

To protect its investment, Landlord will want full replacement casualty coverage to pay the replacement value of the Building in the event of loss. In addition, rental interruption insurance is desirable to prevent a cash flow problem if the Property is damaged and rental payments stop.

2. Tenant's Perspective

Tenant wants to be sure its insurance obligations under the Lease are not excessive when compared to similar buildings in the market. Tenant will likely resist obtaining terrorism risk insurance, particularly if the cost thereof is excessive relative to the perceived terrorism risk.

3. Lender's Perspective

To ensure continued income to the Property, Lender will focus on adequacy of casualty coverage and rental insurance payments. Lender should also seek the right to increase the amount of insurance required by Tenant if it does not consider Landlord's limits sufficient.

C. COMPROMISES AND ALTERNATIVES

Although the amount and scope of coverage may vary, a requirement that Tenant maintain some adequate level of insurance should not be controversial.

D. COMMENTS

None.

E. TYPICAL PARAGRAPH

3.   **Casualty and Liability Insurance.** Tenant shall, at its expense, secure and maintain (a) General Liability Insurance written on a so-called "Comprehensive" Commercial General Liability Form with a primary single-limit coverage of _____ ($ _____), naming Landlord as an additional insured under each such policy; (b) insurance against loss or damage by fire, lightning, and other risks from time included under "extended coverage," special risk, or all-risk or special form casualty insurance covering the Building with Landlord as a named insured and with a standard mortgagee clause in favor of any mortgagee of Landlord, in the amount of one hundred percent (100%) of the then-current replacement cost of the Premises, adjusted annually, containing all insurance coverages ordinarily covered thereby; (c) to the extent available, terrorism risk insurance in the amount of one hundred percent (100%) of the then current replacement cost of the Premises; and (d) rental interruption insurance in an amount at least equal to Net Rent for at least twelve (12) months or more as Landlord or any mortgagee of Landlord's interest may require. Tenant shall deliver to Landlord duplicate certificates of such insurance prior to the Commencement Date and shall deliver new certificates at least thirty (30) days prior to the expiration of the existing coverage. Such certificates shall provide that in the event of termination or material change in coverage, Landlord shall be given thirty (30) days' advance written notice sent by mail to the address of Landlord. Such insurance shall be obtained from insurers satisfactory to Landlord and licensed to do business in the State.

PARAGRAPH **4**

Licenses and Permits

A. DESCRIPTION AND SCOPE

This Paragraph seeks to ensure that all required licenses for operation are obtained and maintained. Failure to be licensed could cause a shutdown of operations, harming reputation and increasing risk of a Lease default.

B. ANALYSIS

1. Landlord's Perspective

Landlord wants to be sure Tenant can operate for its intended use, but Landlord has no incentive to obtain or maintain permits for such use.

2. Tenant's Perspective

Tenant has a natural incentive to ensure it can do business as proposed, and that there is no frustration of its essential purpose in leasing the space.

3. Lender's Perspective

Lender wants to make sure operations are conducted in accordance with law to avoid enforcement actions or harm to this Property's reputation. Lender wants Tenant to accept responsibility for obtaining business permits.

C. COMPROMISES AND ALTERNATIVES

This Paragraph could be deleted in some jurisdictions if there exists no implied warranty of fitness for use under a Lease and Tenant would be bound regardless of absence of permits.

D. COMMENTS

Although operating permits are reasonably the Tenant's responsibility, Landlord should be prepared to disclose the uses permitted under the local zoning code for the location of the Property.

E. TYPICAL PARAGRAPH

4.   Licenses and Permits. If any governmental license or permit shall be required for the proper and lawful conduct of Tenant's business or other activity carried on in the Premises, and if the failure to secure such license or permit might or would, in any way, affect Landlord, then Tenant, at Tenant's expense, shall duly procure and thereafter maintain such license or permit and submit the same for inspection by Landlord. Tenant, at Tenant's expense, shall, at all times, comply with the requirements of each such license or permit.

Multiple-Tenant Building Rules and Regulations

A. DESCRIPTION AND SCOPE

This Paragraph sets forth the need for a uniform set of Rules and Regulations for the Building that is occupied by multiple tenants.

B. ANALYSIS

1. Landlord's Perspective

In a multitenant building, no one tenant will have control over the entire Building; therefore, a uniform set of Rules and Regulations for each Tenant will create a more efficient maintenance program of the Building.

2. Tenant's Perspective

Tenant wants the maximum allowance of use possible of its leased space without having to adhere to strict rules and regulations every time a minor alteration or action is needed.

3. Lender's Perspective

By setting a standard maintenance program, for a multitenant building, Lender will not have to be concerned about deferred maintenance.

C. COMPROMISES AND ALTERNATIVES

This Paragraph might also deal with Tenant's proportionate share of any operating and maintenance costs.

D. COMMENTS

None.

E. TYPICAL PARAGRAPH

5.   Multiple-Tenant Building. In the event that the Premises are part of a larger building or group of buildings (the "Building") then Tenant agrees that it will abide by, keep, and observe all reasonable rules and regulations that Landlord may make from time to time for the management, safety, care, and cleanliness of the Building and grounds, the parking of vehicles, and the preservation of good order therein as well as for the convenience of other occupants and tenants of the Building. The violations of any such rules and regulations shall be deemed a material breach of this Lease by Tenant.

Reservation of Easements

RISK RATING: 4

A. DESCRIPTION AND SCOPE

This Paragraph sets forth the ability of Landlord to grant a right-of-way over or an easement in or to a portion of the Building or Premises needed for public utilities, access, or any other reason that the Landlord deems necessary.

B. ANALYSIS

1. Landlord's Perspective

Landlord desires great flexibility to grant easements and rights of way concerning the Property in order for Landlord to develop the Property or any contiguous property owned by Landlord or an affiliate.

2. Tenant's Perspective

Tenant should be sure that any easement or a right of way over a portion of the Property does not interfere with the operation of the Tenant's business.

3. Lender's Perspective

A Lender, like Landlord, would see the benefit of having the ability to grant easements as it sees fit in order to maximize the Property's potential and thereby maintain an effective cash flow.

C. COMPROMISES AND ALTERNATIVES

Tenant may want to make sure that the granted rights do not adversely affect Tenant's use of portions of the Property other than the Premises.

D. COMMENTS

None.

E. TYPICAL PARAGRAPH

6.   Reservation of Easements. Landlord reserves to itself the right, from time to time, to grant such easements, rights, and dedications that Landlord deems necessary or desirable and to cause the recordation of parcel maps, easements, and restrictions, so long as such easements, rights, dedications, maps, and restrictions do not unreasonably interfere with the use of the Premises by Tenant. Tenant shall sign any of the aforementioned documents upon request of Landlord, and failure to do so shall constitute a material breach of this Lease.

PART 4

Forms

FORM OF LETTER OF INTENT

[Insert Date]

[Landlord]
[Landlord's Address]

RE: [**Property Name and Address**]

Ladies and Gentlemen:

Set forth below are the proposed terms for a lease between _____ ("Tenant") and _____ ("Landlord"), for space at the above referenced property.

Landlord:	[Insert Name of Landlord]
Area and Premises:	Approximately _____ rentable square feet on floors ___ through ___ of the building known as _____.
Lease Term:	_____ (__) Years
Rental Rate:	$_____ per rentable square foot.
Security Deposit:	No security deposit rent will be required of Tenant.
Operating Expenses:	Tenant will pay its pro rata share of all increases in Real Estate Taxes & Operating Expenses over a 2_ _ _ Base Year.
Tenant Improvements:	Landlord will provide Tenant $_____ per rentable square foot as a tenant improvement allowance.
Right of First Offer:	Tenant shall have a recurring first right of offer on contiguous space and floors in the building. Should Tenant exercise a right of first offer, the rental rate shall be the then fair market rental value for such premises. All other terms shall be the same as the initial premises, including the expiration date that shall be coterminous with the initial premises. Base years operating expenses and taxes shall be the first full calendar year the expansion space is occupied.

Renewal Option(s):   [Two] _____ (__) year renewal options at 95% of fair market rental value.

Assignment and Sublease: Tenant shall have the right to sublet or assign all or part of the premises with Landlord's prior consent, which shall not be unreasonably withheld or delayed. Consent shall not be required for assignment or sublease to any subsidiary or affiliate of Tenant, or in the event of a change in ownership.

Building Access: Tenant's employees shall have access to the premises 24 hours per day, 7 days per week, 365 days per year.

Building Hours of Operation: [8:00 a.m. to 6:00 p.m.] Monday through Friday.

Maintenance & Janitorial: Landlord to provide five day per week janitorial service. Landlord will also assume the responsibility for maintaining all common area and building mechanical and HVAC systems including those in the premises.

Nondisturbance: Landlord to provide Tenant with an acceptable Subordination, Nondisturbance, and Attornment Agreement from the existing and any future mortgage lender on the property.

Real Estate Commission: It is understood that _____ and _____ are recognized as the sole brokers in this transaction. Landlord and Tenant understand and agree that they will be compensated on the basis of a full-market real estate commission paid by the Landlord that they will share equally.

Lease: Landlord will provide Tenant with a draft of the proposed of Lease, and Landlord and Tenant will use best efforts to complete and execute the Lease on or before _____.

Substantial Completion: Landlord will make a good-faith effort to deliver the building and premises in a condition suitable for tenant fit out to commence no later than _____. In the event Landlord does not complete the building and premises on or before _____, Tenant shall have the right to terminate the Lease.

Rent
Commencement: Rent shall commence ___ months after the building is complete and the premises are delivered to Tenant for completion of Tenant's improvements.
Parking: Landlord shall provide Tenant with parking spaces in the building at a rate of ___ spaces per 1,000 rentable square feet leased by Tenant. The parking fees for such spaces will be the average rate paid by the other tenants of the building.

This letter of intent is nonbinding on Landlord and Tenant and is only intended as the basis for the preparation of a Lease Agreement between the parties. Neither Landlord nor Tenant shall have any obligations or liability until such time as a definitive Lease Agreement is executed and delivered by both Landlord and Tenant.

Sincerely,

FORM OF NOTICE OF LEASE AND FORM OF LEASE COMMENCEMENT DATE AGREEMENT

Form of Notice of Lease

Caveat: Set forth below is a form of Notice of Lease. Each state has its own statutory minimum requirements for a recordable Notice of Lease or Memorandum of Lease. This form should therefore be adapted to include the statutory requirements of the jurisdiction where this Notice of Lease will be recorded.

NOTICE [MEMORANDUM] OF LEASE

THIS NOTICE OF LEASE, made as of the ___ day of _____, 2_ _ _, by and between _____, ("Landlord") and _____ "Tenant").

1. The name and address of Landlord is:

    _____

    _____

    _____

2. The name and address of Tenant is:

    _____

    _____

    _____

3. Landlord and Tenant have entered into a lease executed on the _____ day of _____, 2_ _ _, (such instrument being hereinafter called the "Lease").
4. The Lease commencement date is _____. The expiration date of the Lease is _____.
5. Pursuant to the Lease, Landlord has leased to Tenant certain premises located at _____ (hereinafter called the "Premises").
6. Tenant has the option to extend the term of the Lease for _____ (___) years. [Tenant has no option to extend the term of the Lease.]
7. The Lease does [does not] contain any option by Tenant to purchase the Premises.
8. Landlord and Tenant shall keep a copy of the Lease on file at their respective addresses as set forth above.

Nothing in this Notice of Lease shall be deemed to have changed or modified any of the terms, covenants and conditions as stated in the Lease.

IN WITNESS WHEREOF, the parties hereto have entered into this Notice of Lease as of the day and year first above written.

WITNESS: LANDLORD

_____   By: _____

_____   TENANT:

_____   By: _____

STATE OF _____)
                             :   ss.
COUNTY OF_____)

The foregoing instrument was acknowledged before me this _____ day of
_____, 2_ _ _, by _____, a _____ of _____, a
_____, on behalf of the _____.

                    Notary Public
                    My commission expires: _____

STATE OF _____)
                             :   ss.
COUNTY OF _____)

The foregoing instrument was acknowledged before me this _____ day of
_____, 2_ _ _, by _____, a _____ of _____, a
_____, on behalf of the _____.

                    Notary Public
                    My commission expires: _____

Form of Lease Commencement Date Agreement

COMMENCEMENT DATE AGREEMENT

This Commencement Date Agreement dated _____, 2_ _ _ shall be attached to and made a part of that certain Lease Agreement dated as of _____, 2_ _ _ (the "Lease") entered into by and between _____ ("Landlord"), and _____ ("Tenant").

Tenant does hereby agree that possession of the Premises has been accepted by Tenant as of _____, 2_ _ _.

The Tenant Improvements to the Premises required to be constructed and finished by Landlord have been substantially completed.

Base Rent shall commence as of _____, 2_ _ _.

The Lease Commencement Date is hereby agreed to be _____, 2_ _ _. The term of this Lease shall end on _____, 2_ _ _, unless sooner terminated as provided in the Lease.

Terms not otherwise defined herein shall have the meanings provided for in the Lease.

LANDLORD: TENANT:
[_____]   [_____]

By: _____   By: _____
　　Its   Its

FORMS OF SUBORDINATION, NONDISTURBANCE, AND ATTORNMENT AGREEMENTS

Subordination, Nondisturbance, and Attornment Agreement
(Landlord or Lender Form)

THIS AGREEMENT is made as of this _____ day of _____, _____ by and among
_____, a _____ corporation having an office and place of
business at _____ ("Lender") a _____ having an
address at _____ ("Landlord"), and _____, a
_____ with offices at _____ ("Tenant").

WHEREAS, Tenant has entered into a certain lease (the "Lease") dated _____
with Landlord covering premises (the "Premises") within a certain building known as
_____ located on the real property more particularly described in
Exhibit "A" attached hereto and incorporated herein; and

WHEREAS, Lender has agreed to make a loan (the "Loan") to Landlord to be evidenced
by a promissory note issued by Landlord to Lender (the "Note") and to be secured by a
Mortgage/Deed of Trust and Security Agreement (the "Mortgage/Deed of Trust") and
by an Assignment of Rents and Leases (the "Assignment") encumbering, inter alia, the
Premises; and

WHEREAS, it is to the mutual benefit of the parties hereto that Lender make such loan
to Landlord; and

WHEREAS, it is a condition precedent to obtaining the Loan that the Mortgage/Deed
of Trust be a lien or charge upon the Premises unconditionally prior and superior to
the Lease and the leasehold interest of Tenant thereunder; and

WHEREAS, Tenant acknowledges that the Mortgage/Deed of Trust, when recorded,
will constitute a lien or charge upon the Premises that is unconditionally prior and
superior to the Lease and the leasehold interest of Tenant thereunder; and

WHEREAS, Lender has been requested by Tenant and by Landlord to enter into a
nondisturbance agreement with Tenant;

NOW, THEREFORE, in consideration of the premises and mutual covenants hereinafter contained, the parties hereto mutually covenant and agree as follows:

1. The Lease and any extensions, renewals, replacements, or modifications thereof, and
   all of the right, title and interest of Tenant hereunder in and to the Premises are and

shall be subject and subordinate to the Mortgage/Deed of Trust and to all of the terms and conditions contained therein, and to any renewals, modifications, replacements, consolidations, and extensions thereof.

2. Lender consents to the Lease and, in the event Lender comes into possession of or acquires title to the Premises as a result of the foreclosure or other enforcement of the Mortgage/Deed of Trust or the Note, or as a result of any other means, Lender agrees that, so long as Tenant is not then in default hereunder or under the Lease and so long as Tenant is then in possession of the Premises and is open and operating its business therein, Lender will recognize Tenant and will not disturb Tenant in its possession of the Premises for any reason other than one that would entitle Landlord to terminate the Lease under its terms or would cause, without any further action by Landlord, the termination of the Lease or would entitle Landlord to dispossess Tenant from the Premises.

3. Tenant agrees with Lender that if the interest of Landlord in the Premises shall be transferred to and owned by Lender by reason of foreclosure or other proceedings brought by it, or any other manner, or shall be conveyed thereafter by Lender or shall be conveyed pursuant to a foreclosure sale of the Premises, Tenant shall be bound to Lender under all of the terms, covenants, and conditions of the Lease for the balance of the term thereof remaining and any extensions or renewals thereof that may be effected in accordance with any option therefore in the Lease, with the same force and effect as if Lender were the landlord under the Lease, and Tenant does hereby attorn to Lender as its landlord, said attornment to be effective and self-operative without the execution of any further instruments on the part of any of the parties hereto immediately upon Lender's succeeding to the interest of Landlord in the Premises. Tenant agrees, however, upon the election of and written demand by Lender within twenty (20) days after Lender receives title to the Premises, to execute an instrument in confirmation of the foregoing provisions, satisfactory to Lender, in which Tenant shall acknowledge such attornment and shall set forth the terms and conditions of its tenancy.

4. Tenant agrees with Lender that if Lender shall succeed to the interest of Landlord under the Lease, Lender shall not be (a) liable for any action or omission of any prior landlord under the Lease; or (b) subject to any offsets or defenses that Tenant might have against any prior landlord; or (c) bound by any rent or additional rent that Tenant might have paid for more than the current month to any prior landlord; or (d) bound by any security deposit that Tenant may have paid to any prior landlord, unless such deposit is in an escrow fund available to Lender; or (e) bound by any amendment or modification of the Lease made without Lender's written consent; or (f) bound by any provision in the Lease that obligates the landlord to erect or complete any building or to perform any construction work or to make any improvements to the Premises or to expand or rehabilitate any existing improvements or to restore any improvements following any casualty or taking; or (g) bound by any notice or termination given by Landlord to Tenant without Lender's written consent thereto; or (h) personally liable under the Lease and Lender's liability under the

Lease shall be limited to the ownership interest of Lender in the Premises. Tenant further agrees with Lender that Tenant will not voluntarily subordinate the Lease to any lien or encumbrance without Lender's written consent.

5. In the event that Landlord shall default in the performance or observance of any of the terms, conditions, or agreements in the Lease, Tenant shall give written notice thereof to Lender, and Lender shall have the right (but not the obligation) to cure such default. Tenant shall not take any action with respect to such default under the Lease, including, without limitation, any action in order to terminate, rescind, or void the Lease or to withhold any rental thereunder, for a period of ten (10) days after receipt of such written notice by Lender with respect to any such default capable of being cured by the payment of money, and for a period of thirty (30) days after receipt of such written notice by Lender with respect to any other such default (provided, that in the case of any default that cannot be cured by the payment of money and cannot with diligence be cured within such 30-day period because of the nature of such default or because Lender requires time to obtain possession of the Premises in order to cure the default, if Lender shall proceed promptly to attempt to obtain possession of the Premises, where possession is required, and to cure the same and thereafter shall prosecute the curing of such default with diligence and continuity, then the time within which such default may be cured shall be extended for such period as may be necessary to complete the curing of the same with diligence and continuity).

6. Landlord has agreed in the Mortgage/Deed of Trust and in the Assignment that the rentals payable under the Lease shall be paid directly by Tenant to Lender upon the occurrence of a default by Landlord under the Mortgage/Deed of Trust. Accordingly, after notice is given by Lender to Tenant that the rentals under the Lease should be paid to Lender, Tenant shall pay to Lender, or in accordance with the directions of Lender, all rentals and other monies due and to become due to Landlord under the Lease, or amounts equal thereto. Tenant shall have no responsibility to ascertain whether such demand by Lender is permitted under the Mortgage/Deed of Trust or the Assignment. Landlord hereby waives any right, claim, or demand it may now or hereafter have against Tenant by reason of such payment to Lender, and any such payment to Lender shall discharge the obligations of Tenant to make such payment to Landlord.

7. Tenant declares, agrees, and acknowledges that:
    a. Lender, in making disbursements pursuant to any agreement relating to the Loan, is under no obligation or duty to, nor has Lender represented that it will, see to the application of such proceeds by the person or persons to whom Lender disburses such proceeds, and any application or use of such proceeds other than those provided for in such agreement shall not defeat the subordination herein made in whole or in part; and
    b. it intentionally and unconditionally waives, relinquishes, and subordinates the Lease and its leasehold interest thereunder in favor of the lien or charge upon said land of the Mortgage/Deed of Trust, and that in consideration of this

waiver, relinquishment, and subordination, specific loans and advances are being and will be made by Lender to Landlord and, as part and parcel thereof, specific monetary and other obligations are being and will be entered into by Landlord and Lender that would not be made or entered into but for said reliance upon this waiver.

8. This Agreement shall bind and inure to the benefit of the parties hereto, their successors and assigns. As used herein, the term "Tenant" shall include Tenant, its successors, and assigns; the words "foreclosure" and "foreclosure sale" as used herein shall be deemed to include the acquisition of Landlord's estate in the Premises by voluntary deed (or assignment) in lieu of foreclosure; and the word "Lender" shall include the Lender herein specifically named and any of its successors, participants, and assigns, including anyone who shall have succeeded to Landlord's interest in the Premises by, through or under foreclosure of the Mortgage/Deed of Trust.

9. All notices, consents, and other communications pursuant to the provisions of this Agreement shall be in writing and shall be sent by registered or certified mail, return receipt requested, or by a reputable commercial overnight carrier that provides a receipt, such as Federal Express or Airborne, and shall be deemed given when postmarked and addressed as follows:

If to Lender:

_____
_____
_____
_____

with a copy to:

_____
_____
_____
_____

If to Tenant:

_____
_____
_____
_____

with a copy to:

_____
_____
_____
_____

If to Landlord:

_____
_____
_____
_____

with a copy to:

_____

_____

_____

_____

or to such other address as shall from time to time have been designated by written notice by such party to the other parties as herein provided.

10. This Agreement shall be the whole and only agreement between the parties hereto with regard to the subordination of the Lease and the leasehold interest of Tenant thereunder to the lien or charge of the Mortgage/Deed of Trust in favor of Lender, and shall supersede and control any prior agreements as to such, or any, subordination, including, but not limited to, those provisions, if any, contained in the Lease, which provide for the subordination of the Lease and the leasehold interest of Tenant thereunder to a deed or deeds of trust or to a mortgage or mortgages to be thereafter executed, and shall not be modified or amended and no provision herein shall be waived except in writing signed by the party against whom enforcement of any such modification or amendment is sought.

The use of the neuter gender in this Agreement shall be deemed to include any other gender, and words in the singular number shall be held to include the plural, when the sense requires. In the event any one or more of the provisions of this Agreement shall for any reason be held to be invalid, illegal, or unenforceable in any respect, such invalidity, illegality, or unenforceability shall not affect any other provision of this Agreement, but this Agreement shall be construed as if such invalid, illegal, or unenforceable provision had never been contained herein. This Agreement shall be governed by and construed in accordance with the laws of the State of _____.

WITNESS:_____   LANDLORD:_____

_____   By: _____

_____   TENANT: _____

_____   By: _____

          LENDER:_____

          By: _____

STATE OF _____)

          :   ss.

COUNTY OF_____)

The foregoing instrument was acknowledged before me this _____ day of
_____, 2_ _ _, by _____, a _____ of _____, a
_____, on behalf of the _____.

> Notary Public
> My commission expires: _____

STATE OF _____)

                     :   ss.

COUNTY OF _____)

The foregoing instrument was acknowledged before me this _____ day of
_____, 2_ _ _, by _____, a _____ of _____, a
_____, on behalf of the _____.

> Notary Public
> My commission expires: _____

STATE OF _____)

                     :   ss.

COUNTY OF _____)

The foregoing instrument was acknowledged before me this _____ day of
_____, 2_ _ _, by _____, a _____ of _____, a
_____, on behalf of the _____.

> Notary Public
> My commission expires: _____

Subordination, Nondisturbance, and Attornment Agreement
(Tenant Form)

THIS AGREEMENT is made as of this _____ day of _____, 2 _ _ _ by and among _____, a _____ corporation having an office and place of business at _____ ("Lender") a _____ having an address at _____ ("Landlord"), and _____, a _____ with offices at _____ ("Tenant").

WHEREAS, Tenant has entered into a certain lease (the "Lease") dated _____ with Landlord covering premises (the "Premises") within a certain building known as _____ located on the real property more particularly described in Exhibit "A" attached hereto and incorporated herein; and

WHEREAS, Lender has agreed to make a loan (the "Loan") to Landlord to be evidenced by a promissory note issued by Landlord to Lender (the "Note") and to be secured by a Mortgage/Deed of Trust and Security Agreement (the "Mortgage/Deed of Trust") and by an Assignment of Rents and Leases (the "Assignment") encumbering, inter alia, the Premises.

NOW, THEREFORE, in consideration of the premises and mutual covenants hereinafter contained, the parties hereto mutually covenant and agree as follows:

1. The Lease shall be subject and subordinate to the Mortgage/Deed of Trust and to all of the terms and conditions contained therein.

2. Lender consents to the Lease and, in the event Lender comes into possession of or acquires title to the Premises as a result of the foreclosure or other enforcement of the Mortgage/Deed of Trust or the Note, or as a result of any other means, Lender agrees that, so long as Tenant is not then in default hereunder or under the Lease beyond any applicable notice and grace period, Lender will recognize Tenant and will not disturb Tenant in its possession of the Premises for any reason.

3. Tenant agrees with Lender that if the interest of Landlord in the Premises shall be transferred to and owned by Lender by reason of foreclosure or other proceedings brought by it, or any other manner, or shall be conveyed thereafter by Lender or shall be conveyed pursuant to a foreclosure sale of the Premises, Tenant shall be bound to Lender under all of the terms, covenants, and conditions of the Lease for the balance of the term thereof remaining and any extensions or renewals thereof which may be effected in accordance with any option therefore in the Lease, with the same force and effect as if Lender were the landlord under the Lease, and Tenant does hereby attorn to Lender as its landlord, said attornment to be effective and self-operative without the execution of any further instruments on the part of any of the parties hereto immediately upon Lender's succeeding to the interest of Landlord in the Premises.

IN WITNESS WHEREOF, the parties hereto have executed this Agreement as of the date first above written.

TENANT: LANDLORD:

_____   _____

LENDER:

_____

FORMS OF TENANT ESTOPPEL LETTERS

Tenant Estoppel Letter (Lender or Landlord Form)

Date: _____   Loan Commitment No. _____

[Lender Name]
[Lender Address]

Re: _____ (Property name and location)

To [Lender]:

The undersigned ("Tenant") understands that _____ ("Lender") has made or will be making mortgage loan (the "Loan") to _____ ("Landlord") on the Property described above. In connection with the Loan, Lender will be receiving an assignment of all leases and rents with respect to the Property and will be acting in reliance upon this letter.

By signing below, Tenant certifies to and agrees with Lender as follows:

1. Tenant leases a portion of a[n] _____ [office building/shopping center/warehouse/other property type] located at _____ [street address, city and state] and known generally as _____ (the "Property")

2. The lease (the "Lease") between Tenant and Landlord regarding Tenant's premises (the "Premises") is dated _____ and is unamended except as follows:

   _____

   [insert date of Lease amendments]. The Lease, together with the amendments, is referred to herein as the "Lease," and is the complete statement of Landlord and Tenant regarding the Premises.

3. The Lease provides:
   A. Current monthly fixed or base rent:_____
   B. Additional Rent: _____
   C. Percentage Rent: _____
   D. Commencement Date: _____
   E. Expiration Date (exclusive of extension or renewal periods): _____
   F. Extension or Renewal Periods: _____
   G. Security Deposit:_____

351

4. Tenant has accepted and is now in sole possession of the Premises. Any construction, build out, improvements, alterations, or additions to the Premises required under the Lease have been completed in accordance with the Lease and Landlord has paid to Tenant all tenant improvement allowances and has paid all other tenant inducements due as of the date of this Tenant Estoppel Letter.

5. Tenant has not subleased or licensed any part of the Premises or assigned the Lease.

6. As of the date of this Tenant Estoppel Letter, the Lease is in full force and effect and there is no violation of or default under the Lease on the part of Landlord or Tenant. There is no present offset of rent and Tenant has no knowledge of any circumstances that would give rise to any credit or set-off against the obligation for present or future rentals under the Lease.

7. Tenant will, concurrently with the giving of any notice to Landlord, give Lender written notice (at the above address) of any default by Landlord under the Lease. Lender will have a reasonable opportunity, before the exercise of any rights Tenant may have pertaining to the Lease, to cure any such default by Landlord.

Sincerely,

[TENANT]:

[_____]

By: _____
    Its

Tenant Estoppel Letter (Tenant Form)

Caveat: Tenant's sole obligation is to execute such Tenant Estoppel Letter as is required by the terms of the Lease. If the Lease does not require a certain provision requested by a Landlord or Lender, then Tenant is not legally obligated to execute a Tenant Estoppel Letter containing the objectionable provision. The Tenant Form of Tenant Estoppel Certificate set forth below is based on the requirements of Paragraph 33 of the Description and Analysis of Lease Paragraphs as set forth in Part I of this Lease Manual.

Date:_____

[Lender Name]
[Lender Address]

Re: _____ (the "Property")

To [Lender]:

By signing below, the undersigned "Tenant" certifies to _____ ("Lender") that to the actual knowledge of Tenant:

1. The lease (the "Lease") between Tenant and Landlord regarding Tenant's premises (the "Premises") is dated _____ and is unamended except as follows:
   _____
   [Insert date of Lease amendments]. The Lease, together with the amendments, is referred to herein as the "Lease."

3. The Lease provides:
   A. Monthly Amount of Annual Base Rent: _____
   B. Date Rent Paid To: _____
   C. Rent Commencement Date: _____
   D. Lease Commencement Date: _____
   E. Expiration Date: _____
   F. Security Deposit:_____

4. All conditions under this Lease to be performed by Landlord have been satisfied and all contributions by Landlord to Tenant on account of Tenant's improvements have been received.

5. Tenant has not assigned the Lease.

6. As of the date of this Tenant Estoppel Letter, the Lease is in full force and effect, and there is no violation of or default under the Lease on the part of Landlord or Tenant. There is no present offset of rent.

7. No Annual Base Rent has been paid to Landlord more than one (1) month in advance.

Sincerely,

[TENANT]:

[_____]

By: _____
    Its

FORM OF LANDLORD'S WAIVER OF LIEN RIGHTS

Waiver of Lien

THIS WAIVER OF LIEN is made and entered into as of the _____ day of _____, 2 _ _ _, by _____, a _____ ("Landlord") in favor of _____, a _____ ("Seller").

WHEREAS, Landlord and _____ ("Tenant") entered into a lease dated _____, 2 _ _ _, (the "Lease") with respect to certain premises located at _____ (the "Premises"); and

WHEREAS, Tenant granted a lien in favor of Landlord in all of Tenant's personal property located at the Premises to secure Tenant's obligations under the Lease (the "Lien"); and

WHEREAS, Tenant has purchased from Seller the personal property described in *Schedule A* attached hereto (collectively, the "Property") and Seller has provided financing to Tenant in connection with the purchase and Tenant has granted to Seller a lien upon the Property.

NOW, THEREFORE, for and in consideration of the sum of One Dollar ($1.00) and other good and valuable consideration, the receipt of which is hereby acknowledged, Landlord does hereby waive and release the Lien as it applies to the Property.

Nothing herein contained shall affect the Lien except as to the Property herein released therefrom.

IN WITNESS WHEREOF, Landlord and Seller have executed this Waiver of Lien as of the date first above written.

WITNESSES:

_____   LANDLORD:

_____   By:_____
                                          Its

_____   SELLER:

_____   By: _____
                                          Its

Index

357

About the Author

Rodney J. Dillman is General Counsel and Secretary of Babson Capital Management LLC. Mr. Dillman also is Corporate Vice President and Associate General Counsel of Massachusetts Mutual Life Insurance Company. He is the Chief Investment Lawyer for MassMutual and manages the Investment Law Group of the MassMutual Law Division. Prior to joining Babson/MassMutual in 2000, Mr. Dillman was a Partner at Day, Berry & Howard LLP in Hartford, Connecticut. He attended Duke University, earning his JD in 1978, and Kent State University, obtaining a B.S in Education and an M.A. in Economics. Mr. Dillman has been a member of the American Bar Association since 1979. He also is a member of the Connecticut and Massachusetts Bar Associations, as well as the American College of Real Estate Lawyers, the American College of Investment Counsel, and the Association of Life Insurance Counsel.